Simon Hudson, PhD
Editor

# Sport and Adventure Tourism

"Hudson provides an interesting and informative book which covers a multitude of sport and adventure tourism niche markets. The book is suitable for students studying tourism, recreation, and leisure as well as industry practitioners. It is very readable and accessible, and all chapters provide useful information for further research through the use of bibliographies and links to Web sites. Overall, the book makes a useful contribution to the evolving study of sport and adventure tourism."

**Dr. Brent Ritchie**
*School of Service Management,*
*University of Brighton,*
*United Kingdom*

"As we move into the new millennium Sport Tourism has come to the forefront as one of the fastest growing sectors of sport and tourism industries worldwide. *Sport and Adventure Tourism* is an inimitable publication that brings together experts from this newly developing field and examines the relationship between sport and adventure tourism. The book incorporates the most recent information and real-world case studies. The publication is rich in knowledge and provides the reader with innovative models, useful resources, and invaluable references for further study and research. The section on virtual sport tourism is unique and adds a new twist to the sport tourism knowledge base. *Sport and Adventure Tourism* is a welcome guide to enhance the newly developing Sport Tourism sector."

**Wayne G. Pealo, PhD**
*Professor, Recreation*
*and Tourism Management,*
*Malaspina University College*

*More pre-publication*
*REVIEWS, COMMENTARIES, EVALUATIONS . . .*

"This book is easy to read, interesting, and informative. It fills a niche in the literature on sport tourism—many of the chapters provide an in-depth look at one particular segment of sport tourism, such as snow skiing or golf tourism. The book will provide students with information about many of the specific components that comprise sport tourism and can be used alongside a more general sport tourism text.

**Heather J. Gibson, PhD**
*Associate Director,*
*Center for Tourism*
*Research and Development,*
*University of Florida*

The Haworth Hospitality Press®
An Imprint of The Haworth Press, Inc.
New York • London • Oxford

# Sport and Adventure Tourism

# Sport and Adventure Tourism

Simon Hudson, PhD
Editor

The Haworth Hospitality Press®
An Imprint of The Haworth Press, Inc.
New York • London • Oxford

The Haworth Press, Inc., 10 Alice Street, Binghamton, NY 13904-1580.

Cover design by Jennifer M. Gaska.

**Library of Congress Cataloging-in-Publication Data**

Sport and adventure tourism / edited by Simon Hudson.
    p. cm.
Includes bibliographical references and index (p. ).
ISBN 0-7890-1275-8 (alk. paper)—ISBN 0-7890-1276-6 (alk. paper)
1. Sports and tourism. I. Hudson, Simon.

G155.A1 S627 2002
338.4'791—dc21

                                                  2001051686

# CONTENTS

# ABOUT THE EDITOR

**Simon Hudson, PhD, MBA, BA, DipM,** is Associate Professor in the Tourism Management Group at the University of Calgary, Alberta. Dr. Hudson has extensive teaching, consulting, and lecturing experience in the tourism field, with an emphasis on marketing, and operated his own successful tour business for several years. He is the author of *Snow Business* and numerous journal articles and sits on the editorial boards of the *Journal of Teaching in Travel & Tourism,* the *Journal of Travel Research,* and the *International Journal of Tourism Research.*

# CONTRIBUTORS

**Paul Beedie** is the course leader for Leisure and Recreation Studies at De Montfort University, Bedford, United Kingdom. He is a qualified teacher with strong vocational qualifications who joined the De Montfort faculty seven years ago. He has held full-time positions in schools, an outdoor education center, and a college. In his latter post he created and organized an innovative one-year course in adventure recreation. His research has included conference presentations and publications in *Outdoor and Adventurous Activities, Risk Management,* and, most recently, *Adventure Tourism.*

**Ross Cloutier** is the founder of the Adventure Programs Department at the University College of the Cariboo in Kamloops, British Columbia, and has been instrumental in the development of business, legal, and risk management curriculum. He has written two books for the adventure tourism industry, *The Business of Adventure* and *Legal Liability and Risk Management in Adventure Tourism.* Cloutier is a professional mountain guide and has studied outdoor recreation, outdoor pursuits, and has an MBA in international business. He was the climbing leader for a Mt. Everest Canada expedition undertaken by Canadians in 1991. In addition to his active role at the University College of the Cariboo, Cloutier works as a consultant to government, school districts, businesses, and law firms in the area of outdoor education and adventure tourism risk management.

**Donald Getz** is Professor, Tourism and Hospitality Management, at the University of Calgary. Getz is interested in a broad range of tourism and recreation-related areas. In particular, he specializes in the study of tourism management, including research, planning, and marketing; event tourism, including festivals and special events management; programming and impact assessment; leisure services management; and recreation development, planning, management, and marketing. Getz has authored three books and numerous journal articles. In 1992,

Getz cofounded and is now editor in chief of the scholarly research journal *Event Management.*

**Michael Hall** at the time of this writing, was Professor and Head of the Department of Tourism, University of Otago, New Zealand. The co-editor of *Current Issues in Tourism,* he has published widely in the fields of tourism, heritage, and environmental history. He is currently undertaking research in tourism and gastronomy, particularly with respect to wine and food tourism and the restructuring of rural economies.

**Gayle Jennings** is Associate Dean (Research), in the Faculty of Business and Law, Central Queensland University, Australia. Prior to this position she was a senior lecturer in tourism studies, and was employed by a Commonwealth agency responsible for natural resource management. In addition, Jennings has been a lecturer in education, an educational consultant, and a teacher. Her research interests include tourism, sociology, and Asian studies, as well as research methodologies. Specifically, she is interested in marine and national park tourism, special interest tourism, rural tourism, and the impacts of tourism on host communities and settings. Jennings has also written a textbook for use in courses teaching tourism research.

**Joseph Kurtzman** holds a PhD in sports management and is Director, Sports Tourism International Council. He is also editor of the *Journal of Sport Tourism* and a reviewer for the *Journal of International Sport Management.* He has taught sports management and tourism management at the university level, and has numerous research publications to his name. His most recent presentation was at the Post-Olympic Conference, Canberra, Australia, as a keynote speaker.

**Lisa Delpy Neirotti** is Professor of Sport, Event, and Tourism Management at The George Washington University. In addition to speaking at various conferences, writing professional articles, and consulting with corporate sponsors and sport commissions, Delpy Neirotti co-authored *The Ultimate Guide to Sport Event Management and Marketing* published by McGraw-Hill. Delpy Neirotti also serves on the editorial boards of *Sport Marketing Quarterly* and *Sport Travel* magazine and writes a monthly column for the latter. Delpy Neirotti conducts market research and arranges for meetings with administrators, sponsors, athletes, and volunteers of the Olympic Games as well as tours of venues and auxiliary facilities. She has attended ten Olympic Games and hundreds of other major sports events.

**Mark Readman** is Senior Lecturer and Head of Sports at Buckinghamshire Chilterns University College. A graduate of the master's program in recreation management at Purdue University, Indiana, he spent several years working for sports travel businesses in the United Kingdom before running a golf travel company. Readman has lectured and consulted in many aspects of sports management but specializes in sports development and golf studies. In addition, he started the first degree course in golf management, the success of which has led to similar courses in football, rugby, and cricket management.

**John Zauhar** has a doctorate in business administration and is Associate Director for the Sports Tourism International Council. His professional and academic interests lie in the sports tourism field, and he has had several publications in leisure, recreation, and tourism; historical perspectives in sports tourism; festival management; recreation and the law; and international winter tourism.

# Foreword

Sport and adventure tourism can be identified as a true sign of our times. Families, teams, and individuals are on the move. Motives differ: for some it is the competition; others seek interaction with like-minded travelers; and more are lured as spectators. For many, the experience of the travel itself is enough. In every case, however, money is spent. Such spending has a beneficial effect on local economies, helping to support perhaps millions of employees of companies serving travelers' needs. This book has been created to define this rapidly growing industry.

As noted, some of us travel to compete or to participate in adventure activities. For cities, destinations, airline companies, car rental agencies, hotels, restaurants, shops and stores, manufacturers of equipment, producers of clothing, and other peripheral businesses, our travel is their opportunity. Most of us do not think about it that way.

Here is an example: In the summer of 1955 my mother, father, brother, and I (and Fritz, the family dog) set out for Alaska from Cleveland, Ohio. We packed two tents and our gear in a station wagon. For six weeks we camped our way to Fairbanks, Anchorage, Valdez, and points in between. We did not think about participating in the sports travel market. However, as will be demonstrated herein, our activity (camping) was technically a "soft" sport tourism adventure. The trip itself turned out to be very much of a "hard" adventure, due to more than 4,000 miles of gravel road, some of which was totally washed away and needed to be bulldozed back into place during one two-day delay. These days, a trip like that could become an article in an outdoor adventure magazine!

There are many examples today of sport affecting industry. Is it not true that "soccer moms" helped to create the minivan market? How else to transport everyone to a weekend of games? What is the value of the minivan market to automobile manufacturers? Contemporary sport and adventure tourism has had an impact throughout the business world.

Our patterns of travel are important to all associated businesses, so much so that we now define sport and adventure travel itself as an industry. It has demonstrable economic importance and value throughout the world.

This book will prove invaluable to anyone wishing to understand the dynamics behind the explosion in sport and adventure tourism.

*Don Schumacher*
*Executive Director*
*National Association of Sports Commissions*
*President Don Schumacher and Associates, Inc.*
*Cincinnati, Ohio*

# Preface

Almost 700 million people traveled to a foreign country in 2000, spending an estimated US$476 billion. Research clearly shows that the idea of holidays for rest and relaxation has shifted to more health-related and quality-of-life experiences, including active and sports-oriented trips. In industrialized countries, sport tourism contributes between 1 and 2 percent to the gross domestic product (GDP), and the contribution of tourism as a whole is between 4 and 6 percent. Although it is difficult to measure the impact of sport and tourism patterns worldwide, growth rates for the sport tourism industry are estimated at about 10 percent per annum.

In previous decades, academics and practitioners have treated sport and tourism as separate spheres of activity, and integration of the two disciplines has been rare. In terms of popular participation and many aspects of practice, however, they are inextricably linked. These links have been strengthened in recent years due to several new influences and trends. These include the common contribution of sport and tourism to economic regeneration; the heightened sense of the benefits of exercise for health; and the increased media profile of international sport and sporting events. Major sporting events have become important tourist attractions, and events such as the Olympic Games can bring long lasting benefits to a host city in terms of infrastructure improvements and increased tourism. Likewise, tourism has served as an incubator for new sports disciplines such as volleyball and snowboarding which have developed into competitive events as they have grown in popularity.

Sport tourism—sometimes referred to as "sports tourism"—refers to travel away from home to play sport, watch sport, or to visit a sports attraction, and includes both competitive and noncompetitive activities. For the purposes of this book, it consists of two broad categories of products: sports participation travel (travel for the purpose of participating in sports, recreation, leisure, or fitness activities); and sports spectatorial travel (travel for the purpose of spectating sports, recreation, and leisure or fitness activities or events).

In the past few decades, sport and tourism professionals have realized the significant potential of sport tourism and are aggressively pursuing this market niche. To exploit sport tourism better, professionals must understand and appreciate the synergy of both the sport and tourism fields. For potential practitioners, degrees in sport tourism are now running at bachelor, master, and doctorate levels at colleges and universities in America, Canada, the United Kingdom, New Zealand, Australia, and Dubai, and certificate programs in sports tourism management are also available for practitioners worldwide.

The *Journal of Sport Tourism,* a quarterly publication, stimulates scholars, professionals, and academics to write and share sport tourism articles while providing further opportunities to develop the body of knowledge of the profession. Conferences dedicated to sport tourism have also started to appear. The Sports Tourism International Council initiated annual sport tourism conferences in 1993, and in February 2001, the World Tourism Organization hosted its first conference on the subject in Barcelona, Spain, attracting some 800 delegates.

Adventure tourism is increasingly recognized as a discipline in its own right. The adventure market is generally split into two categories: hard and soft. The first, sometimes called extreme, attracts "danger rangers," as it involves strenuous physical exertion with risk to life and limb. This includes activities such as rock climbing, heli-skiing, or white-water kayaking. The second, which includes activities such as snow-coach exploration of glaciers, aims at nonadrenaline addicts and families. In Canada alone, there are now forty colleges that run adventure programs for students. Conferences dedicated to adventure tourism are also increasingly common. In Canada, for example, Kamloops, British Columbia, has hosted two national conferences on the adventure tourism industry.

Despite this obvious increase in interest in the subject of sport and adventure tourism, surprisingly little literature exists that addresses the links between sport, adventure, and tourism, and it is hard to find data and quality case studies about individual sports tourism activities. We also have little understanding about the nature and extent of tourism generated by the staging and promotion of sporting events. This book, *Sport and Adventure Tourism,* is an attempt to fill this void. It is written by experts from around the world; hence, it has an international dimension that makes it unique.

The book begins with an introduction to sport and adventure tourism written by Lisa Delpy Neirotti from The George Washington University. The second chapter, contributed by John Zauhar of the Sports Tourism International Council, takes a fascinating and unique look at the history of sport tourism. Chapter 3 is written by Donald Getz from the University of Calgary and covers sport event tourism, perhaps the largest component of sport tourism in terms of tourism numbers and economic impact. In Chapter 4, Simon Hudson from the University of Calgary provides an in-depth analysis of winter sport tourism, and Chapter 5, written by Gayle Jennings of Central Queensland University, examines marine tourism. Chapter 6 is devoted to world golf tourism written by Mark Readman of Buckinghamshire University, England. Chapters 7 and 8 are dedicated to the rapidly growing area of adventure tourism. Paul Beedie of De Montfort University in the United Kingdom writes about the growth of adventure tourism, while Ross Cloutier from the University College of the Cariboo focuses on the business of adventure tourism. Chapter 9 describes the growing area of health and spa tourism, contributed by Michael Hall of Otago University, New Zealand. Chapter 10 is written by Joseph Kurtzman and John Zauhar of the Sports Tourism International Council, and explores the future by examining and analyzing the development of sport tourism in terms of virtual reality.

Nine chapters end with a list of references, some have related Web sites, and the book includes eight quality case studies. I hope readers will enjoy the book as much as I enjoyed collating it. I am sure it will not be the last book dedicated to this rapidly growing area of tourism, but I intend it to be the most readable.

# Acknowledgments

Obviously I am indebted to all the authors who contributed to making this such an interesting and state-of-the-art book. When I set out to write this book, I intended to find the world's top experts in each particular segment of sport and adventure tourism. Not a single author declined the offer to contribute, and it has been a pleasure to work with all of them.

I would also like to thank my wife Louise for her editorial assistance; Whistler Resort, and Marty von Neudegg from Canadian Mountain Holidays (CMH), for their help in writing the case studies for Chapters 4 and 8; and Patrick Thorne from Snow24, who helped me to ensure that my skiing statistics were up-to-date and accurate.

## Chapter 1

# An Introduction to Sport and Adventure Tourism

Lisa Delpy Neirotti

World tourism arrivals are projected to grow at 4.3 percent per year and to reach 1.6 billion by 2020. In this same period, worldwide tourist spending is expected to grow at 6.7 percent per year and to reach US $2 trillion (WTO, 2001). One of the fastest-growing areas contributing to these staggering statistics is sport tourism.

Although sport tourism is a relatively new concept in terms of contemporary vernacular, its scope of activity is far from a recent phenomenon. The notion of people traveling to participate and watch sport dates back to the ancient Olympic Games, and the practice of stimulating tourism through sport has existed for over a century. Within the past five years, however, sport and tourism professionals have begun to realize the significant potential of sport tourism and are aggressively pursuing this market niche.

This sparks the question of whether sport tourism is a new, recreated, or agglomerated field. For many tourism entities, a travel market focused entirely on participating or watching sport is a unique and exciting concept. For recreational managers, the opportunities and impacts related to noncompetitive sport participation have been recognized for years. Thus sport tourism is considered a redesigned marketing tool. In the sport industry, sport tourism is seen as a way to capitalize on the growth and interest in both noncompetitive and competitive sport by aligning forces with sport, recreation and tourism professionals, and organizations. For instance, the more people that participate at a recreational level, the more sport equipment they tend to purchase, the more likely they are to continue to participate at a competitive level, and their propensity to watch sport may also increase. Ultimately, all of these increases related to participating, competing, and watching sport impact the tourism industry in one way or another.

The purpose of this chapter is to identify and define the different facets of sport tourism and to illustrate how influential this market segment can be, not only for the tourism and sport industries but for local, regional, and national economies.

## *DEFINING SPORT TOURISM*

Broadly defined, sport tourism includes travel away from one's primary residence to participate in a sport activity for recreation or competition, travel to observe sport at the grassroots or elite level, and travel to visit a sport attraction such as a sports hall of fame or water park (Gibson, Attle, and Yiannakis,1997).

Sport, in itself, is defined in various ways and from different perspectives. For example, in North America, the terminology of sport is often narrowly associated with competitive play involving concepts of time, space, and formalized rules (Mullin, Hardy, and Sutton, 1993). Other definitions (Brooks, 1994; Goldstein, 1989; Zeigler, 1984; Chu, 1982), however, provide more comprehensive interpretations incorporating noncompetitive elements such as recreation and health. The popular international slogan "Sport for All" refers to one's personal engagement in any physical activity, be it passive, such as walking, or highly active, such as playing competitive basketball (Palm, 1991). The word *sport* is, in fact, a derivative of *disport,* which means to divert oneself. The word *sport* carries the original implication of people diverting their attention from the rigors and pressures of everyday life (Edwards, 1973). Although escape for diversion purposes may still be a motivation for a sport activity, sport today employs a far more engaging concept, encompassing both spectators and participants who seek fulfillment of a wide variety of human needs and wants.

Tourism, like sport, lacks a common definition. International organizations, such as the World Tourism Organization (WTO), the World Travel and Tourism Council (WTTC), and the Organization of Cooperation and Development (OECD), have long labored over the task of developing both supply-and-demand–side definitions of tourism. From a demand side, tourists are generally defined according to one or more of the following categories: purpose of trip, time away from home, distance traveled, mode of travel, or geography (domestic, regional, or international travel). From a supply side, both the WTTC and WTO have developed systems for categorizing businesses and organizations depending on whether their revenues are totally or partially derived from tourist spending. Central to all discussions, though, is the acknowledgment that tourism represents an amalgamation of services and goods for a human activity that takes place beyond a specific distance from one's home or place of permanent residence (Heath and Wall, 1992; Inskeep, 1991; Laverty, 1989; Mill, Alstar, and Morrison, 1985; Theobold,1984; Weiler and Hall, 1992).

Due to its universal appeal (McPherson and Curtis, 1989), sport is regarded as the world's largest social phenomenon. Similarly, tourism has been suggested by the WTO, the WTTC (1996), other research organizations, and scholars to be the largest economic activity in the world. The research problem is not which is larger, bigger or greater, but rather to gauge the extent to which they interact and facilitate each other's growth and dimension.

Within the context of this book, sport tourism is presented as a subset of overall tourism, incorporating several tourism subcategories. The contributing categories include adventure tourism, health tourism, nature tourism, spectator tourism, competitive tourism, recreational or leisure tourism, educational tourism, and business tourism.

## *SPORT TOURISM: THE SUPPLY SIDE*

To better understand the supply-side development of sport tourism Kurtzman and Zauhar (1997) have identified five major areas: attractions, resorts, cruises, tours, and events. Following is a discussion of each of these areas.

### *Attractions*

Sport tourism attractions are destinations that provide the tourist with things to see and do related to sport. Attractions can be natural (parks, mountains, wildlife) or human-made (museums, stadiums, stores). General characteristics represented in this core area of sport tourism include visitations to: (a) state-of-the-art sport facilities and/or unique sports facilities that generally house sports events, such as stadiums, arenas, and domes; (b) sport museums and hall/walls of fame dedicated to sport heritage and to honoring sport heroes and leaders; (c) sport theme parks including water parks, summer ski jumps, bungee jumping; (d) hiking trails developed for exploring nature; and (e) sport retail stores.

Aside from the attraction of Broadway shows and shopping on Madison Avenue, over 50,000 New York City visitors tour Madison Square Garden (Goldwater, 1997). Likewise, the MCI Center in Washington, DC, is positioned as a year-round tourist destination complete with 100,000 square feet of adjoining shopping, entertainment, and dining facilities, a National Sport Gallery, and the Sportcasters Hall of Fame and Museum (Kaetzel, 1997).

There are currently 135 members of the International Association of Sports Museums and Halls of Fame ranging from local museums such as the San Diego Hall of Champions Sports Museum to the International Olympic Museum, Library, and Study Center. The National Baseball Hall of Fame and Museum in Cooperstown, New York, the International Hockey Hall of Fame and Museum in Toronto, Canada, and the Japanese Baseball Hall of Fame and Museum in Tokyo, Japan, attract the most visitors—each reporting over 300,000 per year (Cober, 1997).

Although retail stores are not frequently considered sport tourism attractions, the Bass Pro Shop in Springfield, Missouri, is recognized as the number one tourist attraction in Missouri, accounting for 3.5 million visitors per year. This outdoor sport retail outlet measures 350,000 square feet. Visitors travel from across the globe to explore the vast array of sporting goods as well as a thirty-four-feet high waterfall and four massive aquariums, the largest being 30,000 gallons complete with bass and other freshwater fish (Bass Pro Shop, 2002).

## Resorts

Sport tourism resorts represent well-planned and integrated resort complexes with sports or health as their primary focus and marketing strategy. In many situations, these vacation centers have high standard facilities and services available to the sport tourist. This is one of the main industries for small countries such as Belize.

The sport tourism resort category includes amenity and destination spas (Spivak, 1997); golf and tennis resorts; water and snow sport resorts (Packer, 1997); and nature retreats with a focus on outdoor adventure and exploration. Generally speaking, these resorts are furnished with state-of-the-art sport equipment and facilities and offer visitors various levels of activity opportunities and educational programs lead by instructors with a great deal of expertise and personal visibility. These resorts do vary, however, extending from high level international standards specializing in specific and highly developed skills to campground services focusing on recreational sporting activities.

Meeting and convention planners have also found sport tourism resorts to be ideal locations. Not only are these resorts attractive to attendees (meeting attendance becomes a sort of reward) but the environment also serves a purpose. For many groups, sport activities have become a very important component of the meeting agenda as they help build camaraderie and team spirit, and offer excellent networking opportunities. Others believe that the relaxed atmosphere of a resort keeps delegates from getting bogged down or frustrated with the meeting and even allows for more open thinking—bad news or change tends to be accepted more readily. "People come here for a meeting and they walk away feeling rejuvenated," exclaims Andrea Cook, Human Development Manager at Chateau Elan Winery and Resort in Raselton, Georgia (Farris, 1997, p. 13).

The variety of sports offered at a resort also reduces the stress of a meeting planner in terms of planning free-time activities or events for accompanying family members. In fact, some resorts such as the Marriott's Griffin Gate Resort in Lexington, Kentucky, employ an entire recreational department responsible for customizing sports-based events for meetings of all types. Other resorts such as Saddlebrook Resort in Tampa, Florida, have built extravagant sport facilities. The Saddlebrook Sports Village is centered around a 3,300 square-foot, glass-enclosed state-of-the-art fitness center, around which there are soccer and softball fields, one sand and two grass volleyball courts, a regulation-size basketball court, a boccie ball court, and an open-air pavilion that can be used for classes and group activities (Farris, 1997).

An extension of the sport resort category is sport camps. The American Camping Association estimates that there are more than 8,500 day and resident camps in the United States which serve a total of 6 million campers per year. In terms of economic impact, approximately 65 to 70 percent of campers remain in residence and over 500,000 adults are employed by summer camps alone (Coutellier, 1997).

Currently there are over 2,800 youth sport camps and 2,000 adult camps listed on the Kids Camps and Grown Up Camps World Wide Web sites (<http://www.kidcamps.com> and <http://www.grownup camps.com>). These Web sites as well as others (<http://www.peter-sons.com>, and <http://www.us-sportscamps.com>) provide an excellent overview of the various types of sport camps available. In the summer of 2002, a total of 45,000 campers registered for 450 Nike Junior sport camps. The greatest increase in interest was for field hockey camps. Nike also sponsored twenty-six adult tennis camps, eight adult golf camps, and thirty family golf camps (Nike Sport Camps, 2002).

Sport camps are hosted at resorts, universities, and in the wilderness, and offer organized, intensive training sessions in just about every sport imaginable. There are camps for traditional sports such as baseball, basketball, golf, soccer, tennis, volleyball, figure skating, swimming, gymnastics, hockey, sailing, as well as more adventurous camps that lead participants down white-water rapids, over rugged canyons, or off steep cliffs (hiking, biking, paddling, horseback riding, or climbing). There are also multisport camps such as the Nike sports camps in the United States. Although sport camps are commonly considered an activity for youth, in recent years the number of family and adult camps has been increasing. Fantasy sport camps have been especially successful in capturing the adult market.

Fantasy sport camps provide an opportunity for adults to train with their favorite sport stars, with the coach of a popular team, and/or at a famous sport locale. For example, Major League Baseball runs a one-week camp in Huntington Valley, Pennsylvania, at which participants can play alongside famous players (Schlossberg, 1996). The price tag for the week: $4,500. Upper Deck, a corporation that produces baseball cards, ran a weekend camp at the Iowa site of the film *Field of Dreams*. Participants paid $2,400 for the weekend. The Los Angeles Dodgers Baseball Fantasy Camp, held at their 450-acre Dodgertown Complex in Vero Beach, Florida, includes six nights lodging, five days of instruction, three meals a day, use of all recreational facilities including twenty-seven holes of championship golf at Dodgertown's two golf courses, a welcome cocktail party, and an instructors versus campers finale game under the lights in Holman Stadium, all for $3,995. For sample listing of baseball fantasy camps visit <http://www.HiHard1.com>.

## Cruises

The sport tourism cruise category incorporates all boat-related trips that have sports or sporting activities as their principal market strategy. Many ships built today resemble hotels and resorts and have unique sports installations. They also utilize guest sports celebrities as a marketing tool. To further satisfy the sport tourist, cruise ships often arrange special transportation to provide guests opportunities for golf, tennis, snorkeling, waterskiing, etc., in unique and varied water environments. Other planned activities include provision of on-board sport competitions and/or modified games (e.g., a golf driving range on deck), and special presentations or clinics from invited sport celebrities. Cruise-and-drive programs also exist, whereby tourists board private vehicles and are taken to desired sports destinations. Private yachts that sail directly to the sport destination of your choice can also be chartered. The use of watercraft for sporting activities (e.g., recreational and competitive sailing, jet skiing) is another important dimension in this category.

## Tours

Sport tourism tours bring visitors to their favorite sport event, facility, or destination throughout the world. These tours may be self-guided or organized depending upon access, location, and nature of the activity. For example, many ski tour packages provide air travel, accommodation, local transportation, and ski lift tickets with no special guide or amenities. In contrast, some companies specialize in travel packages that fly fans to an away game, put them up in a hotel for a few nights, provide tickets to the contest, arrange for a cocktail party and pregame briefing with media, schedule a postgame reception with players and coaches, and then return fans safely home. This type of tour is especially appealing to sport aficionados who want to follow their team on the road, take in a major event such as the Super Bowl or Indianapolis 500, and for those who dream of walking the fairways of Augusta National during the Masters golf tournament.

Sport tours may include visitations to sport museums and stadiums as well as events or games in multiple locations lasting anywhere from one to two weeks. Some sport tour companies cater to common interest groups while others specialize in corporate incentive programs, educational tours to a specific conference or location, or outdoor adventure challenges. Some of the more established sport tour companies include Roadtrips, Sports Travel and Tours, Benchwarmer Sports, Broach Tours, and Golden World Travel. Since most of these companies are privately held, business statistics are difficult to gather. However, one company stated that they serve over 5,000 customers and average $2.5 million dollars in revenue per year (Wilson, 1997).

Also included in this category are companies that serve youth teams and professional sports teams, arranging for all their travel and accommodation needs. On average, parents of an elite youth sports participant spend between $1,500 to $5,000 per year on related sport travel (Delpy, 1997b). The National Collegiate Athletic Association (NCAA) spends $33.4 million on travel per year ($29.3 million related to sport championships and $4.1 million for business purposes) (Renfro, 1997). Each major league baseball team spends approximately $2 million on travel per year (Smith, 1997).

### Events

The sport tourism event category refers to those sports activities that attract a sizable number of visiting participants and/or spectators. Visitor types vary depending on the sport event, and some are obviously more spectator driven than others (e.g., Olympic Games versus the National Amateur Shuffleboard Championship). Furthermore, these sport tourism events have the potential to attract nonresident media and technical personnel such as coaches and other sports officials. High-profile sport events such as the Super Bowl, Olympic Games, or World Cup are often referred to in the literature as tourism hallmark events (Ritchie, 1984) and mega events (Getz, 1991).

In some instances, such as the Hong Kong Dragon Boat Festival, sports tourism events may have a cultural, religious, or even ritual association (Sofield and Sivan, 1994). According to professor Robert Rinehart, the Super Bowl is "a modern ritual of pilgrimage in which people attend to reunite with their friends and experience the event in concert with others of similar interest" (Rinehart, 1992). Furthermore, Rinehart's study of the 1992 Super Bowl in Minneapolis, Minnesota, found that individuals attended the game "to be seen, to enjoy the hoopla, to support the team, and to continue a ritual." For many, the sport event experience is a recurring, life-shaping experience.

As far as economic impact, the sport event category of sport tourism receives the most notoriety as it is increasingly common for organizers to calculate the amount of new dollars or hotel room nights an event generates. According to Martha Mitchell of the Rockford Convention and Visitor's Bureau in Illinois, "Sports is the largest growth area as far as hotel room nights for Rockford. In 1987, 3,600 room nights were attributed to sporting events and by 1994 there were 49,287. We've only reached the tip of the iceberg. Every day we uncover new potential" (Sheahan, 1995, p. 5). Although there are numerous examples of the economic impact of various sport events (as provided in Table 1.1), a lack of consistent methodology makes many of these figures suspect.

Events designed to attract large numbers of spectators can bring thousands, even millions, of dollars into a local economy (Mules and Faulkner, 1996). However, smaller participatory events, such as tournaments or marathons, can also be advantageous, particularly for smaller cities or less populated regions. Since participatory events often make use of existing infrastructure and volunteer labor, they can be relatively inexpensive to host, thereby yielding high benefit-to-cost ratios (Allen, 1993). Furthermore, participatory sport events have been shown to be an effective way to attract new visitors and to generate return visits. This is because participatory sport events, similar to sport resorts, target consumers who seek opportunities to share their holidays with others who share an interest in a particular sport (Green and Chalip, 1998).

In terms of scope, an analysis of twenty-two tourism event schedules from seven world geographic regions indicated that sports tourism activities in 1994 represented 34 percent of all scheduled tourism events. This same study also showed that 42 percent of scheduled event days were sports tourism related (Research Unit, Sports Tourism International Council, 1994). Soar International, a Vancouver-based firm specializing in sport information and event management, estimated that there are more than 150,000 sport events in Canada every year (Gaudreault, 1997). The National Association of Sport Commissions (NASC) in the United States has over 200 cities or regions

TABLE 1.1. Economic Impact of Sport Events

| Event | Impact ($) | No. Visitors (participants/ spectators) | Misc. Info |
|---|---|---|---|
| Natl. Girls 12/Under Soccer | 750,000 | 3,500 | — |
| YMCA Age Group Swim | 1.0+ million | 1,200 | 1,000 room nights |
| Junior Natl. Women's Volleyball | 4.9 million | 6,240 (249 teams) | 3 days, 4,462 room nights |
| FL State HS Girls' Basketball | 1.0 million | — | 4 days |
| NY State HS Swim | 343,200 | 400 | 475 room nights |
| Atlantic 10 Swim | 772,200 | 900 | 750 room nights |
| Natl. Jr. Olympic Wrestling | 1.0 million | 8,000 (2,000/6,000) | 4 days |
| Natl. Indoor Champ. Archery | 400,000 | 2,500 (700/1,800) | 3 days |
| ASA Women's Champ. Slow Pitch | 450,000 | 3,800 (300/3,500) | 3 days |
| Super Series Skeet and Trap Shooting | — | 400 | Avg. spent/person $500 |
| Sr. World Series Softball | 1.8 million | — | 4,907 rooms, minimum 1 night |
| U.S. Natl. Champ. Croquet | 35,000 | 300 (50/250) | 3 days |
| U.S. Fed. Natl. Champ. Cycling | 400,000 | 2,700 (700/2,000) | 4 days |
| U.S. Natl. Champ. Volleyball | 800,000 | 4,000 (1,200/2,800) | 3 days |
| U.S. Classic Field Hockey | 1.65 million | 11,200 (1,200/10,000) | 3 days |
| U.S. Champ. Figure Skating | 3.0 million | 20,020 (20/20,000) | 4 days |
| U.S. Champ. Gymnastics | 5.0 million | 8,000 | 5 days |
| U.S. Nationals Swim | 800,000 | 1,000 | 2,200 room nights |

| Event | Impact ($) | No. Visitors (participants/ spectators) | Misc. Info |
|---|---|---|---|
| U.S. Olympic Trials Boxing | 1.2 million | 3,150 (150/3,000) | 7 days |
| U.S. Champ. Shuffleboard | 25,000 | 242 (142/100) | — |
| National Masters Swim | 640,000 | 800 | 1,200 room nights |
| National Masters Track and Field | — | 1,200 | — |
| Nike World Masters Games | 100 million | 55-75,000 (25K/30-50K) | 100 countries |
| IHRA Series Drag Racing | — | 600 teams | 4 days |
| CA Rodeo | 6.1 million | 53,172 | 100 percent hotel occupancy |
| Arizona Golf | 1.0 billion | — | — |
| FL Spring Training Baseball | 350 billion | 1.8 million | — |
| Paintball World Cup Tournament | — | 1,500+ | ESPN |
| Police Olympic Games | 7-10 million | 10,800 (5,400/5,400) | 6 days |
| German Sport Holiday | 5.1 million DM (3.3 million U.S.) | — | 30 percent domestic |
| U.S. Olympic Congress | 3.2 million | 1,400 | — |

*Note:* Data were collected from a number of different sources. Methodologies vary greatly.

as members and maintains a database of various sport events complete with information on the length of events, number of hotel/motel room nights for the last two events, number of participants, facility specifications, and bid application information such as decision schedule, contact person, and rotation pattern if applicable. The purpose of the NASC is to promote information sharing and cooperation among America's public and private sector sports commissions. In addition to the database, NASC organizes an annual convention and publishes a newsletter. For many cities, sport is seen as a new niche market, and they receive encouragement to obtain major sport events, particularly from hotels, as they see a major impact from such events on their off-season and weekend business.

An excellent example of how a city, or in this case a country, can maximize exposure through a sport event is in the case of Sydney, Australia, and its hosting of the 2000 Summer Olympic Games. Shortly after Sydney was awarded the right to host the 2000 Summer Games, the Australian Tourist Commission (ATC) prepared the Olympic Games tourism strategy and worked tirelessly to ensure that every possible opportunity was maximized. Over 1,000 individual projects were implemented, beginning in 1994, that resulted in tremendous returns for Australian tourism, the ATC, and Australia as a whole. A few of these programs and benefits include:

1. The ATC's media relations program included hosting more than 5,000 international journalists and generated an additional US$2.1 billion in publicity for Australia between 1997 and 2000.
2. The ATC's partnerships with major Olympic sponsors, such as Visa, McDonalds, Kodak, and Coca-Cola generated an additional US$170 million in publicity for Australia.
3. An additional $A96.3 million of new business was generated in 2001 by the ATC's "New Century. New World. Australia 2001" campaign to capture meetings, incentive, convention, and exhibition (MICE) business for Australia as a result of hosting the Summer Games. In terms of hosting meetings, Australia moved from seventh in 1999 with a 3.8 percent market share to fourth in 2000 with a 5.3 percent share, pushing down France and Italy. In the three months following the Games, Sydney attracted eleven events, double the number of events won in the same period the previous year, and the Sydney Convention and Visitor's Bureau 2000/2001 calendar of meetings and events showed a 10 percent growth in number of events over the previous year.
4. Research indicates that 88 percent of the 110,000 international visitors who came to Australia for the Olympic Games are likely to return to Sydney as tourists. In addition, research in the United States after the Games reveals that the event has increased the likelihood of Americans spending their next holiday in Australia. Approximately 50 percent of Americans surveyed said media coverage during the Games had increased their inter-

est in vacationing in Australia. During the Games there was a 600 percent increase in traffic to the ATC's Web site. In December 2000, tourism was up 23 percent over 1999, with a record 565,000 international visitors. This was the highest figure ever for any month.

Overall, it is estimated that the Games will have injected $A6.1 billion into the Australian economy and will be responsible for attracting an additional 1.7 million visitors to the country between 1997 and 2004. The ATC recognizes, however, that there is a twelve-month window of opportunity to capitalize on the Games and has implemented an extensive post-Games strategy focused on converting the enormous interest in Australia into visitor arrivals.

## A PROFILE OF THE SPORT TOURISM INDUSTRY

Based on the readership of *SportsTravel Magazine,* Schneider Publishing estimates that sports-related travel and tourism accounts for at least $118.3 billion in the United States alone. The breakdown includes:

- Team and participant travel at $6.1 billion
- Corporate incentive travel at $2.1 billion
- Family and spectator travel at $47.3 billion
- Adventure and fantasy travel at $62.8 billion

Furthermore, the readers of *SportsTravel* book 12.1 million sports-related hotel room nights annually, with each of its reader's organizations spending an average of $852,037 on travel each year. Nearly all subscribers (99 percent) expect their volume of travel to either stay the same or increase during the next year (Schneider Publishing, 1999).

In 1999, Travel Industries Association of America (TIA) profiled travelers who attend sport events and found that two-fifths (38 percent) of U.S. adults are sports event travelers. This equates to 75.3 million U.S. adults who attended an organized sports event, competition, or tournament in the past five years as either a spectator or participant while on a trip of fifty miles or more, one way, away from home. Men outnumbered women as sport event travelers, but both sexes expressed similar interest in baseball, football, basketball, and auto/truck racing, which were reported as the preferred sports events attended during travel. Professional and amateur sport events were attended equally while traveling. High school and college sports were the most popular among amateur events. Attending a sport event was the primary purpose of 76 percent of sports event travelers, with 84 percent traveling to watch a particular sport. In fact, 25 percent of all sport event travelers attended events to watch their children or grand-children participate. When looking at all U.S. resident trips in 1997, 6 percent included sports events as a trip activity, ranking tenth among trip activities (shopping, participating in outdoor activities, and visiting historical places are the top three activities; see Figure 1.1). Sports event travelers are more likely than other American travelers to be younger, have children, and be employed full-time. They are also more likely than other U.S. travelers to travel during the fall. In general, sport event travelers stay in hotels, motels, or bed-and-breakfast inns significantly more than travelers overall, but are more likely to take shorter trips of two to three days. More than half (55 percent) of all sports event travelers spend $250 or less on their trip, which is similar to all U.S. travelers who average $414 per trip.

## *ADVENTURE TOURISM*

The Adventure Travel Society reports that adventure tourism is growing at an annual rate of 10 to 15 percent with most of this growth occurring in existing markets such as Costa Rica, parts of Mexico, and Peru. Most adventure travelers are North Americans, but an in-creasing number are Japanese, Thai, and Western European. Inde-pendent travelers are a significant and growing segment of adventure travelers, but not much analysis is available as of yet. In addition, the number of seniors and women who are adventure travelers continues to increase. In fact, more women than men went sailing and back-packing in 1998 (Adventure Travel Society, 2000).

Based on a study conducted by TIA (1998), one half of Americans said they were adventure travelers (98 million out of 197.7 million to-tal U.S. adults) with 46 percent stating that they had participated in soft adventure activities, and 16 percent in hard adventure activities

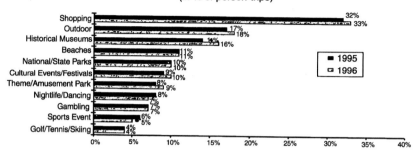

FIGURE 1.1. Activities in which U.S. resident travelers participated, 1995-1996 (in percentage of person-trips).

during trips in the last five years. Figures 1.2 and 1.3 identify the most popular hard and soft activities.

Hard adventure travelers are more likely to be men than soft adventure travelers (60 percent of hard adventurers versus 51 percent of soft adventurers); single (40 percent versus 26 percent); young, eighteen to twenty-four years old (24 percent versus 18 percent); college educated (82 percent versus 73 percent); with higher household incomes of $75,000 per year or more (25 percent versus 19 percent).

Results also showed that certain groups of people shared common interests. Women tended to participate in horseback riding and sailing more than men. Generation Xers participated in waterskiing more than any other group, while baby boomers hiked more, and mature persons identified most with bird/animal watching and photo safaris.

Furthermore, the 1998 TIA report examined trip profiles of adventure travelers and found that both hard and soft adventurers averaged three activity vacations in the past five years, but hard adventure travelers tended to focus on one activity per trip while soft adventure travelers participated in multiple activities during their trip.

In addition, hard adventurers traveled more frequently with friends and acquaintances (48 percent hard adventurers versus 30 percent soft) or alone (4 percent versus 2 percent), compared to soft adventurers who traveled more often with spouses (60 percent soft versus 42 percent hard) and children or grandchildren (41 percent versus 18 percent). Hard adventurers also spend more than soft adventurers,

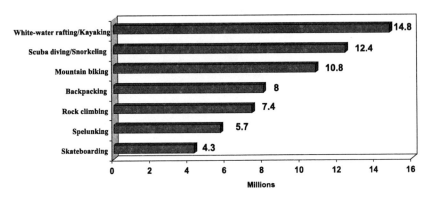

FIGURE 1.2. Hard adventure activities on trips in last five years (*Source:* Travel Industry Association of America, Inc., 1998).

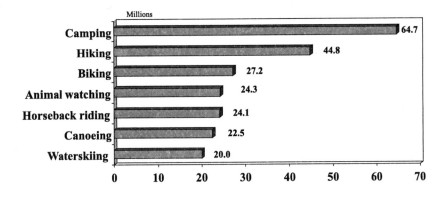

FIGURE 1.3. Soft adventure activities on trips in last five years (*Source:* Travel Industry of America, Inc., 1998).

with the average cost of a trip being $1,275 versus $820. Six percent of hard adventurers spend $5,000 or more compared to 2 percent of soft adventurers. Almost twice as many hard adventure vacations cost $1,000 or more (30 percent versus 17 percent) while more soft vacations cost less than $250 (42 percent versus 31 percent).

As far as where adventure travelers live within the United States, 57 percent reside in western states. Men, Generation Xers, and Westerners are more likely to call themselves adventure fanatics. In terms of cross recreators, it appears that off-road bicyclists participate in more adventure activities (11.6 activities out of 35 possible activities) compared to other groups. Wilderness campers, canoe/kayakers, and skiers also participate in a high number of activities (11.3, 10.8, 10.5 out of 35 activities respectively).

When making decisions to travel, 31 percent of those on short, one to two night trips within a week of traveling, compared to 9 percent of those on longer trips. In addition, about one quarter (24 percent) of destination visitors made reservations directly with their lodging facility while 12 percent used a central reservations number and 9 percent consulted with a travel agent or tour operator. The majority of spectators who travel to mega sport events such as the Olympic Games also make decisions relatively close to the event (68 percent decide one year or less). Furthermore, three primary motivations influence adult skiers' and boarders' choice of destination, which include friends (34 percent); ease of getting to resort (25 percent); and previous experience (31 percent). The Internet has also soared as a source of information about ski resorts. Ninety-two percent of active skiers and riders indicate that they have access to the Internet, and 59 percent of all downhillers indicate that they accessed the Web site of the resort they were visiting prior to their trips (Leisure Trends Group, 2000).

The most common motivators for outdoor recreation are fun, relaxation/getaway, health and exercise, family togetherness, stress reduction, experience nature/environment, and the thrill/challenge of learning. The most common barriers to outdoor recreation are time, lack of interest, money, and lack of instructional programs at recreational areas (Recreation Roundtable, 1995).

## THE FUTURE OF SPORT TOURISM

Based on the description of the five supply-side categories of sport tourism (resorts, cruises, attractions, tours, and events) one can see the scope and diversity of this burgeoning field. A study of North American convention tourism bureaus observed that sport accounted for 25 percent of all tourism receipts (Research Unit, Sports Tourism International Council, 1994). In addition, the Sports Tourism Index

(STIX) calculated that the direct contribution of sports tourism activities to overall tourism was 32 percent (Research Unit, Sports Tourism International Council, 1997). Considering that sport tourism activities can take place in urban and nonurban settings, indoors or outdoors, and in all types of climatic conditions and seasons, the opportunity for growth appears unlimited. Furthermore, the array of sport tourism activities appeals to a variety of tourists, from the traditional to the high adventure traveler. In addition, interest in sport activities is on the rise, as is money spent on such activities. As reported in the *Recreation Executive Report,* as leisure time becomes more scarce, spending on recreation increases in order to make the most of available time (Jensen, 1997b). Currently, recreational expenditures in the United States exceed $350 billion annually with a growth rate of 8 to 10 percent per year (Beresford et al., 1995). Dive travel alone "accounts for nearly $2 billion a year, comprising 80 percent of the total dive market," states Laurie Wilson, a business development specialist with expertise in dive travel marketing (Levine, 1996, p. 15). This figure is reasonable considering that diving is a year-round sport and that the average diver travels at least three times a year.

The effect of Title IX, Education Amendments of 1972 (a federal law in the United States that prohibits sex discrimination in any educational program or activity at any educational institution that is a recipient of federal funds), is finally apparent with more women participating in sport activities (Women's Sport Foundation, 1997). As examples, the number of women in sport hunting has doubled in ten years; the growth of women participating in shooting sports, such as targets, clays, and skeet, has grown at a rate of 15 to 20 percent a year (Jensen, 1997b); in golf, women account for 40 percent of new golfers each year (National Golf Foundation, 1997); and the number of women entering yacht races is rapidly increasing—in the Whitbread yacht race alone there are two all-women crews among forty-one teams (Jensen, 1997b).

As the population ages, the amount of leisure time available increases. Although a negative relationship continues to exist between participation in sport and age, research is indicating an upward trend toward greater physical activity among seniors. Currently, 10 percent of outdoor or adventure travelers are sixty-five years or older (U.S. Travel Data Center, 1994), indicating that the senior market is wide open and ready for sport tourism.

Another emerging population segment is the disabled population of which there are an estimated 49 million Americans (Jensen, 1997a). The 1990 Americans with Disabilities Act (ADA) has allowed more disabled individuals to lead physically active lifestyles, and as such they take part in a variety of activities and events. Facilities and event organizers, however, must strive to accommodate any special needs of this population segment.

Sport-related meetings and trade shows should also not be overlooked. There are over 300 single and multisport organizations in the United States alone, each supporting at least one annual membership, coaching, or executive meeting (*Sport Market Place Directory*, 2002). For example, the NCAA annual membership convention registers over 2,000 delegates for four days (Renfro, 1997). Academic courses and programs geared toward preparing sport tourism professionals are also growing. Based on one study, sport tourism modules, courses, certificates, and degrees are offered in the United States, Belgium, Canada, the United Kingdom, Australia, and South Korea. Programs have also been instituted in France, Germany, and a number of other countries. These programs are offered in various academic departments including physical education, recreation, sports management, tourism, hospitality, and leisure (Swart, 2000).

Overall, sport tourism is viewed as a strong market by organizations such as the Travel Industry Association (TIA), Washington, DC, which reports an increase in the time travelers will spend outdoors (1999). During the summer of 1997, 75 percent of travelers were expected to visit a beach or lake, and 45 percent (up from 40 percent in 1996) planned to camp, hike, or climb, while 38 percent were expected to fish (Jensen, 1997a). In addition, of the 100 million American adults who have not taken an adventure trip in the past five years, 28 percent indicate that they are very or somewhat likely to do so in the next five years. The WTO also recognizes the importance of sport tourism and in March 2001 teamed with the International Olympic Committee to host a conference on the subject. Further proof of the growing interest in sport tourism is the growth of TEAMS: Travel, Events, and Management in Sports conferences and trade shows. In 1997, The George Washington University organized the first conference, which approximately 150 people attended. In 2001, the number of attendees grew to over 500 with the assistance of

*SportsTravel Magazine,* which partnered with the university to stage the event.

To better exploit sport tourism, professionals must understand and appreciate the synergy of both fields, sport and tourism, as they approach the next decade. As an example, travel agents will need to be professionally grounded in sport tourism offerings and learn as much as possible about their customers. For dive travel, Wilson suggests that travel agents understand the nuances of the field, ask questions, and direct clients to the right products (quoted in Levine, 1996, p. 17). She recommends agents inquire of prospective dive clients:

1. Are you certified or do you want to be?
2. What types of dive vacations do you like?
3. What time of year do you like to travel and for how long?
4. Are you traveling with a nondiver or child who is too young to dive?
5. What nondiving activities do you like?
6. Do you have your own dive equipment or do you need to rent?
7. What is your budget?

Wilson also recommends that travel agents form an alliance with a local dive shop or dive travel specialist who can serve as an outside consultant.

Figure 1.4 helps to illustrate the integral elements of sport tourism. To begin work in sport tourism, it is necessary to recognize its different categories as well as those that are either directly or indirectly a part of sport tourism. All those who have a stake in the outcome of a sport tourism development campaign should also be identified and involved.

In terms of development, basic planning should include a facility audit to determine the feasibility of pursuing the various opportunities. This would include a list of existing and required infrastructure. The benefits associated with each sport tourism category should also be defined and prioritized. Along with facility restrictions, goals and priorities should be established to help determine the type of sport tourism endeavors to pursue (e.g., high-profile events may create more community goodwill and media attention than net economic impact). Next, gatekeepers need to be identified, as these individuals or groups are key to attracting sport tourists and events to any area. At

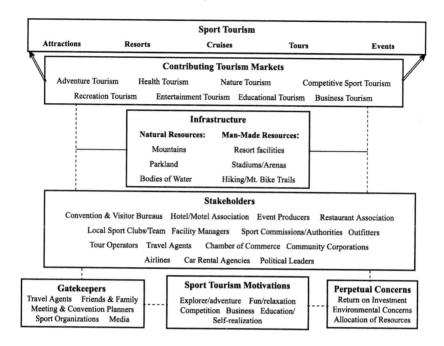

FIGURE 1.4. A dynamic model for sport tourism.

the same time, the needs and interests of end users or sport tourists must be considered in order to market and package sport tourism activities appropriately. Finally, larger issues should be continually addressed to maintain the positive benefits and growth of sport tourism.

Figure 1.4 provides a dynamic model for sport tourism providers to better understand, evaluate, and maximize their fit within the entire tourism spectrum.

## *SUMMARY*

Sport tourism is a growing segment of the tourism industry and includes travel to play sport, travel to watch sport, and travel to sport attractions. The definition and scope of sport tourism is not exact, and priorities should be established as many tourism sectors contribute to this market. Studies conducted by TIA have profiled the sport event and adventure traveler while other organizations such as the Adventure Travel Society and the Recreation Roundtable continue to collect data on their constituency groups. As the sport tourism industry continues to grow and be recognized, more academic programs will develop and add to the body of knowledge and professionalism of this important tourism sector.

# REFERENCES

Adventure Travel Society (2000). <http://www.adventuretravel.com>.

Allen, L.R. (1993). The Economic Impact of Sport and Physical Education. Paper presented at the Conference on American Sport Policy for the 21st Century, New Orleans, Louisiana.

Bass Pro Shop (2002). Press Release.

Beresford, L., Chun, J., Page, H., and Phillips, D. (1995). Tred Track. *Entrepreneur,* December: 110-111.

Bregman, K. (1997). Co-Owner KidsCamps. Personal communication, August 13.

Brooks, C.M. (1994). *Sports Marketing: Competitive Business Strategies for Sports.* Englewood Cliffs, New Jersey: Prentice-Hall.

Chu, D. (1982). *Dimensions of Sports Studies.* New York: John Wiley and Sons.

Cober, T. (1997). Executive Director, International Association of Sport Museums and Halls of Fame. Personal communication, August 12.

Connor, M. (1997). American Dragon Boat Association, Burlington, IA. Personal communication, August 18.

Coutellier, C. (1997). Director of Professional Development, American Camping Association. Personal communication, August 13.

Delpy, L. (1997a). *A Profile of the 1996 Summer Olympic Games Spectator.* Paper presented at the 12th Annual North American Society for Sport Management Conference. San Antonio, Texas.

Delpy, L (1997b). Unpublished research. George Washington University.

Edwards, H. (1973). *Definitions and Clarifications in Sociology of Sport.* Dorsey, CA: Homewood.

Farris, A. (1997). Sports and Resorts: A Winning Meeting Combination. *Convention South,* 13(10): 1-20.

Gaudreault, G. (Ed.) (1997). *Canada Communique,* Newsletter. Summer, Ottawa, Ontario.

Getz, D. (1991). *Festivals, Special Events, and Tourism.* New York: Van Nostrand.

Gibson, H., Attle, S., and Yiannakis, A. (1997). Segmenting the Active Sport Tourist Market: A Life Span Perspective. *Journal of Vacation Marketing,* 4(1): 52-64.

Goldstein, J.H. (1989). *Sports, Games, and Play.* Hillsdale, New Jersey: Lawrence Erlbaum.

Goldwater, B. (1997). Vice-President, Facilities Presentation, Madison Square Garden, New York. Personal communication, August 14.

Green, B.C. and Chalip, L. (1998). Sport tourism as the celebration of subculture. *Annals of Tourism Research,* 25: 275-291.

Heath, E. and Wall, G. (1992). *Marketing Tourism Destination.* New York.

Howard, D.R. and Crompton, J.L. (1995). *Financing Sport.* Morgantown, WV: Fitness Information Technology.

Inskeep, E. (1991). *Tourism Planning: An Integrated and Sustainable Development Approach.* New York: Van Nostrand.

James, C. (1995). Survey of Barbados: Sporting Holidays. *Financial Times,* London Edition, April 26, p. 39.

Jensen, M. (Ed.). (1997a). Quoted in *Leisure Industry Report* (Newsletter), 17(3), Washington, DC.

Jensen, M. (Ed.). (1997b). Quoted in *Recreation Executive Report* (Newsletter), 27(3), Washington, DC.

Kaetzel, D. (1997). Managing Director/Marketing Centre Group, Maryland. Personal communication, August 13.

Kanner, B. (1995). Exotic Locations Fail to Send Many Vacationers. *Advertising Age,* 66(20): 32.

Kurtzman, J. and Zauhar, J. (1997). A Wave in Time—The Sports Tourism Phenomena. *Journal of Sports Tourism,* 4(2): 10-17.

Laverty, P. (1989). *Travel and Tourism.* Suffolk: Elm Publications.

Leisure Trends Group (2000). National Skier/Boarder Opinion Survey, 1999-2000. Boulder, CO: Leisure Trends Group.

Levine, J. (1996). If You Want to Sell Dive Travel, Learn to Do It Well. *Travel Agent Dive Vacations Supplement,* May 27, pp. 15-18.

Lipsyte, R. (1997). Wish Upon a Star, Then Be One. *The New York Times,* July 27, p. 15.

McPherson, B. and Curtis, J. (1989). *The Social Significance of Sport.* Champaign, Illinois: Human Kinetics.

Mill, R., Alstar. C., and Morrison, M. (1985). *The Tourism System: An Introductory Text.* Englewood Cliffs, New Jersey: Prentice-Hall.

Mules, T. and Faulkner, B. (1996). An economic perspective on special events. *Tourism Economics,*14(2): 314-329.

Mullin, B.J., Hardy, S., and Sutton, W.A. (1993). *Sport Marketing.* Champaign, Illinois: Human Kinetics.

National Golf Foundation (1997). Personal communication and fact sheet.

Nike Sport Camps (2002). Personal communication, May 13.

Packer, J. (1997). Everything You Ever Wanted to Know About Ski and Snowboard Tourists But Were Afraid to Ask. *Journal of Vacation Marketing,* 4(3): 22-32.

Palm, J. (1991). *Sport for All: Approaches from Utopia to Reality*. Schorndorf, Germany: Verlag Karl Hofmann.

Pitts, B. and Stotlar, D. (1996). *Fundamentals of Sport Marketing*. Morgantown, WV: Fitness Information Technology.

Recreation Roundtable (Newsletter) (1995). *Recreation in the New Millennium: A Report on Recreation Motivations and Satisfaction Levels by the Recreation Roundtable*. Washington, DC.

Reid, T.R. (1994). *Ski Japan*. New York: Yodansha International.

Renfro, W. (1997). Director of Constituent Relations, NCAA. Personal communication, June 13.

Research Unit, Sports Tourism International Council (1994). Sports As an Economic Generator. *Journal of Sport Tourism*, 1(2): 21-33.

Research Unit, Sports Tourism International Council (1997). STIX—Sports Tourism Impact Index, As an Economic Generator, *Journal of Sport Tourism*, 3(4): 13-14.

Rinehart, R. (1992). An Analysis of the 1992 Super Bowl in Minneapolis, Minnesota, presented at the 1992 National Association for Sport Sociology annual conference, Toledo, OH.

Ritchie, B. (1984). Assessing the Impact of Hallmark Events, *Journal of Travel Research*, 23(2): 2-11.

Schlossberg, H. (1996). *Sport Marketing*. Cambridge, MA: Blackwell.

Schneider Publishing (1999). Economic Impact of Sports-Related Travel and Tourism. *Sports Travel Magazine*, 3(10): 10.

Seghers, M. (1995). Mississippi Coast Tourist Officials to Lure Out-of-State Fishermen. *Sun Herald*, September 3: C-10.

Sheahan, T. (1995). Unpublished research paper for Edelman Public Relations.

Smith, D. (1997). Owner, Destination Network. Personal communication, June 13.

Sofield, T. and Sivan, A. (1994). From Cultural Event to International Sport—The Hong Kong Boat Race. *Journal of Sport Tourism*, 1(3): 5-22.

Spivak, S. (1997). Health Spa Development in the U.S.: A Burgeoning Component of Sport Tourism, *Journal of Vacation Marketing*, 4(1): 65-77.

*Sport Market Place Directory* (2002). Phoenix, Arizona: Franklin Covey.

Swart, K. (2000). An Assessment of Sport Tourism Curriculum at Academic Institutions, *Journal of Sport Tourism*, 6(1).

Theobold, W. F. (1984). *Global Tourism—The Next Decade*. Oxford, England: Butterworth Heinemann.

Travel Industry Association of America (1998). *Adventure Travel Report 1997*, February.

Travel Industry Association of America (1999). Profile of Travelers who Attend Sports Events, May.

U.S. Travel Data Center (1994). *Outdoor/Adventure Travel*. Unpublished prepared for the Travel Industry Association of America. Washington, DC.

Vinoker, M.B. (1988). *More Than a Game—Sports and Politics.* New York: Greenwood.

Walt Disney World Sports (1997). A Complete Sports Community Being Created at Walt Disney World Resort. Press release. Orlando, Florida.

Weiler, B. and Hall, M (1992). *Special Interest Tourism.* Toronto, Canada: Halsted Press.

Wilson, S. (1997). Owner, Sports Tour, Inc. Personal communication, June 16.

Women's Sport Foundation (WTTC) (1997). Title IX Media Helper. Long Island, NY: Women Sport Foundation.

World Tourism Organization (WTO) (2001). Statistics. <http://www.world-tourism.org>.

World Travel and Tourism Council (1996). *Travel and Tourism's Economic Impact: Special Report,* March. London, England.

Zeigler, E. F. (1984). *Ethics and Morality in Sports and Physical Education—An Experiential Approach.* Chicago, Illinois: Stripe.

Chapter 2

# Historical Perspectives of Sport Tourism

John Zauhar

## INTRODUCTION

It is imperative to provide a foundation for defining sport tourism using categories of sporting activities rather than relying on philosophical description. Sport and tourism individually are two very different categories; but they conjoin in five distinctive areas: attractions, resorts, cruises, tours, and events.

From a historical perspective, the study of sport tourism should always be approached with an awareness of the different social, cultural, technological, and transportation circumstances of the era. For instance, travel time is variable depending on the available modes of transportation. Also, attitudes toward travel products are determined by the benefits and attributes of the sport that could be viewed very differently 100 or more years later. Thus, sport tourism throughout ancient and modern eras should be viewed, analyzed, and judged in terms of all these facets. This chapter therefore covers the historical perspectives of sport tourism from the Greek civilizations, through the vitality and passion of the Renaissance, to the mega events of the twentieth century.

## GREECE: THE FOUNDATION

Museums worldwide have archeological materials and artifacts that relate to Greek sport. Among the art and objects of antiquity, evidence has been found relating to athletic events, horse racing, weight lifting, boxing, wrestling, pole vaulting on horses, field events, and torch parades. Although they subscribed to slavery, ancient Greeks believed in the dignity and rights of the human being. They affirmed and emphasized courage, honor, love, and enjoyment of the beauty of the physical world. Throughout the history of Greece, people lived in separate communities called *city states*. The majority of these states were found along the coasts. At times, there were 140 city states in Greece holding athletic events. Participants came from all parts of Greece and beyond the borders of the country.

Most of these festivities included athletic contests in veneration of certain gods such as Prometheus and Hermes. Various factors contributed to the indulgence of Greeks in sporting events and physical activity. Among the most prominent were geography, climate, social appreciation, and political drive. In essence, the propensity to strive linked the participants to gods. Their obsession with victory, especially in athletic ventures, was a distinguishable and discernible feature.

Greeks valued recognition. They idolized danger and pain. Much of their daily life was spent in physical revelry. Their motto, in sum, was live to fight and fight to live. They admired speed in running, skill in wrestling, bodily strength, physical beauty, eloquence, and form. The Greeks showered their victors with various gifts: oils, iron, silver, gold, and money. The value of prizes varied with contests and the first prize usually represented five times the value of the second prize.

At the outset of the Greek civilization, sports prepared citizens for soldiering. Athletics were associated with military events, and it was thought that painful trials and contests raised participants to higher virtue. In time, amateur athletes diminished in number and professional performers took over. Professionalism led to event specialization for the sake of winning. Athletics became a career. As such, physical fitness among the citizenry was no longer a viable goal. Consequently, hero worshipping was redirected. Athletes began to hire trainers and coaches, and the number of idle passive onlookers gradually increased. More time and interest were devoted to observing contests. Celebrations became forms of rest, recreation, and manifestations of patriotism. Women were, to a large degree, excluded from certain games, not only as participants, but also as spectators.

To attract tourists, particularly from other parts of the Greek territory and beyond, certain services were required. At the outset, travel by land was strenuous. Roads offered little in terms of amenities. People were obliged to travel in groups with many slaves for safety purposes and for baggage conveyance. Groups of city states came together for many festivals particularly the Olympic Games, the Pythian Games, and the Isthmian Games. These games polarized tourists. At any one time, there was a large block of travelers. Some arrived days prior to the scheduled activities; others lingered after the closing ceremonies. As such, incidental attractions were organized to entertain and distract these people. Many visitors had ample time to arrive early and enjoy the atmosphere and excitement before returning home. Historical records mention tens of thousands of visitors, not including active participants. Hence, vendors of essential and non-essential services, such as food, drink, souvenirs, guided tours, transportation, and the like, became omnipresent. In time, an abundance of inns offering rest and necessities were established at the places of the events, and along roadways for the comfort of travelers. Some had sufficient amenities; others simply offered sleeping quarters. Nonetheless, this hospitality trend diminished the risks and perils of travel to some degree. Such improvements assisted in the promotion and promulgation of sport tourism.

## THE PERSIAN EMPIRE: THE SOIL AND THE SOUL

In the mid-sixth century B.C., the Persian Empire incorporated the territory between Europe and Asia. The Empire included a mosaic of peoples and a number of dynasties. Most inhabitants earned their livelihoods by hunting and tilling the land. Gradually, they developed expertise in handicrafts. Hunting was the favorite sport. This activity was practiced in open territory as well as in closed hunting parks stocked with lions, tigers, pheasants, ostriches, and the like, surrounded by walk trails. The game of polo, played with a light ball of willow root, competed in popularity with hunting. Ladies of the court are said to have played the game with great skill. Usually, two teams with four or six players competed. Furthermore, literature of the era reveals feats of horsemanship, archery competitions, javelin throwing, and conquests of wild boars. Athletic clubs were subsidized by the government. Champions traveled to different urban sites and challenged local talents—a sport tourism experience. Moreover, Persian King Cyrus instituted horse races, and competitions were divided according to nationalities. Hence, sport tourism ventures were popular and quite frequent throughout the Persian Empire.


## THE ETRUSCANS: CAUSAL INFLUENCE

In the course of the first millennium B.C., Etruscan culture developed in and around the central and northern regions of the Italian peninsula. Sports activities, participants, and spectators during the Etruscan era are depicted mostly in tombs. For example, the Tomb of Bighe has detailed illustrations of equestrian events with an assembly of spectators—patrons seated on platforms with seats lined with red coverings and surrounded by a canopy. Activities included boxing, jumping, and discus throwing. The Tomb of the Monkey shows wrestling with a referee present, and the Tomb of the Augurs portrays a woman wrestler among men. In other tombs, races of horseback riders are represented, some even riding sidesaddle.

Many vessels are also decorated with men and women athletes. Some relief carvings depict bloody, wounded athletes. Killings apparently were an accepted form of Etruscan entertainment for participants as well as spectators. At times, prisoners of war were used to perform at games and without question, they were considered an important element at festivals.


## ROME: THE ARISTOCRATIC EXPRESSION

The city of Rome was built in the eighth century B.C., and was a regional center. The expansion of the Roman Empire truly began after the Etruscans were driven out of the peninsula. Rome's dominance was felt in all geographic directions, and by the second and first centuries B.C. the Romans were masters until their collapse at the end of the fifth century A.D. In the middle of the fourth century B.C., the Roman Empire occupied approximately 2,400 square miles. In 280 B.C., its territory covered some 31,700 square miles, and later extended to around 48,000 square miles. At its peak, the Roman Empire embraced between 100 and 120 million people.

To keep inhabitants and travelers quiescent, entertainment was organized and offered to the masses. Oftentimes, individuals seeking high office sponsored entertainment programs. On other occasions, the State took appropriate measures to finance special games, festivals, and/or athletic contests. Truly, sports spectators of Rome, Alexandria, Antioch, and Constantinople were frequently and repeatedly involved because of politics.

Romans had a natural love of excitement and they lived, as some writers have expressed, for senseless amusement. Throughout Roman history, numerous holidays were satiated with action programs lasting from twenty-four hours to seventeen days. On occasion, one-day events were divided into morning games consisting of fights with wild beasts; midday festivities concentrated on the execution of criminals or enemies of the state; afternoon amusements included gladiator combats. The latter, apparently, were among the biggest crowd attractions and pleasers. Spectators frequently yelled with great emotion: "Hit! Strike! Kill!" Gladiator violence was not only considered legitimate but sacred. Supplying gladiators for festive events and games was quite profitable. In fact, many gladiator schools throughout the land were established. The emperor Caligula alone had twenty thousand gladiators in training from different parts of the Empire, strictly for entertainment purposes. Gambling among spectators was also profitable. Even Ovid recommended that women gamble on races, probably to enhance the sport's attractiveness and retention.

Chariot races were quite popular in Roman society. At some competitions, Samnites contended with large shields; Britons vied in war chariots. Other spectator participatory sport activities included wrestling, boxing, boating, horseback riding, ball games, hunting, and bowling.

In fact, sport entertainment occurred throughout Rome. In urban centers, spectacles were appreciated and applauded, and games were instituted. As onlooker passions for sports activities grew, travel from different parts of the world became a regular feature. In truth, the State controlled leisure activities, so much so that, in the fourth century, a total of 176 days were set aside for festivities. The underlying principle was to consolidate all parts of the Roman Empire through sports and festive entertainment.

## BYZANTIUM: A GLITTERING CIVILIZATION

As Rome declined, Constantinople, the capital of the eastern half of the now split empire, rose in prominence between A.D. 326 to 565. In the course of these centuries, the Roman concept of bathhouses had spread throughout Europe. Centers for passive care of the body (spas) were established, and these attractions for social life were customary. In A.D. 430 Constantinople boasted eight public and 153 private baths. Byzantine peoples also participated in a wide range of sports activities, either as contestants or as spectators. Skill at horsemanship was a predominant feature, and chariot racing was the most popular sport. Crowds seeking excitement filled the stands every race day and displayed loyalty to sporting associations or circus factions by wearing the color schemes that were associated with specific teams. During program intervals, spectators, local and foreign, remained seated to be entertained by a variety of performances. Athletes often hired small bands of claqueurs to produce loud orchestrated applause and to ensure audience appreciation of the spectacle at hand. Reliefs dating to the Byzantine era depict races, onlookers, and reward monies being presented to the victors.

During A.D. 393 to 433, the Olympic Games ended. Edicts against pagan practices were overbearing. Furthermore, changing tastes contributed to the end of the Games. Wild beast fights and exhibitions as mock forms of entertainment also diminished and dwindled. Difficulties in obtaining animals, and care costs also led to the disappearance of animal spectacles. Furthermore, Barbarian attacks, earthquakes, and floods destroyed athletic centers, particularly the site of the Olympic Games.

## THE CRUSADES: PICTURESQUE AND EVENTFUL

The commercial ambitions of Italian cities, coupled with a weakening of the Byzantine Empire and general oppression, caused thousands of Christians to pledge themselves to a battle cry of serving God—in essence, a Holy War. On the First Crusade (1095 to 1099), 12,000 people set out from France; another 5,000 set out from Germany. These numbers included peasants, serfs, prisoners, adventurers, merchants, knights, women, and children. Through travel, crusaders transmitted and acquired diverse concepts, lifestyles, and sports activities of land variety and vastness, customs, traditions, and values. Whenever there were moments of peace or friendly exchanges, special celebrations, feasts, and tournaments were organized. Strolling players performed in marketplaces or city squares. Riding, hunting, and tournaments were the pastimes of Crusade nobility.

When at peace, these knights and their entourages went into the countrysides for fishing and hunting where beautiful orchards, vineyards, and olive groves were to be found. They also hunted foxes and practiced falconry, the art of training falcons to hunt in cooperation with a person. As considerable monies were spent on horses, owners and riders selected pasturelands around urban settings as parade grounds for horse displays and horsemanship. During peaceful lapses, foreigners joined in these spectacles. Whenever scheduled, ladies were invited to observe the pageantry and mock battles. Bathouses (spas) were occasions for amusement and social contacts.

Many men, women, and children died from hunger, thirst, exposure, and disease during these times. Thousands of artworks were stolen, mutilated, or destroyed. However, the crusaders helped stimulate the zest for exploration and travel.


## THE ISLAMIC SCENE: RESOURCES OF THE EARTH

Historians describe the Islamic civilization as a union of earthly resources. People raised cattle, horses, camels, goats, elephants, and dogs. They also grew varieties of grains, vegetables, and fruits. Land transport was chiefly by camels, horses, mules, and men. Throughout the era, commercial interests and entrepreneurship developed— domestic as well as foreign. Religion influenced and molded everyday living, and morals, laws, and traditions were based on religious teachings.

The upper classes, amid splendor, lived a life of luxury and sport. They would gather in town plazas to watch polo competitions and horse races. Common people upheld their daily chores, toils, and services. Yet on festive occasions they would enjoy the sporting elements organized and offered. Pleasure boats, passenger vessels, and barges were quite common to the Islamic scene as were public parks and private and public baths. In the tenth century Bagdad had 27,000 baths. Most dancers, singers, and actors for entertainment purposes were slaves. Other activities that were enjoyed by the rich, the lower classes, and the slaves included cock fighting, juggling, boxing, wrestling, running, javelin throwing, gymnastics, fencing, croquet, and weight lifting.

## EUROPE: THE RECOVERY

Between A.D. 1095 and 1300, many countries within Europe were politically unstable. Hostile populations were noted, particularly in what are now Scandinavia, Germany, Poland, Russia, Spain, Portugal, Italy, France, England, and the Balkans. Sports activities during this period tended to be specific to social status or class. The peasantry, for example, enjoyed soccer; the middle class burghers participated in crossbow contests; and knights and squires savored tournaments. Typical sites for contests and tournaments were meadows and open fields. Oftentimes, whenever a tournament or trial by combat was held, masses of people would line the highways to regale and feed on the pomp and pageantry—formidable occasions of sport tourism for people near and afar. Teams of knights from England, Brittany, Normandy, and Anjou traveled together throughout Europe and, in many circumstances, participated as specific representative groups or partners in games lasting several days. The games resembled wars, and around A.D. 1200, war simulations and mimicries became the major attractions. It was a time of more pageantry and less combativeness.

Throughout this recovery period in Europe, specific sports activities can be said to have influenced tourism. For instance, in Italy, horse racing was gaining great popularity. In England, the first recorded horse race took place in A.D. 1174. In France, large crowds gathered in open air to watch tennis matches, and in A.D. 1351, tennis became an open-air game in England, attracting players and enthusiastic onlookers.

The public steam bath was also introduced throughout Europe—although the Church frowned upon public baths as leading to immorality. Nonetheless, among the Slavic peoples, steam bathing was to be found in many villages, towns, and cities. In A.D. 1308, Poznan, Poland, had twelve commercial steam baths in various districts of the city and Cracow had eleven such facilities. It is assumed that travelers took advantage of such establishments.

In many European countries, festivals were organized to celebrate various occasions, such as the agricultural season, specific guilds, special patron saints, and the like. Christian feasts drew immense crowds, and glorified the pageantry of tournaments featuring knightly initiatives. In addition, men and women of this period developed a taste for travel, visiting strange lands, historical sites, and legendary monuments.

## THE RENAISSANCE PERIOD

The Renaissance period (A.D. 1300 to 1576) produced a more secular spirit, revived a new interest in classical civilization, and increased respect for literature. People were fascinated by human achievements, believing that humankind possessed the elements and power to shape its own destiny. Politically, mercantile dignitaries and military dictatorships were cast aside. Morally, the era left human instincts free. The Italian cities were the forerunner of this new mentality. Because of the geographical crossroads of the Italian peninsula, the movement spread across land, sea, and mountain to France, Germany, Flanders, Holland, and England.

Society was in transition during the Renaissance. Transformation of sport to spectacle was becoming popular. Sports activities typically found during the Renaissance period were archery contests, hunting, horse racing, falconry, footraces, boat regattas, tennis, and boxing. The role of the spectator increased as sports activities became tamer, more civilized, and less spontaneous. This approach changed the nature of sites, facilities, and lead time for necessary organizational preparations. In Italy, the highly formalized game of *calcio* attracted hordes of spectators. The annual meet, *The Schuetzenfeste,* provided occasions for many to watch and enjoy the festivities. Guilds of archers participated from Artois, Brabant, Flanders, Picardie, northern France, and German-speaking Europe. Villages competed against other villages. A game that involved kicking, throwing, and carrying a ball across open fields, narrow streets, and small waterways that included both the participants and spectators was quite common. At times, it was difficult to distinguish the players from the onlookers. The invention of the printing press encouraged the rapid spread of tournament and contest information, and games could be announced well in advance.

## THE ENGLISH ENCHANTMENT: KNOWLEDGE TO REASON

From 1538 to approximately 1638, England progressively gained power and prestige at home and abroad. During this period, England's industries developed, commerce flourished, theological questions were debated, and music, arts, and architecture excelled. By the fifteenth century, hunting, longbow shooting, and fishing were popular among English city dwellers. Other pastimes, particularly for onlookers, included wrestling, bull baiting, and cock fighting. Nobles, on the other hand, embraced deer, fox, and hare hunting with greyhounds followed by men and women on horseback. The English promulgated that noble youths should complete their education by traveling—as did the Romans, who sent their youths to Greece. Philosophies differed as to the definition of education. Francis Bacon (1561 to 1626) upheld that youth should meet important, influential, and prestigious people rather than pursue specific knowledge. Those affiliated with James I endorsed travel for particular social elements and cultural endeavors. The middle-ground proponents stressed the importance of both knowledge and social skills. This travel to educate became to be known as the "Grand Tour." Sport tourism flourished in Europe during this period. In Spain for instance, bullfighting was a favorite spectacle attracting people from diverse areas of the country. Dueling, although illegal, was also quite popular. In France, tennis was the rage. The Dutch, on the other hand, devoted themselves to the sport of golf.

Between 1643 to 1715, the countries of Europe were in various stages of upheaval and turmoil. During this period, sport tourism did not necessarily enjoy its previous fervor and influence. Nonetheless, in England, sports did somewhat flourish. People traveled to watch cockfighting, bear and bull baiting, wrestling, pugilism, and tightrope walking. Generally speaking, animal sports appeared to be national pastime draws, particularly for the lower classes. Distance travel for this social class was quite limited. Some aristocrats, however, did travel to enjoy such amusements. Bowling, tennis, and cricket progressively gained favor and fervor. With the system of royal highways being improved, high society drove in carriages, on pleasant afternoons, from one destination to another. The poor classes began to travel in stagecoaches. As such, roadside inns became more accommodating, inducing people to travel more and to enjoy new experiences. On the south bank of the Thames, Vauxhall Gardens became a fashionable resort, particularly for the wealthy. Also in the 1700s, people in England began forming fishing clubs and holding casting competitions.

## THE EIGHTEENTH CENTURY: DOMINATED BY WAR

Western Europe, from approximately 1715 to 1756, evolved gradually while conflicts between religion and ideology continued. The perspectives of this half-century era lie in the development of the Industrial Revolution, in the collapse of feudalism in France, in the transformation of peripheral nations, and in the triumph of certain philosophies.

Throughout these tumultuous years, sport tourism prospered. Cricket, bear baiting, bull baiting, cockfighting, and boxing thrived, particularly among the rich. Practically all sports contests were accompanied by betting and spectator crowds were abundant. The pleasures of Vauxhall Garden and Ranelagh consisted of promenades, fireworks, and acrobats, as well as onlooker sites for regattas, rowing, festivals, and barges on the Thames. In 1739, when the Thames froze, Londoners staged a carnival of dancing on ice.

In France in the 1720s, French men and women, bored with domestic chores and everyday routines, flocked to promenades, malls, and dance halls while the rich went hunting and the bourgeois feasted. There were also favorite resorts for carriage rides, walks, and Easter parades at the Bois de Boulogne, the Jardins des Tuileries, and the Jardins du Luxembourg.

In Italy in the eighteenth century, up to 30,000 tourists from all parts of Europe and the Orient flocked to the carnival season in Venice. Summer sports programs included races and regattas. Many cities throughout Europe followed suit and initiated the carnivalesque activities. Bowling of one kind or another was a popular pursuit in Europe, especially in Germany. It became an integral part of German social life and was commonly practiced by many on almost all festive occasions. Wealthy citizens built private alleys to entertain their guests. Individual cities arranged public bowling competitions and contests. From Germany, the sport of bowling spread to other coun-tries such as England, Scotland, and Holland.

During the eighteenth century, bullfights rivaled religion in Spain. Skillful and brave toreadors were the idols of all classes. The colorful entrance, the dramatic exits, the capes, and the richly embroided cos-tumes made bullfighting a symbol of Spanish culture and a great en-ticement to spectators. Dancing was also a major passion, sprouting variations that became famous all over Europe. As an example, mas-querade balls sometimes attracted 3,500 dancers from various parts of the country.

Sport tourism was also growing outside of Europe at this time. Captain Cook and his crew upon reaching Hawaii in 1778 were amazed to see men skimming across the ocean waves on long wooden boards. The Hawaiians are said to have been surfing since the tenth century as attested by numerous legends, chants, and specialized vo-cabulary. Apparently, surfing displays and fierce competitions in rid-ing out the swells were very prominent. Contests included several heats. The winners received prizes, and losers were obliged to surren-der their possessions and even their personal freedom.

In the United States, particularly in the South (Virginia, South Carolina), cricket activity and competition blossomed during the end of the eighteenth century and the beginning of the nineteenth, attract-ing active and passive participants. Horse racing also came to North America from England. The first horse race in the United States took place in Long Island, New York, at the Newmarket. Furthermore, as America's harness racing evolved from a local pastime to an inde-pendent sport, trotting races were arranged for public enjoyment pur-poses.

In North America around 1730, impounding big herds of buffalo became a community sport for Western Canadian Indians. Old women and men would travel a mile or more out of their villages observe the spectacle. Sioux Indians played field hockey with a soft ball made of elk or moose hair covered with buckskin, while the Chilean Indians used hard balls for this game (Mapuche). Among the North American natives, lacrosse was known as *bagataway*. Usually, this game was a battle between 500 warriors or more on either side. Spectators who wished to join the fray were most welcome, and the natives were delighted to give displays and play for special onlookers of white settlers. Europeans were very anxious to play lacrosse. Records detail a number of early matches between natives and French Canadians.

Furthermore, Natives Americans were well acquainted with wrestling long before white men came to the New World. Wrestling became popular among the early American pioneers, and many accounts exist describing matches between the two groups.

## THE NINETEENTH CENTURY:
## THE STEPPING-STONES

In nineteenth-century Western Europe, revolutions failed, nationalism was on the rebound, and idealism prospered as a philosophy. France became the most populous and prosperous nation in Europe. England challenged this prosperity by creating the second phase of the Industrial Revolution. England claimed the seas as a territorial extension.

In many nations there was an underlying current of unrest. Many countries fought and sought control; some scrambled for African territories. Others, through force, gained power through territorial occupation. New areas of the United States of America and Canada were gradually being settled. Throughout these upheavals, turmoils, and recovery periods, sports activities, development, and tourism were prevalent and becoming increasingly imbedded into different facets of life. The nineteenth century witnessed a tremendous growth of sports clubs, associations, and federations throughout the world. In fact, these sports formations, through team structures, league affiliations, and competitive spectacles helped increase active as well as passive participatory interests. They also contributed to solidify fan intensity and longevity among all levels of society. Furthermore, sports scenarios began to change significantly with the development of the railroad. This transportation mode permitted people to travel more readily from one sports destination to another, thus impacting directly on the sport tourism movement.

Athletic events, contests, and competitions in the nineteenth century gradually became highly rationalized, specialized, and professionalized. Athletes began spending more time training and perfecting skills, and onlookers qualified their sports enthusiasm through the appreciation of athletic achievements and excellence. This role delineation between athlete and spectator was induced and facilitated by communications, sports writings, and sports periodicals. This distinction, however, did not restrict the general public from participating in sports on an amateur and recreational level, nor did it eliminate the imitation and emulation elements found among enthusiasts.

The popularity of certain sports in the nineteenth century was based on social class structure. Some sports, such as horse racing, because of their required expertise and equipment costs, were quite fashionable among the richer populations. Certain sports transgressed all levels of society. Soccer, for example, attracted tens of thousands of spectators from all walks of life and social strata. Women also performed in athletics. For instance, in France and in England, some women from the working class boxed and wrestled. Some performed on stages, in barns, or in backrooms. Female pugilism was also common in the United States (New York). In Pittsburgh (1888), women competed in a six-day bicycle race to the delight of 1,500 spectators. Such competitions also took place in Great Britain and France.

In the United States, athletic clubs were a common feature, particularly among the middle class. Most clubs, however, did not accept females as members. As such, some women formed clubs of their own. In 1905, the Coca-Cola Company published an advertisement depicting a man with golf clubs and a girl with a tennis racket in her hand. Women were finding their active way into summer resorts and country clubs.

In England in the nineteenth century, horse racing was the premier spectator sports event. Virtually all populations got to the racecourse at least once a year. Prizefighters, on the other hand, could easily attract 10,000 spectators. Pugilists came from all over the country and national loyalties were commonly stressed. In 1880, crowds attending cricket matches grew in numbers as the railroad facilitated travel throughout England, promoting new recreational opportunities. Cricket in the nineteenth century was associated with the upper classes, whereas soccer was the people's sport. In the 1870s, soccer crowds numbered around 20,000 per game. In the 1800s, formal rowing races attracted many spectators. Competitions between the Universities of Oxford and Cambridge began in 1829. Ten years later, the Henly Regatta was held on the Thames River. The Harvard/Oxford race of 1869, an international touristic venture, drew an estimate of one million spectators along the banks of the Thames.

In the United States, specific occurrences in the nineteenth century fostered the development of and accentuated the sport tourism phenomenon. The following are some milestones.

1823    The first international horse race attracted 50,000 spectators in New York.

1835    The first yacht race was recorded in New York. Today, circuits include the Southern Ocean Racing competitions, the Whitbread Round, and the World Race—a transatlantic and transpacific competition.

1868    The American Skating Congress held races. Later, in 1927, the Amateur Speedskating Union was formed to organize races and serve as a governing body.

1869    The Cincinnati Red Stockings baseball team traveled around the country, directly and indirectly enticing the formation of the National Association of Baseball Players with nine teams in different cities—to be followed by the National League in 1876, and the American League in 1901.

1876    The bicycle captured America after its exhibition at the Philadelphia Centennial. This was followed by the Yellow Fellow Transcontinental Bicycle Relay from San Francisco to New York. The bicycle, an English invention, played a key role in the development of harness racing, flying, motorboating, motorcycling, and automobiles.

1885    The first automobile race took place in Chicago, Illinois. Today, many types of auto racing include Formula One, Indy car, stock car, and drag racing, attracting millions of spectators, domestic as well as foreign.

1892    Basketball made its first appearance in front of some 200 attendees. Today, this sport is played in more than 100 nations with millions of onlookers.

1895    The first professional football game was played between Latrobe YMCA and the Jeannette Athletic Club. In 1920, a fourteen-team American Professional Football Association was formed, changing its name to the National Football League two years later. Here again, tourists account for many among the spectator followership.

1895    The American Bowling Congress was organized with ten leagues. Today, more than 2.5 million bowlers compete in over 100,000 leagues.

American sports have flourished, particularly within the educational system. Growth in interest, enthusiasm, and competitiveness, has resulted in highly skilled professionalism with a significant following. However, two sports, tennis and golf, have gained prestige and popularity in the United States through country clubs. Many of these clubs were founded toward the end of the nineteenth century. Among the most prominent were the Brookline Country Club in Boston (1882) and Tuxedo Park of New Jersey (1885).

In Western Canada, canoeing, sleighing, snowshoeing, horse racing, and dancing were common sports activities in the nineteenth century. Trials of strength were also quite popular, such as wrestling, running, jumping, putting the stone, and throwing the hammer. Among the favorite sports were tobogganing, skating, and sailing. Intertown sports competitions grew; return trips by steamship companies along certain routes were offered. Later, railway companies adopted similar practices to entice tourist interest in sports travel. Around 1852 covered rinks were sprouting in Canada, starting with Quebec City, then in Montreal, followed by other municipalities. This skating innovation produced gala balls on ice, tournament races, skating competitions, and shinty, hurley, and bandy—all attracting great numbers of spectators, as well as participants from near and far. By 1900, a professional hockey league was organized which included American and Canadian players. This sports formation later developed into the National Hockey League consisting of five teams vying for the Lord Stanley Cup.

Accessibility to waterway plans and waterways helped establish aquatic activities at the early stages of Canadian historical development. The earliest organized regattas were found in the Maritimes

(1880), particularly in Newfoundland. Crews from St. John's rivaled oarsmen from Halifax, Boston, and New York. Later, Halifax (1826) and Quebec City (1830) organized similar regatta competitions. Sailing regattas were also popularized by the Halifax Yacht Club in 1837.

Race meetings throughout the nineteenth century were also very fashionable, particularly in large urban centers. Racing horses on the ice of the St. Lawrence River and other rivers became a trendy winter sport. Towns would be all but deserted during such races. In 1844, the Montreal Olympic Games (not modern) were held with a variety of competitive activities such as snowshoeing, racquets, and lacrosse, for club members as well as nonmembers. All of these activities attracted local and domestic participation, some requiring much travel displacement.

The nineteenth century was the genesis of sport in Australia. Unification of divided communities was the goal of organized activity. Transportation modes increased participation; visiting ships encouraged sport competition; and the construction of sophisticated sports facilities fostered spectator interests. Australia became, in essence, the home of every sport. For instance, Australia was the first country to conceive the idea of international croquet contests in 1868. Rowing races, sailing contests, and swimming competitions particularly belong to the Australian way of life. From 1850 to 1890, rowing developed into international competitions. Nine and ten-pin bowling followed (1855) in various parts of Australia, and, regattas, with few events, were loosely organized. Nonetheless, sports activities did attract large crowds. A good example of large spectatorship could be traced to the Hobart Town Regatta where, in 1838, 5,000 people attended.

Many other countries, through their particular sports interests, expressions, and happenings, enhanced, directly or indirectly, the overall concept of sport tourism during the nineteenth and twentieth centuries. Mexico is a good example. Mexico greatly encouraged balloon flights in the nineteenth century. These events attracted large crowds and allowed customers special ringside seats. Animal parachute drops, acrobatics, and aerialists were oftentimes featured to enhance the balloon excitement. By 1908, advertising slogans began to appear on balloons and balloonists began to tour the provinces. Today, the biggest hot air balloon festival in the world is held in Gatineau, Quebec, which attracts 300,000 spectators and participants from more than twenty countries.

Although early fiestas in Mexico included classical Spanish style matadors, Mexicans developed their own approach to bullfighting on two distinctive levels: first, as a gentleman's pastime, and second, as a professional spectacle to be found in challenges, contests, and shows. When bullfighting was banned in early 1890, Mexico's professional bullfighters came north to the United States, and joined popular traveling shows such as the Vincente Oropeza. This contributed to the establishment of the American rodeo, not to mention the Canadian Calgary Stampede, which draws participants and spectators from far and wide.

## MEGA INTERESTS OF THE TWENTIETH CENTURY

The sport tourism movement took on an added importance in the twentieth century through the blooming of specific endeavors catering to athletes and sports enthusiasts. Key influences on sport tourism were the Olympic Games, halls of fame, sport cruises, sport resorts, and sport tours.

Very few cultural phenomena attract as much attention as the Olympic Games. Prior to the 1896 Olympics held in Athens, Greece, few reported Olympic festivals were held. With the suggestion that the first modern Olympics be held in Athens, there were initial, and growing, pains. Problems with travel, accommodations, program design, spectator comfort, conflicting athletes, and publicity were omnipresent and rampant. With time, organizers gained experience and streamlined administrative decisions, thus rendering the Olympics more conducive to the sport tourism phenomenon. Table 2.1 of selected Summer Olympic Games demonstrates the increasing number of participants over the years.

The Winter Olympics have also proven to be a great boost to sport tourism. Beginning in 1924, in Chamonix, France, 258 athletes participated representing sixteen nations. The 1994 Games in Lillehammer, Norway, saw 1,717 athletes from sixty-four different countries and counted approximately 100,000 spectators daily.

Another popular phenomenon of the twentieth century proved to be halls of fame. The need to recognize and honor sports individuals

TABLE 2.1. The Summer Olympics

| Year and Site | Male Participants | Female Participants | Number of Countries |
|---|---|---|---|
| 1896 (Athens) | 200 | 0 | 14 |
| 1900 (Paris) | 1,066 | 11 | 26 |
| 1924 (Paris) | 2,956 | 136 | 44 |
| 1952 (Helsinki) | 4,407 | 519 | 67 |
| 1988 (Seoul) | 6,270 | 2,186 | 159 |
| 1996 (Atlanta) | 6,797 | 3,613 | 197 |
| 2000 (Sydney) | 6,582 | 4,069 | 200 |

and teams has created these highly specialized museums that come in all sizes, forms, and shapes—stables, saloons, walkways, locker rooms, and full-fledged museum structures. Their beginnings can be pinpointed to the Helms Athletic Foundation of Los Angeles, which created halls of fame for a number of sports in 1936. Today, sports shrines of every conceivable nature can be found complete with souvenir shops, adventure rooms, galleries, dressing rooms, gardens, patios, screen projections, important objects, computerized settings, dinner banquet facilities, and the like. Examples include:

- Australian Gallery of Sport
- Central Museum of Sport and Physical Education (Bulgaria)
- Sports Museum (Beijing)
- Olympic Museum (Cyprus)
- Musée du Sport Français (France)
- Wimbledon Lawn Tennis Museum (Great Britain)
- Sports Museum (Korea)
- Lahore Museum (Pakistan)
- Sports Hall of Fame (Philippines)
- Olympic Museum of Lausanne (Switzerland)
- Musée Sportif (Turkey)
- National Art Museum of Sport (United States)
- Olympic Glory Museum (Russia)

Cruises as we know them today began in the 1920s. The impact of World War I, immigration restrictions, and the American Prohibition Act altered seaway thinking and marketing procedures. Shorter trips were planned; weekend tours were offered. Ships became floating speakeasies. Liquor was legal, gambling was permitted, and exotic ports became accessible. The art of mass travel began moving into the tourist industry. The Great Depression and World War II hampered tourism, but momentum revived around 1960.

Today, sport cruises are gaining in popularity. Many ships are equipped with swimming pools, tennis courts, basketball nets, health club facilities, and water sports equipment such as sailboats, motorboats, water skis, snorkeling, and fishing gear. The stimulation of traveling with people who share similar interests adds to cruise popularity. Many offer educational ventures such as clinics, special instructional sessions, conferences, lectures, and sport site visitations.

Adventure cruising was pioneered in the late 1960s by Lars-Eric Lindblab (Sweden), who wished to open up parts of the world that tourists had neither visited nor seen before. In this type of endeavor, passengers take an active role in every aspect of the expedition whether in the Artic, the Chilean Fjords, or East Africa. New cruise vessels are equipped with unique stern platforms allowing for water sports amenities. These platforms are lowered when ship is at anchor facilitating sailing, swimming, snorkeling, scuba diving, sunfishing, jet skiing, windsurfing, or hitching a Zodiac ride. For those preferring shoreline excursions, specialty companies or local operators offer all types of sports activities relative to the area, climate, topography, time of day, and port time duration. These activities can be as diversified as gondola rides, helicopter ascents, museum visitations, guided trail hikes, spectator sports activities, kayaking, or rollerblading. Available statistics indicate that over three million people worldwide take cruises yearly, visiting more than 300 ports of call. To determine what portion of these cruise tourists have been enticed by sports activity is rather difficult to speculate. Nonetheless, it is safe to say that a good number enjoy the sports offerings included in their travel package deals.

Just as sport cruises have grown in number, so too have the number of sport resorts. The original spa concept gradually changed in the twentieth century from a medical visitor center to a more elaborate accommodation, catering, and entertainment destination. The idea of a resort hotel was born in the eighteenth and nineteenth centuries in Europe. Palatial hotels were built along the French Riviera, in the Swiss Alps, and at various mineral springs throughout the continent.

The morphology of resorts was shaped by the attractiveness of beaches and mild climate, by railway lines, motorcars, and water-crafts. Resort hotels such as the Banff Springs Hotel in Canada and the Greenbrier Hotel in the United States (West Virginia) are good examples.

Inventions, sport equipment design, sportswear composition, and economic practices have influenced summer and winter sport resort centers. For instance, helicopters have introduced new skiing possibilities; the growth of boating has altered the design of water basins, islets, and river flows; existing and popular sports facilities, such as golf courses, have been exploited to promulgate the resort concept.

Sun and surf have always been natural attractions, and organizations have capitalized on this public desire. For instance, in 1936 Butlins holiday camp opened in Skegness, England, with organized fun, entertainment, and games. In 1949, in Majorca, Spain, the first Club Med opened. Today, with over eighty clubs around the world, Club Med offers many sporting activities. Many winter resorts and centers have also been developed into self-contained destinations that offer sports and recreational facilities as well as food and accommodations. The use of mountains, hillsides, and gulleys for winter sports activity is relatively recent. The development of the ski lift in the 1930s helped in the creation of winter resorts (Chamonix and Zermatt). Gradually, hotels, apartments, and villas colonized the surrounding winter terrain.

Sport tourism is also used to promote countries as a whole. Australia, for example, realizing that modern tourists are more sophisticated and more knowledgeable, aspires to sell the country's personality and people. Special interest activities are tailored to one's desires and aspirations. Hundreds of different experiences are offered within yearly thematic campaigns. The Malaysian Sports Tourism Council is similarly promoting Malaysia as a world class destination for international sporting events. Portugal is another nation that has concocted tourist promotion in terms of selling the country as a whole and as a sports destination.

Sport tours have also provided an impetus to the sport tourism movement, and sport tour operators emerged in the late 1960s. Tour components are purchased in advance and combined into a single entity and sold to the consumer as a package deal. Independent tours offering individual freedom of movement can also be arranged by travel counselors. Today's sport tours encompass, to a large extent, the following selected experiences: heritage site tours; sports study tours; nature tours; facility tours; event tours; game safaris; sports participation tours; training tours; walking/fitness tours; cycling tours; excursions; outdoor expeditions; and adventure tours.

## *CONCLUSION*

Throughout history, sport has proved to be a great motivator for travel and tourism. From the initial formative years of sport development, the sport tourism phenomenon has grown into a mass worldwide tourism framework, implicating a gamut of sports activities and contests. In studying the past, one sees that the sport tourism movement does have its cycles, trends, and significant emerging factors and facets. A study of the history of civilization reveals that sports have always been a viable cultural characteristic. From antiquity to modern times, sport participants, spectators, and travel are always associated in varying degrees with sport tourism. Destination distances fluctuate in terms of opportunities, modes of transportation, economic means, and discretionary free time. Generally speaking, sports environments throughout history have spurred and stimulated people to journey different distances to satisfy innate or acquired physical, emotional, cultural, social, or intellectual needs.

Chapter 3

# Sport Event Tourism: Planning, Development, and Marketing

Donald Getz

## *INTRODUCTION*

Events are a major component of sport tourism, and perhaps the most significant in terms of tourist numbers and economic impact. Sport event tourism is internationally recognized as a substantial and highly desirable niche market. Numerous American cities have established sport commissions to cultivate this form of travel; Australian states all have their special purpose event development corporations; and destinations around the world are competing furiously for sport events.

This chapter defines sport event tourism, examines its nature and value with a focus on impact evaluation, profiles the sport event tourist, highlights forces and trends shaping this sector, and suggests goals and strategies. A planning, development, and marketing process is presented and a case study of Seminole County Florida is included. Issues and research needs are identified in the conclusions. The overall purpose of this chapter is to assist destinations in getting the most from sport event tourism and to help them develop appropriate and sustainable strategies.

---

Special thanks are expressed to Jack Wert, Executive Director of Seminole County Convention and Visitor's Bureau for case study material.

*49*

## WHAT IS SPORT EVENT TOURISM?

From the destination's perspective, sport event tourism is the development and marketing of sport events to obtain economic and community benefits. To the consumer, it is travel for the purpose of participating in, or viewing, a sport event.

From the event organizer's perspective, tourists might be one of several target markets to attract, and to event sponsors (companies and organizations who pay to participate in events for their own marketing purposes), the tourism market is only one of several within which relationships are forged. Many stakeholder groups can be involved with sport events, therefore tourism goals must be complimentary to those relating to sport and community development, corporate marketing, and the physical environment.

It might be necessary for some sport event tourism stakeholders to reconceptualize events as tourism products. To become a product for sale, the event has to be attractive to specified target segments, high in quality, priced right, packaged carefully to meet the needs of travelers, and integrated with other tourism and hospitality services. Events oriented exclusively to competitors' needs or to local community preferences will not necessarily work well as tourism products.

### Unique Aspects of Sport Event Tourism

Sport event tourism is somewhat unique. Consider the following special characteristics:

- Many sport events are "biddable," that is, they can be attracted to a destination.
- Special events can attract more tourists than regularly scheduled games.
- Corporate sponsors love sport events.
- Major sport events can be catalysts for new facilities and new or improved infrastructure.
- When sport facilities are built, they become permanent event venues.
- Major sport events can be catalysts for attracting training sessions and other types of events, such as meetings and exhibitions.
- There is potential for various sport events year round.

- Sport events appeal to everyone: there are seniors or masters games, numerous Little League events, and events for every spectator regardless of gender, age, or physical ability.
- Community pride and entertainment are associated with successfully hosting sport events.
- Sport events can reflect and enhance culture and local traditions, helping to create a unique and attractive sense of place.
- Media coverage and its impact on developing a sport destination image can be more important than actual visitor spending.
- Sport events can assist in destination branding by providing powerful, active lifestyle images and making cultural themes come alive.
- Sport events are an effective means of securing tourism benefits in rural areas and small towns that might have limited attractiveness otherwise.

## Types of Sport Events

There is enormous variety in the sport events sector. Tourism marketers might automatically think of sport mega events (i.e., an event of unusually large size or impact) such as the Olympics or World Cup (soccer), but much benefit can be realized through small, amateur sporting events as well. As a way of categorizing these events, the following criteria are suggested:

1. Regularly scheduled meets and their playoffs contrast sharply with rare mega events; annual special events in the sport sector are popular, including sport festivals and major invitational competitions.
2. Many sports require specialized indoor or outdoor venues or facilities, while others occur in more or less natural settings.
3. Multisport events are typically much more complicated and expensive to produce than single-sport events.
4. Amateur sports contrast greatly with professional team events.
5. Drawing power, or tourist attractiveness, varies greatly. Most sport events are local to regional; some are national; and a very few are global in their appeal. Elevating an event in this hierarchy takes effort and money.

6. Target markets can also be used to differentiate sport events, depending on their focus or mix of competitors/participants, spectators, or broadcast audiences; all three have tourism potential.

Destinations contemplating sport event tourism might not be able to compete in bids for all these types of events. A balanced portfolio, however, is a worthwhile goal.

### Scale and Benefits of Sport Event Tourism

One measure of the significance of this market is provided by Walt Disney's Wide World of Sports resort in Orlando, Florida, featuring facilities for thirty-two sports (Helin, 1997). Disney has realized that sport events are big business, and that people are willing to travel long distances for participation and viewing. Other indicators include the expanding number and size of international events such as the World Police and Fire Games (held in 1997 in Calgary, Alberta, attracting 8,600 competitors and 20,000 visitors) and the World Masters Games held in Brisbane, Australia, in 1994, which attracted 23,203 entries and 2,000 supporters from sixty-nine countries (cited in Getz, 1997: 119). Mega events such as soccer's World Cup hosted by France in 1999 had a cumulative global television audience of 37 billion viewers over thirty-three days, and a live audience of 2.5 million spectators (Sports Business Market Research, Inc., 2000, p. 323). In the United States, the Super Bowl has become a mega tourist event, with Tampa Bay hosting over 100,000 visitors for Super Bowl XXXV in 2001, plus 800 million worldwide television viewers. It was so big that the host city established a special task force to organize the event. The 2000 Super Bowl in Atlanta was reported to have generated an estimated economic impact of $285 million (Sports Business Market Research, Inc., 2000).

*Street and Smith's Sport Business Journal* (1999) estimated the annual U.S. market for spectator sports was over $22 billion, while sport-related travel was worth over $44 billion. A study of 100 sport events by the American Coalition for Entertainment and Sports Sponsorship concluded that these events pumped $1.8 billion of direct spectator expenditure into the local host economies, without using multiplier analysis (Sports Business Market Research, 2000). However measured, sport tourism is definitely big business.

The benefits of any niche market strategy are usually expressed in terms of economic impacts that stem from an injection of visitors' money into the local economy. In particular, convention and visitors bureaus and other Destination Marketing Organizations (DMOs) seek to use events to generate new demand for local commercial accommodations and other businesses, to stimulate demand in off-peak seasons, to generate favorable publicity, and even to make money (Getz, Anderson, and Sheehan, 1998). Commercial accommodation operators look specifically for bed nights to be generated, and airlines such as Air New Zealand explicitly create and sponsor events to fill seats. The travel and hospitality industry, as a rule, is not interested in peak-season events because they usually displace regular business.

Some American cities benefit more from sport event tourism, according to Tourism Industry Association of America (1999) data. The biggest winners appear to be Charlotte, North Carolina, with 19 percent of its tourists attending sport events, and Indianapolis, Indiana, at 17 percent. Sport event tourism is not just for large cities; everyone can compete. Eriksen (1997), for example, reported on the success of Boulder, Colorado (population under 100,000), which annually attracts 38,000 to its 10K run, and Ames, Iowa, population 25,000, which pulls in 15,000 participants and 30,000 spectators to its annual Iowa Games Sports Festival. It is also a particularly attractive market for resorts, given their built-in orientation toward recreation and sport, and for individual hotels that can develop sport event packages.

Benefits might also accrue in the community through increased leisure opportunities, improved facilities, an increased feeling of pride at being host to great events, and a heightened interest in sport and fitness. Media coverage and positive word-of-mouth recommendations from sport event tourists can also improve the destination's reputation and help to create a positive image as a place to visit or in which to host more events.

### Potential Costs and Problems

Sport event tourism does not develop without significant costs, including capital investments, operating and marketing costs, and a number of potentially serious impacts. As noted by Higham (1999), the benefits of mega-event sport tourism have likely been oversold and the costs underreported, especially for externally imposed mega events, such as the Olympics. Higham, therefore, argues for an emphasis on regularly scheduled and participatory sport events.

Bramwell (1997) reviewed sport mega events within the context of principles of sustainable tourism, focusing on the 1991 World Student Games in Sheffield, England. Both costs and benefits were noted, but an overall evaluation was difficult because Sheffield, similar to most event hosts, failed to monitor longer-term impacts. Whitson and Macintosh (1996) warned that sport mega events in particular are beneficial only to the affluent elite and seldom benefit the disadvantaged in society. Indeed, major events tend to displace low-cost housing.

Capital costs for new and improved sport facilities can be high, and there has been an unfortunate tendency—especially in North America—for the public sector to pay for facilities that generate mostly private benefits, such as to professional sport clubs. The cost/benefit evaluation upon which these decisions are based are often flawed, so the case for luring professional sport teams to cities has been controversial, to say the least.

Even though mega events usually generate a legacy of new sport facilities, they carry long-term operational costs that can easily make them "white elephants." In Calgary, Alberta, Canada, however, the large Olympic cash legacy continues to support excellent sport facilities that benefit the community. The problem is that highly specialized sport facilities (especially for winter sports such as ski jumping and luge) will always have very limited use.

Environmental and community impacts of events must be evaluated. The larger the event and the busier the event calendar, the more traffic, noise, and other problems are likely to arise. This argues for specially designed and located sport event venues, at least for major events. The philosophy of "green games" has caught on, especially with the sanction of the International Olympic Committee. However, the contention that sport mega events can be environmentally friendly, with their inherent emphasis on large-scale developments and mass tourism, is definitely open to debate.

It cannot be assumed that all special sport events will generate economic benefits. The "attribution question" must first be answered: Did the event attract visitors who would not otherwise have traveled to the destination? If the event was partially responsible, some of the economic impact can be attributed to it. If the event held visitors longer or resulted in higher spending from travelers who came to the area for other reasons, then some of their spending can be counted.

## THE SPORT EVENT TOURIST

Although there are some useful data on American sport event tourists, little research has been conducted elsewhere on this subject. In particular, we know little about indivuduals'motivation to take sport event trips. Nogawa, Yamaguchi, and Hagi (1996, p. 47) found that "Little attention has been given to the research focusing on tourists whose main purpose of travel was to attend sports events as spectators." These researchers examined the domestic Japanese sport event tourist, while others (Cha, McCleary, and Uysal, 1995) looked at sport as a motivator for outbound Japanese tourists. Tourism Canada (Marshall Macklin Monaghan, Ltd., 1993) used general international pleasure travel data to review the importance of sport spectator tourists in Canada. In general this is a neglected field, and a comprehensive sport event tourism research effort is essential.

### Motivation to Travel for Sport Events

It has been theorized that travel in general is motivated by a combination of seeking and escaping (Iso-Ahola, 1980) in both personal and interpersonal contexts. In the context of sport events this might have two generic dimensions. Sport events away from home can have an appeal based on their uniqueness or their quality that, when combined with escaping from the familiar and routine, generates personal and interpersonal benefits which make it a worthwhile expenditure of time and resources. More specifically, research is needed on particular types of sport events and on the difference between spectating and participating. Important motivational differences are likely to be found when comparing families to individuals or groups of friends, comparing age groups and genders, and racial, ethnic, or cultural groups.

Getz and Cheyne (1997) argued that special event motivation centered on unique benefits and behavior outside a person's normal experiences. Specific to sport events, they found that focus group participants identified important quality factors that can influence a decision to travel to an event, including reputation of the event, caliber of participants (the best in their field), international scope, and the presence of celebrities. Rarity is also a factor. The Olympics are identified as a once-in-a-lifetime opportunity for spectators. Packaging events is important, as many people taking an event trip want a range of leisure experiences. Getting drawn into the excitement of a crowd and the atmosphere in general, can be powerful motivators, especially at international sport events where patriotism is a factor. Social factors are also high, as individuals often leave the decision to attend an event to others in their family or to a group of friends.

One study by Green and Chalip (1998) determined that participants in the Key West Women's Flag Football Tournament sought the opportunity to get together to celebrate their subculture. The place of the event may be much less important than the nature of the event—especially if opportunities are provided for both formal and informal socializing and celebration.

## Who Is the Sport Event Tourist?

Sport event tourists fall into several categories. Many events are spectator oriented and the tourism benefit is mainly to those who travel to view the competition (see Figure 3.1).

Numerous sport events are of the participation variety, primarily involving athletes and often their friends and families. Indeed, some of the biggest impacts stem from events such as marathons, masters games, and amateur sport tournaments at which paying spectators are often a minor element. Events also attract officials, media coverage, and sponsors, and these too are valuable target segments. A related category is the media event, which typically draws small tourist numbers and potentially higher participant numbers, and has a major potential benefit through televised coverage.

Overall demand for sport activities has been rising globally (Priestley, 1995), and travel related to sport events has become substantial, yet the amount of research conducted on sport tourists has been minimal. Douvis, Yusof, and Douvis (1999) reported on available research, finding sometimes contradictory conclusions and a dearth of information on sport spectator tourists. They did conclude that middle-aged males forty to forty-five were especially interested in sport participation tourism, and that college students also represented a substantial target market.

FIGURE 3.1. Spectator-oriented events: Snowboarders in Verbier, Switzerland, gather at an extreme snowboarding competition for the awarding of prizes. (Photo used by permission of Office du Tourisme Verbier.)

They also recommended that researchers pay more attention to differences between racial and ethnic groups as well as examine the relationship between sport tourism and the need for action and levels of stimulation.

Data on international sport event tourists are meager. It has been reported that about 2 percent of foreign visitors to Australia were influenced by an intent to watch or spectate in an organized sport event, although the proportion was as high as 7 percent for Irish tourists in 1998 (Australia: Industry Science Resources, 2000). Almost 7 percent of foreign tourists in Australia actually attended an organized sport event, but almost 30 percent of Irish tourists in Australia did so. Tourism Canada reported that of 33.5 million person trips to Canada by Americans in 1991, about 2 percent included a spectator sport event, as did a similar percentage of overseas visitors (Marshall Macklin Monaghan, Ltd., 1993). From 1990 data, it was revealed that about 5 percent of domestic trips in Canada included a spectator sport event. Data from 1994 revealed that 27 million trips were taken for the purpose of participating in or spectating at a sport event, accounting for over 36 percent of all tourism trips.

One of the best sources on domestic sport event tourism comes from the Tourism Industry Association of America report: "Profile of Travelers Who Attend Sport Events" (1999), using 1997 survey data that examined travel over the previous five years. Highlights of that report follow, with a few other references where comparisons are possible.

## Volume of Sport Event Tourism

Sport event tourism has increased in popularity in the United States alongside other forms of special interest travel. Thirty-eight percent of U.S. adults have been sport event travelers (defined as those attending a sport event and traveling at least fifty miles from home) either as event participants or spectators within the previous five years. Seventy-six percent of these travelers listed the sport event as their primary purpose for their most recent such trip. Fully 84 percent of the most recent sport event trips were to spectate rather than to participate, and 25 percent were to watch children or grandchildren play in the event. Sixteen percent of sport event travelers participated in the event, including a minor portion who both participated and spectated. In total, 6 percent of all resident trips (amounting to 60 million person trips) in 1997 included a sport event, making it the tenth most popular travel activity. Griffiths (1999) reported that Australians are very active sport event tourists, with 1.6 million spectating away from home in 1995. Most of them traveled only within their own state.

## Demographics of the Sport Event Tourist

In the United States, 45 percent of men and 31 percent of women attended sport events while traveling over the previous five years. The dominant segment consists of parents, especially among those on trips made specifically for a sport event, so there is a very large family market to tap. The average age of the sport event traveler was forty-five years, but compared to all U.S. travelers sport event travelers were more likely to be younger, to have children, and to be employed full time. The percentage of sport event travel parties having children was 30 percent, compared to 21 percent overall, but party size was comparable.

Gibson (1998) determined the "active sport tourist" to be male, but also college educated with a higher income. Gibson said these active sport tourists are likely to travel for participation in their favorite pursuits well into retirement.

## Types of Events

The most popular sport events attracting tourists were baseball/softball (17 percent of adults had done so over the previous five years), followed by football (15 percent), basketball (9 percent), auto/truck racing (8 percent), golf tournament (6 percent), skiing/snowboarding (5 percent), soccer (5 percent), and ice hockey (4 percent), while all other sports events attracted 13 percent of adults. Professional and amateur sports were attended equally on respondents' most recent trips. Professional sports attracted 50 percent of the travelers, with the most popular amateur events being high school (14 percent) and college-level sports (13 percent). The other categories of amateur sport events were amateur athletics (12 percent), Little League (5 percent), church/intramural (4 percent), and other (6 percent). Summer is the peak season, followed by autumn. It is very interesting to note that men and women identically ranked the top four types of sport events attended, although females were less interested in golf and hockey. Men definitely traveled more for professional sport events (54 percent of males compared to 45 percent of females). Mothers (the infamous "soccer moms") do support their children's sporting activities.

## The Sport Event Trip

Sport event trips involve about the same amount of spending as all types of trips, although research has determined that this segment tends to purchase sport-related equipment and/or clothes for their trips. Travel is done by car most often, although some use air transport. Overnight travel for sport events is high, with 84 percent of trips being overnight, compared to 82 percent for all U.S. trips. Just over half (52 percent) stayed in commercial accommodation, but their overnight trips were shorter than the average U.S. overnight trip (three nights versus 3.3). Overall, sport event trips were the same average length (3.3 nights) as all trips.

Group tours accounted for only 4 percent of the total person trips among sport event travelers, which is the same proportion as for all U.S. travelers. Party size for sport event trips was found to be slightly higher (2.1 compared to 1.9 persons).

*Special Segments*

There are many clearly identifiable, special sport event tourism segments, each with their own events. Pitts (1999) reported on the gay and lesbian sport tourism industry, finding this target segment to be large and affluent, with its own sport travel industry, media, and events. The Gay Games are an annual, international participation event with substantial economic impact, and many smaller, sport-specific events are growing in popularity. A number of professional groups hold major sport events at the international, national, and regional levels, such as the World Police and Fire Games. This event is won through competitive bidding by cities, and the 1998 event in Calgary, Alberta, Canada, attracted 8,600 participants. Masters Games have become a global phenomenon, involving older adult competitors, as have Paralympic games for persons with disabilities.

## FORCES AND TRENDS SHAPING SPORT EVENT TOURISM

### Media Influence

A major force for growth has been television and especially narrowcasting—that is, aiming broadcasts at specific target audiences. The multiplicity of sport is a cultural phenomenon reflecting leisure trends in general, but it is aided by the desire of the media to cover new, exciting events, by sponsors who pump money into sports to reach their customers, and by destinations that compete with each other to attract events. According to Gratton and Kokolakakis (1997), the biggest single change in sports has been the dramatic rise in revenues from television broadcast rights, and this in part reflects the increase in dedicated sport channels on television. Global live coverage of events helps fuel interest and increase audience numbers for advertisers, while the elevation of athletes to celebrity status generates even more media coverage and oportunities for merchandising.

## *Sponsorship*

Commercial sponsorship of sport events continues to fuel growth, so much so that Delpy (1998) argued that sponsorship was the key to sport event success. The International Events Group (IEG) (1995) estimated that in 1984 event sponsorship in North America was valued at $350 million, but that by 1992 it had mushroomed to $3.2 billion! The success of the 1984 Los Angeles Olympics was a major contributing factor, as is the phenomenon of "relationship" and "lifestyle" marketing (Schreiber and Lenson, 1994), which finds benefit in using events to detect, access, and cultivate specific market segments. The bulk of this money has always gone to sport events but, according to IEG, the proportion has declined from 90 percent in 1984 to 65 percent in 1995. Sponsorship dollars, plus accompanying marketing clout and expertise, have elevated many events in terms of size and quality, while facilitating the creation of several new events. Indeed, some events such as the Super Bowl have become corporate events, being more and more oriented to attracting and hosting the corporate elite.

Delpy (1998) provided advice on how to develop sport event sponsorship, with emphasis on understanding what sponsors want in terms of hospitality/entertaining, relationship building, and leveraged marketing. Building a suitable sponsor base should be a priority for destinations developing sport event tourism.

There is no doubt that sponsorship is driving the event sector, but where is it headed? Many have questioned the impact of sponsorship on the Olympics, particularly because of the high level of commercialism associated with the 1996 Atlanta Olympics. How many other events have changed their orientation or goals because of the demands of sponsorship or because of the new opportunities that sponsors and media partners afford? Are all these changes worthwhile? Many perspectives on this issue are legitimate, so the answers cannot be simplistic. Research into goal displacement and the evolution of the event as a sport and as a sponsorship vehicle is needed; the opinions of many stakeholder groups will be required.

## Urban Renewal and Economic Development

Through the 1980s and 1990s, American cities in particular engaged in urban redevelopment schemes that "put a heavy emphasis on sports, entertainment and tourism as a source of revenue for the cities" (Sports Business Market Research, Inc., 2000, p. 167). According to Gratton and Kokolakakis (1997, p. 13), in the United Kingdom "sports events are currently the main platform for economic regeneration in many cities." Whitson and Macintosh (1996, p. 279) argued that countries and major cities compete for sport mega events to demonstrate to the world their "modernity and economic dynamism"; to those authors, international sport "has become one of the most powerful and effective vehicles for the showcasing of place and for the creation of what the industry calls 'destination image.'" This force reflects the growing integration of news, entertainment, and promotion. Cities have to position themselves as service centers, places for entertainment and shopping, because their manufacturing sectors are no longer vital.

Indianapolis is widely acknowledged as being a sport tourism success story. Rozin (2000) termed it a "classic case" of civic turnaround, based first on the efforts of a newly established Indiana Sports Corporation to attract amateur sport governing bodies after 1978. Massive infrastructure development followed, aided by the private Lilly Endowment, pumping a total of $884 million into sport facilities between 1979 and 1984. This helped make the city attractive for other corporate headquarters. Indianapolis expected to gain some $304 million from sport events in the year 2000.

Numerous cities or regions have established sport commissions or event development corporations that have the mandate to create, bid on, and facilitate sport events. Most destination marketing organizations also engage in bidding. A profile of the Queensland, Australia, Events Corporation is given in Getz (1997). In the United States, the Cincinnati-based National Association of Sports Commissions was established in 1992 and pulls together commissions that had their roots in chambers of commerce or visitors and convention bureaus. Their executive director at the time, Don Schumacher, explained the rationale: "Increasingly, the value of the sports event industry in terms of tourism, economic development and image enhancement is being recognized. In response, communities are forming sports commissions whose purpose is to attract sports events" (Schumacher, 2000). The national association provides a forum for exchange between commissions, national sport governing bodies, event rights holders (i.e., the owners of events), sport marketing firms, and service or equipment suppliers.

## Strategic Event and Facility Development

The competition for events is also stimulated by the trend for cities to build major facilities. Large-scale, multipurpose facilities, such as the Rose Gardens in Portland, Oregon (Deckard, 1995), are constructed to attract or keep professional sports teams, for the benefit of local amateur sports, or as part of urban renewal and economic development strategies. Once facilities are built their continuing use as event venues becomes a financial necessity.

Massive growth in the number of festivals and other special events can also be attributed to strategic planning on the part of many governmental agencies and tourism or economic development organizations. Events created specifically as tourist attractions tend to be better funded and marketed than those operated by volunteers and/or not-for-profit bodies.

## Sport Popularity and Diversity

Sport continues to multiply in variety, each with its own facility requirements and events. What once were only recreational pursuits, such as the many forms of boating or exercising, now have leagues and global events. Some have even become Olympic events. This makes it possible for destinations to specialize or diversify in their appeal, finding competitive advantage within the sport event field. Perhaps more important, there has been substantial international growth in the number and size of mass participation events.

But is sport activity and spectating increasing? Bull and Weed (1999) note that sport participation in several European countries, including Great Britain, continues to grow. Women's sport is certainly more popular, especially in terms of television coverage and audiences (Sports Business Market Research, Inc., 2000). The U.S. National Endowment for the Arts, in July 1998, reported that 41 percent of the adult population attended sport events, up from 37 percent in

1992 (Sports Business Market Research, Inc., 2000). Gibson (1998, p. 159) concluded that "very few Americans are involved on a regular basis [with sport activity] and 60 percent are not regularly active at all." In other words, a small minority does most of the activity, so that participatory sport events are not drawing on the whole population.

## PLANNING, DEVELOPING, AND MARKETING
## SPORT EVENT TOURISM

Destinations wanting to be globally competitive in sport event tourism will have to engage in strategic planning. The Australians, pioneers in event development and marketing, formulated a draft national sport tourism strategy in late 2000. Their planning process identified and assessed key issues, including the following:

- Coordination
- Education and training
- Government regulations
- Infrastructure development
- Evaluation of benefits
- Data and research
- Implementation

A recommended planning process is illustrated in Figure 3.2. Essentially, strategies for supply and demand development are required (including marketing), a formal planning process has to be established, and organizational work must be undertaken. The suggested competitive advantages are either preexisting or follow from strategies, leading to attainment of sport event tourism goals. Nine elements in the planning process are shown in Figure 3.2, but they do not necessarily have to be sequential, and some can be combined. The discussion starts with vision and leadership.

### Vision and Leadership

The logical starting point is for a tourism organization such as a chamber of commerce or convention and visitors bureau to take the lead, perhaps in partnership with sport bodies. Specific organizational issues are examined in this text, but at the earliest stage in the

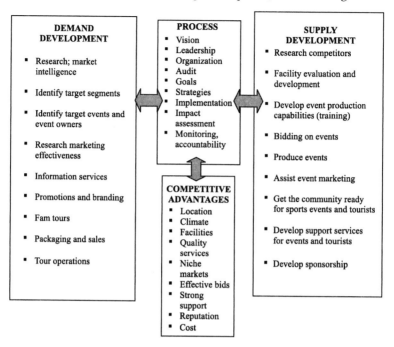

FIGURE 3.2. Sport event planning, development, and marketing process.

process the formulation of a general vision for developing sport event tourism should take priority over the details of planning and implementation. At this early stage it is also necessary to forge relationships where perhaps none previously existed.

## *Destination Audit*

What is your resource base for sport event tourism, and what is its potential relative to competitors? In some cases the major resource or competitive advantage will be climate for all-year events, or perhaps an excellent location relative to essential markets. In other cases it can be superior facilities or proven event management capabilities. What facilities, infrastructure, and services exist for sport events, and what must be added or improved to reach certain target markets? Other resources consist of sport clubs and organizations, specialty tour operators, and services aimed at sport tourists. Having a professional, experienced group of event managers and volunteers is a major asset.

Developing a calendar of existing and planned events is useful, but it should also be determined which events already attract sport tourists and which ones could be marketed better. This leads to matching the current portfolio of events with existing and potential target markets. Remember that target markets consist of spectators, participants, teams, governing sport bodies, media, and sponsors.

Competitor analysis is always important. Competitors are those destinations developing or bidding on the same events, not necessarily your next-door neighbor. Collaboration within a region, as in central Florida (see the case study in this chapter), will likely pay off, as will networking. Belonging to sport and tourism associations will result in a great deal of learning about what works and what does not. Combining resource evaluation with competitor analysis, do a strengths, weaknesses, oportunities, and threats (SWOT) analysis. What are your destination's relative strengths, weaknesses, opportunities, and threats? Identifying a unique selling proposition or distinctive competency should help with strategy development. What does your destination offer or do better than most competitors? Many are constrained by size and have to pursue niche markets. Others can seek to develop the biggest and best capability for a variety of sport events. Also consider ease of access to your destination and to specific venues by automobile and public transport.

### *Organization and Human Resources*

In locations where the subject of sport event tourism is new, a series of community and stakeholder consultations will likely be necessary. For example, the Canadian Tourism Commission (CTC, n.d.) has been operating a "community development process" to encourage cities or destinations to develop sport tourism strategies. CTC also plans to offer a sport event database, national facility standards for hosting events, impact assessment tools, event-related intelligence, and relationship marketing to link sport organizations to the tourism industry.

Partnerships might have to be forged or strengthened. Sport bodies do not necessarily consider tourism, and the two do not automatically mix. Tourism, when it exploits well-established policy or social domains such as the arts or sports, might even be seen as a dangerous interloper. Indeed, converting sport events into tourist attractions, or creating a program to develop sport event tourism, might very well result in the displacement of goals and resources. Consequently, the biggest challenge in many destinations will be to formulate a working partnership.

Having examined policy in the United Kingdom, Weed and Bull (1998, p. 295) concluded there was "a general lack of genuine liaison and partnership between the regional agencies responsible for sport and tourism policy." To foster meaningful partnerships it will be necessary to understand and deal with different organizational cultures and structures. A lack of communication between sport and tourism bodies can also be identified as a barrier to developing sport tourism in South Africa (Swart, 1998).

Hall (1997) reports the creation of Eventscorp in New Zealand, modeled after Australian events development corporations, but with the unique twist of being a joint venture of the New Zealand Tourism Board and the Hillary Commission, which is the lead government agency for sport and leisure. Its primary function is to encourage and assist organizations in bidding on international sport events.

Identification of educational and training needs is important. Event organizers, especially volunteers, might have to be informed of the goals and processes of sport event tourism and especially regarding related marketing needs. Facility managers might be interested in learning more about bidding on events and packaging for tourists. Tourism marketers often do not understand the intricacies of event production or the needs of sport participants and governing bodies. The hospitality and travel trades could benefit from information on target markets and their preferences. The question of who will do the training and provide ongoing information is critical; this is where dedicated sport event agencies will have the advantage.

### Set Goals

The following goals suggest the desired outcomes or benefits of sport event tourism.

- Attract high-yield visitors (spectators, participants, officials, and media).

- Generate a favorable image for the destination (related to destination branding efforts).
- Develop new infrastructure (for both community use and future sport event development).
- Attract government grants and corporate sponsorships (generating additional income for the area).
- Generate an increased rate of tourism growth (compared to the situation without intervention).
- Improve the organizational, marketing, and bidding capability of the community (to sustain sport event tourism).
- Secure a financial legacy for management of new sport facilities (prevent "white elephants" that could drain community resources and generate ill feelings).
- Maximize the use of and revenue for existing facilities (to the benefit of the community and especially its taxpayers).
- Increase community support for sport and sport events (by demonstrating the benefits).

Unintended impacts must also be considered, as not every outcome might be positive or well received. The planning process therefore has to build in an ongoing research and evaluation system.

### Formulate Strategies

Demand and product development strategies can be pursued individually or collectively to develop sport event tourism. They will have to be supported by research, ongoing market intelligence, and monitoring for effectiveness. For each strategy the outcome should be attainment of competitive advantages. The ensuing discussion focuses on supply development strategies, but each of them also entail demand development implications.

### Creating New Events

The potential for creating new sport events seems limitless, but each should be subjected to a rigorous feasibility study including a cost/benefit evaluation before money is invested. Air New Zealand has created a series of international sport events for older adults to help fill off-season seats, but destinations have a problem when it comes to creating events: whose responsibility is it? Without a specially mandated sport commission or tourist organization the job might not get done.

Events should be created only when the desired portfolio is lacking, as reliance on bidding and on existing events can accomplish many goals. Events are created for specific target markets, with existing and planned facilities setting the limits. This is an exercise in product/market matching, and each destination should be able to find one or more niche markets to pursue competitively.

New events are also an excellent way to help brand the destination by reinforcing imagery and themes, and attracting specific target segments. An "adventure" destination, for example, should offer adventure sport events. Branding, and positioning in general, can vary with the target markets, so destinations can strive to be both culturally renowned and a sport resort.

## *Facility Development*

The capacity of venues and visitor services in a community will largely determine the size of events attracted or created. Most sport events require specialized facilities, very few of which can accommodate more than one or a few types of sport. This makes sport tourism development capital intensive, but with the advantage that most facilities have community value as well. Barbados is one country that has deliberately built new facilities for sport event tourism, as well as to enhance its own athletic potential (*Journal of Sport Tourism,* 1997). Specific goals set in 1987 were to reduce tourism seasonality and boost tourist earnings. To accomplish this, the government ministries for sport and tourism were merged, and the Barbados Tourism Authority continues to target sports tourism niche markets and to bid on events. The case study of Seminole County Florida, documented later in this chapter, illustrates a strategy of facility development.

Stevens (1997), referring to the facility development strategy of Cardiff, Wales, argued that sport venues should be built with a number of objectives, including:

- Provide community access
- Meet the technical specifications of events and sport governing bodies
- Meet the requirements of competitors

- Provide offices for sports organizations and administrators
- Incorporate state-of-the-art telecommunications
- Provide for research, education, and training
- Provide medical services

*Assistance to Events*

Many options exist for providing assistance to events and organizations bidding on or hosting sport events. As detailed by Getz (1997), the funding agency has a number of fundamental choices and issues to resolve. First, what type of assistance should be provided? To whom? Under what circumstances and conditions? For what purposes? The Seminole County case illustrates a typical form of assistance directed specifically at the marketing of events to increase their tourist appeal. Another example is from the city of Thunder Bay, Ontario, Canada, which developed an event hosting strategy including application procedures and criteria to receive event development grants. The city also produces a calendar of events, provides a central event contact and directory of contact persons, and a standard bid package.

Many tourism-oriented organizations choose to support only marketing efforts of events, rather than operational grants. Event organizers might not otherwise undertake tourist-specific promotions, familiarity (fam) tours, or packaging. Event organizers also often need help in connecting with corporate sponsors or making sponsorship bids. Bridging the gap between events and tour operators is another valuable way to assist events and enhance their tourism potential.

*Bidding on Events*

Little attention has been paid to event bidding by researchers. Ongoing work by this author suggests that convention and visitors bureaus in North America are very active in bidding, and although conventions and meetings usually predominate, sport events are also highly sought after. Preliminary findings of a survey of North American bureaus reveals that bureaus decide which events to bid on based on the following major criteria:

- Economic impact (usually expressed in terms of visitor spending or yield)

- Room nights generated (bureaus are closely tied to the commercial accommodation sector)
- Season (all events are preferred in otherwise slow demand periods)
- Capacity (availability of hotels and facilities)
- Awareness and positive imagery generated by media coverage and event participants
- Competitive advantages in going after specific events (e.g., local support, track record of successful event hosting, location, cost, etc.)

Note that some of these criteria pertain to desired outputs (i.e., the benefits) and some to process (how to win events). Bids are often competitive with somewhat unpredictable outcomes, but sometimes events can be won through strong relationships with the sport governing body that awards them. Research on Olympic bids by Persson (2000) establishes the bid as a communication process, drawing attention to the nature and effectiveness of the key messages, messengers, and the political or social context of the communication. Not all event bids will be won through technical excellence or outspending the competition.

Bid Regina is a unique group set up specifically to bid on sport and other events for the Canadian city of Regina, Saskatchewan. It works closely with Tourism Regina (a convention and visitors bureau) but mainly encourages and assists event bidding by local associations and clubs. Bid Regina pursues only larger events with city wide benefits and high-profile status. Its coordinator, Brenda Bathgate, expressed its mandate this way: "Bid Regina takes a proactive approach in combining the strengths of all the stakeholders in the community for the purpose of attracting new local, regional provincial, national and international events and conferences to our city" (Bathgate, 2000). In the first years of its operation, success came most often from winning sport events.

Bidding on major events has become very competitive, so there are many losers. Can the bid effort itself be justified, knowing that many losses are likely? This is a particularly important question for Olympic and other global-scale event bids, because the effort can easily cost many millions of dollars over a multiyear period. Some potential advantages of the bid itself can be identified:

- Attracting publicity to the destination
- Mobilizing public support (although opposition can be a negative)

- Attracting interest and resources from sponsors
- Creating partnerships and organizational capability
- Improving infrastructure and venues

Agencies and communities making major bids should do so with a strategy to attain specific benefits. Researchers will have to develop new measures and methods for assessing the value of bid efforts.

## Packaging

Destinations can work with tour companies and transport carriers to package sport events, or do it themselves in partnership with the event organizers and sponsors. For example, the Malaysian Tourism Promotion Board works with Malaysia Airlines to promote sport event packages at the resort of Penang (Aidid, 1997). Types of tours that can be developed include:

- Packages self-organized by sport teams
- Packages self-organized by fans or affinity groups
- Packages by wholesalers sold by travel agents or other retailers
- Special packages assembled and promoted by carriers (air, coach, rail)
- Incentive tours (assembled by specialist tour companies and sold to corporations)
- Packages developed and sold directly by event organizers
- "Hospitality" tours offered by event sponsors to their staff, suppliers, buyers, friends

## An Event Portfolio

Major destinations should ideally possess an attractive portfolio of sport events by type, size, and attractiveness for tourists. The occasional mega event should be balanced by bidding on lesser occasional events and developing periodic local or regional events. Elevating an event from local appeal to one attractive for tourists requires resources. Moving from domestic to international appeal requires a quantum leap in resources and marketing effort, so only a few sport events will achieve that goal. Many communities can never aspire to hosting large and expensive-to-win events, but they can carve out a suitable niche in, say, small-scale amateur sport meets. Thus, the event portfolio has to be customized for each destination, including the choice of sport versus other types of events.

There seems to be a natural temptation for governments and tourism agencies to emphasize mega events at the expense of developing a balanced portfolio. Swart (1998) notes this problem in South Africa where the South Africa Sport Tourism Agency, created in 1997, focused "almost exclusively on mega events such as the Whitbread Round-the-World Yacht Race, the All Africa Games, the Cricket World Cup and the Soccer World Cup" (p. 9). Swart argued for more smaller and regular events.

## *Implementation*

Key elements in any implementation plan include policies and programs to achieve goals and implement strategies, including determination of funding and other resources to be committed, identification of responsibility, a time line, and establishment of performance measures. A formal action plan is a good tool to help outline all the tasks and time lines.

Funding might very well be the big issue. Plans are easier to develop than to implement, so it is wise to ensure that a realistic funding scheme is formulated before a plan is finalized. Several models can be suggested:

- Public sector capital developments for new or improved facilities
- Public sector financial assistance (loans, grants, bid support)
- Private sector investments in facilities, marketing, bidding
- Corporate sponsorship of events

Some degree of public/private partnership makes sense in developing sport event tourism. Major sport facilities and events almost always involve and require some form of public assistance, and this has to be justified on the basis of public benefits to be attained. Organizations such as convention and visitors bureaus and sport commissions are typically bridges between public and private sectors, so their roles in implementation will be critical.

Impediments and unexpected consequences might occur, so the implementation process has to be adaptive. In particular, government laws and regulations pertaining to customs and immigration might impact sport events.

## Impact Assessment, Monitoring, and Accountability

With such large amounts of effort and resources devoted to the sport event sector, demands for accountability have risen. Communities are asking their event agencies and organizers to be accountable for spending public funds and for using community facilities and infrastructure. Wise event managers provide their sponsors and media partners with detailed postevent evaluations and ensure that their concerns are reflected in planning the next event. Sport commissions and tourist bureaus are held accountable to members and governmental partners for money spent on bids.

Many issues and challenges are associated with impact assessment, and the following discussion examines three major elements: economic impact assessment, marketing effectiveness, and the special case of media impacts.

### Economic Impact Assessment

Numerous sport events have been examined as to their economic and other impacts, although many studies are never published. In fact, some event sponsors or development agencies routinely release only favorable results to the public. The practice of event impact assessment is sometimes suspect, as a great deal of exaggeration has accompanied some published results. Many authors have documented the problems and challenges (Getz 1987, 1997; Crompton, 1999; Crompton and McKay, 1994), and recently efforts have been made by researchers to develop a valid, standardized approach (Carlsen, Getz, and Soutar, 2001).

A group of experts were commissioned by the state of New South Wales in Australia to develop a model for assessing the economic impacts of events (Dwyer et al., 2000), and they assessed a large number of sport event studies. Unfortunately, they detected little consistency in research methods, scope, accuracy, and assumptions, which made comparisons, trend analysis, and forecasting extremely difficult. As a consequence, New South Wales now requires uniform impact assessments of any event it sponsors. This problem is global, so that any agency desiring to assess sport event impacts and use that in forecasting (to determine which events to bid on or support) will have to adopt a similar research requirement.

Crompton (1999) examined fourteen sport tournaments and sixteen festivals and spectator events hosted by seven community park and recreation agencies in the United States, with an intent to develop principles and guidelines for economic impact assessments. Results demonstrate that economic benefits accrue mostly from events that attract the largest number of visitors, but without an overnight stay the impacts are minimal. As well, large events (in terms of numbers of participants) can generate lower economic benefits than small events because the impacts stem from travel specifically motivated by the event, not from other purposes. Many events attract "time switchers" who would have come to the destination anyway, and their spending cannot be claimed as a benefit of the event. Crompton concluded that for many communities sport tournaments are likely to generate higher benefits than festivals, especially multiple day sport events.

A number of key issues and problems are involved in the economic impact assessment of events. To attribute tourism benefits to an event, the evaluator must demonstrate that visitors traveled because of the event in whole or in part and did not merely switch the time of a planned visit. Alternatively, it can sometimes be demonstrated through visitor surveys that an event led directly to extra spending at the destination by keeping people there longer or encouraging more spending than planned.

Frequently, tourists attracted to large events displace regular or other potential visitors, which can result in damage to a destination's established tourist traffic and exaggeration of benefits. Analysis is required to determine the extent and duration of displacement.

A financial legacy is usually required to support new facilities, lest they become liabilities to the host community. Although emphasis is frequently placed on the legacy of sport facilities, they are not always useful or accessible to area residents.

Overbuilding of accommodation for anticipated mega event demand is a common problem, resulting in a postevent reduction in occupancy rates and profitability. Temporary additional accommodations can be used instead to offset this risk.

In New Zealand it was observed by the minister for tourism that event tourists to that country spent three times more per day than the average visitor (Hall, 1997). It is a mistake to emphasize high quantity (i.e., the number of tourists attracted or total attendance), as this can lead to overcrowding, displacement of other visitor segments, and negative impacts on the community and environment. Rather, destinations should focus on yield per visitor, the best of which display these characteristics:

- They travel because of the event (new spending results).
- They can be attracted to stay in commercial accommodation during off-peak periods.
- They engage in other destination activities and spend money on a variety of local goods and services.
- They will return and/or spread positive word-of-mouth recommendations.

Irwin and Sandler (1997) undertook research on a variety of American collegiate sport championships and determined that sport event tourists affiliated with participating teams had the greatest yield per person for the destination.

## Evaluating Marketing Effectiveness

Large sums of money are often spent on marketing, and only a pittance is allotted for demonstrating that the money was well spent. Faith in the benefits arising from sport event tourism has to be earned through research into marketing effectiveness and return on investment. The typical measure of return on investment for tourism projects is that of the economic impacts generated. The biggest single issue relating to marketing effectiveness is the hypothetical value of media coverage, because it is difficult to prove that tourism directly benefits.

## Media Impact Assessment

Media coverage of sport events should translate into greater destination awareness and a positive image on the part of viewers, but the connection between media coverage and future demand has not been researched systematically and remains tenuous. The main problem is how to measure the real impact of viewing a sport event, or many events, on viewers' perceptions, images, and travel decisions.

In theory, consumer decisions are built on product awareness, development of a positive image, assessment of potential benefits relative to the competition, and—if purchases are made—ultimately brand loyalty (i.e., repeat visits). Forecasters assume that the greater the event and its media coverage, such as for the World Cup of Soccer or the Olympics, the bigger the so-called "induced" demand will be.

The normal practice for sponsors, and for tourism or event development agencies supporting sport events, is to evaluate media coverage and develop surrogate dollar values for the imputed benefits. This is based mainly on what comparable advertising might cost. According to Paterson (2000), who undertakes such evaluations for clients, there are a number of problems with this process. First, verification of actual media coverage, before the event, during the event, and afterward, in terms of geographic coverage, quantity, and quality, is problematic. Details of sponsor and destination visibility must be quantified, including signage and other content. An audience analysis should also be undertaken to determine the real number of viewers rather than potential reach, and how people actually viewed (or heard) the coverage. Speed and Thompson (2000) also advised that it is not enough to consider exposure alone when selecting and evaluating sponsorships. Market research is needed to demonstrate the fit between events and sponsors and consumer attitudes toward both.

Frequently the destination is not featured in sport event coverage, a problem identified as having reduced the tourism effectiveness of the World Championships in Athletics in Gothenburg, Sweden (Mossberg, 2000). With that in mind, destinations must work to maximize the destination's benefits from sport event media coverage, learn from past experience and other destinations, and integrate sport events with destination branding and marketing. It is important to work closely with sponsors and media people to communicate the destination's goals and desired imagery, including familiarization trips. They should remember that sponsors often use media coverage in their marketing and networking and might produce their own videos. Destinations should discuss ways to incorporate destination imagery and messages into broadcasts and videos.

Identifying target market segments is also important. Golf events are a vehicle for attracting golfers, not necessarily other sports enthusiasts. Research of the target markets should be undertaken to determine what aspect of an event broadcast will have the greatest effect. For example, are golfers motivated to travel because they see an attractive or challenging golf course by its association with professional golfers and celebrities, or by factual information about golfing at that destination?

Planners should work with tour operators and travel carriers to package the event and get them to advertise on the event broadcasts, and be sure they mention periodic and major events in their communications so that the venue and destination become associated with sport events.

Careful attention should be paid to the exact mechanisms by which imagery and messages will be broadcast. Unless there is some specific reason to incorporate them, broadcasters might very well neglect everything but their own advertisers. Can you get destination postcards inserted into the broadcast, not as paid advertisements but as part of the coverage? Are signs placed strategically for maximum visibility? Can TV/video interviewers be enticed to stand in front of your signs or landmarks? Is the destination or venue name featured prominently on screen or through commentary?

There is also a downside to media events. Higham (1999, p. 86) warns there is a "huge potential for negative publicity," such as that surrounding the public transport chaos and bombing in Atlanta during the 1996 Summer Olympic Games. Not all publicity is good, and contingency plans have to be in place to cope with disasters.

## *CASE STUDY: SEMINOLE COUNTY, FLORIDA, CONVENTION AND VISITORS BUREAU*

Many convention and visitor bureaus (CVBs), perhaps most, are involved with event bidding. Some are directly involved with production; others assist the event sector through a variety of means including marketing and funding. When it comes to bidding on events, sports, or other types, the CVB is likely to perform this function for cities. Increasingly, however, many cities and regions have created sport councils specifically to attract and develop sport events and related infrastructure. In the case of Seminole County, Florida, the CVB performs certain functions alongside the county government, and sport event bidding is handled by the Central Florida Sports Authority.

## Marketing Strategy and Sport Events

The Seminole County Tourism Development 1998-1999 marketing plan contains a special events section. The major objectives are:

- Attract festivals and events
- Develop partnerships to create events
- Advertise to niche markets
- Develop promotions and packages for event tourists
- Foster good media relations
- Use trade shows to assist promotion of local events
- Develop pertinent print material and other collateral
- Use direct mail and telemarketing to reach sport teams
- Pursue new grassroots events

## Funding

Seminole County Tourist Development Council and Seminole County CVB (1999) administers funds generated by the tourist development tax, which is really a 3 percent surcharge on commercial accommodation rates. A maximum sponsorship of $25,000 per event is available by way of reimbursement for advertising and promotional expenses. Criteria for sponsoring events have been made explicit in an application for funds:

- Events should be major enough to attract large numbers of visitors from outside the County
- Events must be of two days minimum duration
- At least 100 hotel rooms per day of the event should be generated (this is a guideline)

Applications are judged using a four-category point system:

1. Tourism expansion (measured by room demand, marketing effort to be expended, partnership with the tourist industry, plan to become self-sufficient)

2. Soundness of the proposal (clear, attainable objectives; realistic timetable for implementation; additional sources of funding)
3. Management (track record of organizers; ability to administer and report on funds received)
4. Quality and uniqueness (the event would not take place otherwise; program provided for both residents and visitors)

### The Seminole County Sports Training Center

In 1992, the U.S. Soccer Federation began a search to design and develop a training center for their national teams. They had made a commitment as an organization to bring the U.S. soccer program up to a competitive level in international competition. With the World Cup in 1994 to be held in the United States, they wanted to make a statement to the world.

The U.S. Soccer Federation had never built a training center before, so it looked to areas of the country that had already established a tradition for promoting soccer. Officials for a local, privately owned soccer club, Seminole Soccer, heard about the search for a training center and contacted the Seminole County Convention and Visitors Bureau for assistance.

The Seminole County CVB had a long tradition of supporting Seminole Soccer in four or five national tournaments each year. The club, with 2,000 registered youth players, was the logical demonstration of the community's commitment to furthering the sport of soccer. Bureau and club officials met with U.S. Soccer Federation officials and jointly developed the "ideal training center." The resulting request for proposal (RFP) was a perfect fit for Seminole County. The competition to locate the training center began with twelve locales and narrowed to two—San Diego and Seminole County.

The bureau arranged to bring the U.S. Soccer Federation site selection team to Seminole County and to put on a spectacular multimedia presentation, complete with helicopter tours of the proposed site in a county park on the north perimeter of the Seminole Soccer club. Seminole County eventually won the bid to build the center. It officially opened in 1993 and hosted the Irish National Soccer team for World Cup 1994 training. Since then, teams from Germany, Sweden, Argentina, and the Netherlands have trained at the center. Most recently, the U.S. Women's National Soccer Team trained at the center for its eventual World Championship in the 1996 Olympics and the 1998 Women's World Cup.

The economic impact of the training center for Seminole County has been phenomenal. Each year, the teams who train there spend millions of dollars. They stay in local hotels, they eat in local restaurants, and they shop in local malls. The impact has averaged over $1 million each year from this activity and has easily offset the $3 million investment needed to build the training center.

The center is located in a 120-acre county park some ten miles north of downtown Orlando. It contains the following facilities:

- Six quality grass playing fields (suitable for soccer, field hockey, and lacrosse)
- A 15,000-square-foot conference and training space
- Nine tennis courts
- Four outdoor racquet courts
- One mile-long jogging trail
- A weight training room
- A treatment room
- Two team locker rooms and a separate coaches' locker room
- Laundry facilities

### Aquatic Sports

Lake Brantley High School in Seminole County Florida has a long tradition of excellence in swimming and water polo, despite the lack of a swimming facility on its campus. The school's booster club had always been very successful in raising money and had built a football stadium and a softball facility on the campus in the past. The boosters approached the Seminole County Convention and Visitors Bureau with a request for funding to build an aquatic center. After two attempts, the boosters were successful in acquiring a $150,000 grant from the bureau. The boosters matched that $150,000 through private fund-raising activities, acquired an additional $100,000 from the city of Altamonte Springs, and took that $400,000 commitment to the state of Florida for a matching grant. With the state grant in place, they went to a local banker, who was also an avid swimmer, and received a loan for $200,000 to complete the financing package of $1 million.

The resulting aquatic center became an instant success. National swim meets, water polo matches, and college swim team holiday training have become normal activities at the center. The pool was designed and built by a Seminole County-based, nationally known firm, who also designed and built the Olympic swimming and water polo pools for the Atlanta Olympics in 1996.

The resulting economic impact from the aquatic center for Seminole County has been over $1 million each year. The international reputation of the pool has been enhanced by the teams who trained there for the 1996 Atlanta Olympics—Spain, Russia, and Yugoslavia. The boosters are hard at work to build a cover and add additional seating to the facility to make it even more attractive to northern college teams for winter holiday training.

## Softball

Florida has a long tradition as a hotbed for softball. Youth, adult, and senior leagues are a daily business for softball facilities throughout the state. Seminole County had a strong softball organization in the Metro Orlando Amateur Softball Association. County officials wanted to build a facility that would attract national softball events to the area. They identified a location, just north of a county park on an old landfill. Working with designers and engineers, they created a nationally acclaimed demonstration project that would reclaim the former landfill into a state-of-the-art softball complex (see Figure 3.3). The resulting facility has become a much-sought-after tournament site for regional and national softball events. The annual economic impact from softball events is estimated at $2.5 million.

## Other Field Sports

With the increased interest throughout the country in field hockey and lacrosse, the Seminole County CVB has begun to bid on and host training and competition events at its state-of-the-art soccer complex in these two sports. Field hockey festivals and national championships have been played at the complex. Lacrosse spring training for eastern seaboard high schools and colleges has become a booming business for the complex in March and April each year.

The benefit to the county, first of all, is economic impact. Another benefit is a more flexible use of the fields. Both field hockey and la-

FIGURE 3.3. Seminole County softball complex. (Photo courtesy of Seminole County CVB. Used with permission.)

crosse fields can be laid out in such a way as to move the playing area and to allow more even wear of the turf. Economic impact for Seminole County from field hockey and lacrosse events is estimated at $750,000 annually and growing.

### Regional Sports Promotion

The Seminole County CVB is a founding partner of the Central Florida Sports Commission. This regional organization researches and develops events that will fit the needs and facilities of each of their eight funding partners. The Sports Commission organized and successfully bid on regional events such as Olympic Soccer in 1996, a tae kwon do international competition, U.S. Figure Skating Championships, and the 2000 Amateur Athletic Union (AAU) Junior Olympic Games. These regional events have great economic impact on the counties making up the region. The economic impact of the

2000 Junior Olympics event was estimated to be $2.1 million in Seminole County alone.

## *CONCLUSION*

Sport event tourism is a substantial and growing niche market for destinations. It is somewhat unique in its ability to attract large numbers of high-yield visitors, including spectators, participants, officials, and the media, as well as the potential to generate positive destination imagery through media coverage. With the right vision and plan, sport event tourism can also bring major benefits to area residents through urban renewal, new and more efficiently operated sport facilities, more entertainment and sport participation opportunities, and heightened community pride.

To realize these benefits in an increasingly competitive marketplace, a vision and plan is required. Destinations must identify the best target market segments, decide on appropriate strategies, and forge a number of essential partnerships. Valid monitoring and impact assessment research is required to ensure that goals are being obtained and negative impacts avoided. A great deal of marketing research is necessary to better understand sport event tourist motives and to package and promote events effectively.

This chapter has outlined the planning and development process for sport event tourism, including a case study of one successful sport event tourism destination, Seminole County, Florida. Generally, competitive advantages can be realized through natural environmental and locational advantages, bigger and better sport event facilities, quality programs and services to develop sport events, and better planned, managed, and marketed events. Destinations should develop their own portfolio of sport events, with the occasional mega event at the top of the hierarchy, and a program of periodic and one-time regional events at the base. An overemphasis on large-scale events will likely prove to be detrimental to long-term sustainability of this sector. Bidding on events is an essential element in developing sport event tourism, and dedicated sport or event development organizations are increasingly being established to maximize bidding success.

Although research has certainly documented the economic benefits of sport event tourism, much work is needed to improve our understanding of this sector and its consequences. Priority should be given to better segmentation of the sport event tourist markets, focusing on motives for different types of events and on the desired experiences. In particular, little is known about the international sport event tourist. Evidence suggests that participants are looking for both the sport experience and related socializing, and in many cases the event location might be irrelevant.

Other important issues require research. The influence of media and sponsors on sport events is enormous, but the potential implications are not fully understood. Events are becoming more commercialized and media oriented. Are these harmful trends? Evidence suggests that increasing sport participation is helping to fuel growth in sport event tourism, but it is also apparent that large segments of the population are not involved. Is that exclusivity healthy? Many new, publicly financed facilities have been built as part of sport tourism strategies, but are they true community legacies or mere subsidies for the rich and influential?

As planning for sport event tourism becomes more formalized, such as the draft national strategy for Australia (2000), so too must the research, education, and training components. Creation of centers for sport tourism and sport event management will be highly beneficial. Government and tourist industry support for these initiatives can be justified by reference to the overall benefits that sport tourism generates, as well as to the costs and problems that might accrue through inadequate planning and management.

## *USEFUL WEB SITES*

Queensland Events Corporation: <www.qldevents.com.au>
Indiana Sports Corporation: <www.indianasportscorp.com>
Bid Regina: <www.tourismregina.com/bid_regina.html>
Seminole CVB: <www.visitseminole.com/what/attractions/sports/index.asp>
Central Florida Sports Commission: <www.orlandosports.org>
National Association of Sports Commissions (United States): <www.sportscommissions.org>

## REFERENCES

Aidid, S. (1997). Penang (Malaysia) as a tourism sport center. *Journal of Sport Tourism,* 3(4).

Australia: Industry, Science, Resources, Sport and Tourism Division. (2000). *Towards a National Sports Tourism Strategy*. (Draft) Canberra.

Bathgate, Brenda (2000). Personal communication.

Bramwell, B. (1997). A sport mega-event as a sustainable tourism development strategy. *Tourism Recreation Research*, 22(2), 13-19.

Bull, C. and Weed, M. (1999). Niche markets and small island tourism: The development of sports tourism in Malta. *Managing Leisure*, 4, 142-155.

Canadian Tourism Commission (2001). The Canadian Sports Tourism Initiative. Accessed online <http://www.canadatourism.com/en/c.../partnering/sports_initiative.htm>.

Carlsen, J., Getz, D., and Soutar, G. (2001). Event evaluation research. *Event Management*, 6(4), pp. 247-257.

Cha, S., McCleary, K., and Uysal, M. (1995). Travel motivations of Japanese overseas travelers: A factor-cluster segmentation approach. *Journal of Travel Research*, 34(1), 33-39.

Crompton, J. (1999). *Measuring the Economic Impact of Visitors to Sports Tournaments and Special Events*. Ashburn, Virginia: National Recreation and Park Association.

Crompton, J. and McKay, S. (1994). Measuring the economic impact of festivals and events: Some myths, misapplications and ethical dilemmas. *Festival Management and Event Tourism*, 2(1), 33-43.

Deckard, L. (1995). The future is now in Portland. *Amusement Business*, October 2-8, p. 27.

Delpy, L. (1998). Sport tourism and corporate sponsorships: A winning combination. *Journal of Vacation Marketing*, 4(1), 91-101.

Douvis, J., Yusof, A., and Douvis, S. (1999). An examination of demographic and psychographic profiles of the sport tourist. *The Cyber-Journal of Sport Marketing*, 2 <http://www.cjsm.com/Vol2/douvisyusof24.htm>.

Dwyer, L., Mellor, R., Mistilis, N., and Mules T. (2000). A framework for assessing "tangible" and "intangible" impacts of events and conventions. *Event Management*, 6(3), pp. 175-189.

Eriksen, A. (1997). Small towns with big hearts. *Sports Travel: Team and Event Planning and Management*, 1(3), 22-29.

Getz, D. (1987). Events tourism: Evaluating the impacts. In Ritchie, B., and Goeldner, C. (Eds.), *Travel, Tourism and Hospitality Research: A Handbook for Managers and Researchers* (pp. 437-450). New York: John Wiley and Sons.

Getz, D. (1997). *Event Management and Event Tourism*. New York: Cognizant Communication Corp.

Getz, D., Anderson, D., and Sheehan, L. (1998). Roles, issues and strategies for convention and visitors bureaux in destination planning and product development: A survey of Canadian bureaux. *Tourism Management*, 19(4), 331-340.

Getz, D. and Cheyne, J. (1997). Special event motivations and behaviour. In Ryan, C. (Ed.), *The Tourist Experience: A New Introduction* (pp. 137-154). London: Cassell.

Gibson, H. (1998). Active sport tourism: Who participates? *Leisure Studies,* 17(2), 155-170.

Gratton, C. and Kokolakakis, T. (1997). Financial games. "Sport Management," *Leisure Management,* 17(7), 13-15.

Green, C. and Chalip, L. (1998). Sport tourism as the celebration of subculture. *Annals of Tourism Research,* 25(2), 275-291.

Griffiths, M. (1999). Positioning the Illawara and Southern Highlands region As a sports tourism destination. Report prepared for Illawara and Southern Highlands Toursim (Australia).

Hall, M. (1997). Recent progress of sports tourism in New Zealand. *Tourism Recreation Research,* 22(2), 63.

Helin, K. (1997). A climate for sports. *Sports Travel,* 1(6),16-22.

Higham, J. (1999). Commentary—Sport as an avenue of tourism development: An analysis of the positive and negative impacts of sport tourism. *Current Issues in Tourism,* 2(1), 82-90.

International Events Group (1995). *IEG's Complete Guide to Sponsorship.* Chicago: IEG, Inc.

Irwin, R. and Sandler, M. (1997). An analysis of travel behavior and event-induced expenditures among American collegiate championship patron groups. *Journal of Vacation Marketing,* 4(1), 78-90.

Iso-Ahola, S. (1980). *The Social Psychology of Leisure and Recreation.* Dubuque: Brown.

*Journal of Sport Tourism.* (1997). Sports tourism in the Barbados: The development of sports facilities and special events. *Journal of Sport Tourism,* 3(4).

Marshall Macklin Monaghan, Ltd. (1993). *Spectator Sporting Activities in Canada From a Tourism Perspective.* Report for Tourism Canada, Ottawa.

Mossberg, L. (2000). Effects of events on destination image. In Mossberg, L. (Ed.), *Evaluation of Events: Scandinavian Experiences* (pp. 30-46). New York: Cognizant Communication Corp.

Nogawa, H., Yamaguchi, Y., and Hagi, Y. (1996). An empirical research study on Japanese sport tourism in sport-for-all events: Case studies of a single-night event and a multiple-night event. *Journal of Travel Research,* 35(2), 46-54.

Paterson, J. (2000). Event sponsorship and evaluation: A practitioner's perspective. Unpublished paper presented at Events Beyond 2000: Setting the Agenda. Sydney, Australia: Australian Centre for Event Management.

Persson, C. (2000). The Olympic host selection process. Doctoral thesis, Department of Business Administration and Social Sciences, Lulea University of Technology, Sweden.

Pitts, B. (1999). Sport tourism and niche markets: Identification and analysis of the growing lesbian and gay sports tourism industry. *Journal of Vacation Marketing,* 5(1), 31-50.

Priestley, G. (1995). Sports tourism: The case of golf. In Ashworth, G. and Dietvorst, A. (Eds.), *Tourism and Spatial Transformations: Implications for Policy and Planning* (pp. 205-223). Wallingford, UK: CABI Publishing.

Rozin, S. (2000). The amateurs who saved Indianapolis. *Business Week,* April 10, pp. 126, 130.

Schreiber, A. and Lenson, B. (1994). *Lifestyle and Event Marketing: Building the New Customer Partnership.* New York: McGraw Hill.

Schumacher, Don (2000). Personal communication.

Seminole County Tourism Development (1988/1989). Marketing Plan-Special Events.

Seminole County Tourist Development Council and Seminole County Convention and Visitors Bureau (1999). Application for Funds Fiscal Year, 1999/2000.

Speed, R. and Thompson, P. (2000). Determinants of sports sponsorship response. *Journal of the Academy of Marketing Science,* 28(2), 226-238.

Sports Business Market Research, Inc. (2000). *The 2000 Sports Business Market Research Handbook.*

Stevens, T. (1997). Centre of excellence. "Sport Management," *Leisure Management,* 17(7), 21-22.

Street and Smith's (1999). *Street and Smith's Sports Business Journal,* December.

Swart, K. (1998). Visions for South African sport tourism. *Visions in Leisure and Business,* 17(2), 4-12.

Tourism Industry Association of America (1999). *Profile of Travelers Who Attended Sport Events.* Washington: TIAA.

Weed, M. and Bull, C. (1998). The search for a sport-tourism policy network. In Collins, M. and Cooper, I. (Eds.), *Leisure Management: Issues and Applications* (pp. 277-298), Wallingford UK: CABI Publishing.

Whitson, D. and Macintosh, D. (1996). The global circus: International sport, tourism, and the marketing of cities. *Journal of Sport and Social Issues,* 20(3), 278-295.

Chapter 4

# Winter Sport Tourism

Simon Hudson

This chapter examines winter sports tourism, in particular, down-hill skiing and snowboarding. The first section outlines the history of snow tourism; the next two sections cover the market size and various destinations. Section four gives a short synopsis of ski field location and development. An analysis of the consumer is then followed by predictions for the future of winter sports, and the chapter concludes with a case study of Whistler Resort in Canada. Relevant Web sites and a reference section are found at the end of the chapter.

## EVOLUTION OF THE MARKET

The birth of skiing is commonly associated with the Norwegians. Rock carvings of two skiers hunting elk have been found in Norway that date back to 2000 B.C. Modern skiing is said to have been started in 1820 by Sondre Nordheim, a Norwegian from Telemark (McLennan, 2000). Later in the century, the first winter mountain holidays started in St. Moritz, Switzerland (Cockerell, 1988), and the British upper classes swiftly made skiing a fashionable winter pursuit. In 1905, skiing was included in the Olympic Games although not as a recognized event. This inclusion was in response to a growing interest in skiing as a sport, and a desire on the part of destination managers and developers to keep ski sites operational for the entire winter season. In the process of developing this strategy, the concept of a broader set of physical fa-cilities and a more sustainable market base for skiing is believed to have originated (Williams, 1993).

By the beginning of World War I in 1914, there were at least as many German skiers in Switzerland as there were British. Hotel accommodations were already in good supply, with Switzerland accounting for over 215,000 hotel beds in 1914. Demand was further enhanced as a result of the higher profile that skiing was receiving in potential travel markets. In 1924, skiing was introduced as a formal event at the Olympics in Chamonix, France. It was highlighted again at the 1932 Olympic Winter Games in Lake Placid, New York. These two occurrences helped to place skiing at the forefront of winter recreational activity on both continents and gave a push to its development as a major contributor to winter-based tourism (Liebers, 1963).

Until the 1930s, few ski resorts had any uphill transport capability specifically for skiers. Early railways, ratchet trains, and buses were used primarily for summer visitors, but a few skiers in resorts such as Davos, Zermatt, and Wengen took advantage of them to pursue their new sporting pastime. In 1929, the first mechanically propelled uphill lift designed just for skiers was installed in Canada, and within a few years most ski slopes of any significance in North America and Europe had one or more improved versions of it in place. Trains transporting thousands of skiers to the slopes became commonplace throughout North America in the 1930s. In 1936, Union Pacific developed the first tourism-oriented ski resort in Sun Valley, Idaho, and this became the prototype for world-class ski areas in North America.

It was not until after World War II that skiing in a mass tourism context began to emerge. Skiing played a vital military role in northern combat areas, and its introduction to thousands of returning troops as a form of winter recreation combined with rapid improvements in safer and more comfortable ski equipment, better access to ski destinations brought on by the development of family automobiles, and rising standards of living, helped skiing demand mushroom during the postwar period. By the late 1940s and 1950s, the second phase of ski resort development took place in France with the opening of centers such as Courcheval, Meribel, and Tignes. Along with the availability of on-slope activities for skiing, off-slope amenities began to grow. Ski facilities and services associated with lodging, food, beverages, and entertainment became important components of the ski vacation experience (Tanler, 1966).

The 1960s saw the start of the great ski boom. Europe witnessed the creation of a new generation of fully integrated ski stations, while in North America, larger resorts in New England, Colorado, California, the Canadian Rockies, and eastern townships of Quebec emerged to meet the growing demand for winter vacations. Wooden skis were slowly phased out and replaced by metal and fiberglass; leather boots were replaced by plastic ones.

Although the 1970s was a period of massive market and product expansion, the 1980s was a decade characterized by industry consolidation and product management (Williams, 1993). Influenced by changing demographics, skiing markets began to mature, and by the mid-1980s ski facility supply had outstripped demand in many regions, and many less well-managed ski destinations were experiencing financial difficulties (Kottke, 1990). In response, many ski destinations were forced to address both product and market issues in a more businesslike fashion, which led to a more tourism-focused approach to ski area development. Larger ski centers that included tourism among resident ski options continued to grow, while many small centers without such offerings faltered. Consequently, the number of ski areas dropped by 18 percent in North America between 1980 and 1990. Counteracting this trend, ski area capacity expanded by approximately 51 percent in the same period (Williams, 1993).

During the 1980s' consolidation period, skiing attracted an increasingly formulaic image, but the mold was broken by the invention of snowboarding. Visitors to winter resorts began seeking a variety of niche options. Snowboarding has had a huge impact on the ski industry, and it is estimated that there are 11 million snowboarders worldwide ("Breaking News," 1999). A recent survey of downhillers in North America showed that 28.3 percent were snowboarders, although many more have tried it (35 percent) (National Ski Areas Association, 2001). Growth in snowboarding is attributed to increased numbers of under-twenty-four-year-olds in the market (Spring, 2000). The snowboarding boom, which has had a greater impact on young people, has caused the ski industry to assess its effect on the winter sports market. One of the disadvantages of skiing is that it is technically demanding at a high level of performance and expertise is possible only for those who start the sport at a very young age. However, a snowboarder can learn to stay upright and turn after one morning and tackle powder within a week. Such a high learning curve has led many skiers to cross over to snowboarding, and figures indicate that over 60 percent of snowboarders skied before they adopted snowboarding (Spring, 1997). However, growth in snowboarding has leveled off, and the percentage mix has remained the same for the past few years (Beyrouti, 2000).

Faced with the inevitable rise of snowboarding, skiers and resort authorities in particular are increasingly conciliatory toward snowboarders and their needs. It is now generally agreed in Europe and North America that adherents of the two disciplines must coexist on the same slopes (see Figure 4.1). Those who believe that snowboarders should be confined to particular mountains or pistes (Bray, 1995) are now a minority.

Telemarking—the first type of downhill skiing introduced by the Norwegians—also appears to be experiencing some growth. The telemark turn, designed to be executed in loose-heeled bindings worn with lightweight boots and skis that are comfortable for walking uphill and on flat snow, has come into its own again. Snowshoeing and telemark skiing, both low participation sports, saw a threefold growth between 1998 and 1999 in the number of enthusiasts ("Breaking News," 2000). Heliskiing, in which skiers are flown by helicopter to virgin slopes where they can ski powder snow, has also shown a marked increase in the past decade. During the 1999-2000 season, 92,000 heliskiers opted for this challenging activity in British Columbia and the Yukon (Loverseed, 2000). According to the British Columbia Heli and Snowcat Ski Operators Association, gross revenue from high mountain skiing now generates between $80-$100 million Canadian annually.

## MARKET SIZE

The current ski market is estimated to include some 70 million skiers worldwide ("Breaking News," 1999). Of that number, 77 percent are alpine skiers, 16 percent are snowboarders, and the remainder prefer cross-country skiing. Europe accounts for approximately 30 million skiers, including domestic business (those who ski only within the boundaries of their own country). The United States and Canada generate an estimated 20 million skiers and snowboarders—again primarily domestic—and Japan 14 million. Fewer than 1 million Americans have ever been abroad for a skiing holiday, and some 400,000 of such trips were to Europe. The number of Japanese skiing outside Japan is said to be a mere 50,000, of whom about 7,500 have visited Europe, but this number is increasing. Snow24 maintains a

FIGURE 4.1. Skier and snowboarder together: It is now generally agreed in Europe and North America that adherents of the two disciplines must coexist on the same slopes. (Used with permission, Office du Tourism Verbier.)

database of ski resorts (www.snow24.com), and this data, combined with statistics from Lazard (1996) on lifts and skier visits, is shown in Table 4.1.

Skiing is a mature market in Europe as well as in America, but it continues to evolve in other areas of the world such as Eastern Europe, Korea, and Southeast Asia. The number of skiers in the United States fell for the third consecutive year in 2000 to 7.4 million, while the number of snowboarders dropped 8.8 percent to 3.3 million ("Breaking News," 2000). However, in 2000/2001, the United States' 490 resorts attracted 57.3 million skier/boarder visits. Although the number of skiers stayed the same at 7.4 million, the number of snowboarders increased nearly 20 percent to 4.3 million (National Ski Areas Association, 2001). According to the latest Mountain International Opinion Survey (MINOS) conducted at ski resorts in Austria, Switzerland, Italy, and France, skiing numbers are dwindling in Europe (Spring, 1996b). Although the average number of

TABLE 4.1. Skiing Worldwide

| Country | Resorts | Lifts | Skier Visits (million) |
|---|---|---|---|
| Japan | 460 | 3,600 | 75 |
| France | 390 | 4,143 | 56 |
| United States | 503 | 2,269 | 57 |
| Austria | 604 | 3,473 | 43 |
| Italy | 341 | 2,854 | 37 |
| Switzerland | 288 | 1,762 | 31 |
| Canada | 284 | 1,375 | 17 |
| Germany | 491 | 1,670 | 20 |
| Sweden | 415 | 950 | 12 |
| Norway | 207 | 405 | 8 |
| Czech Republic | 174 | 1,500 | 4.8 |
| Spain | 33 | 294 | 4.3 |
| Australia | 18 | 139 | 2.6 |
| Finland | 117 | 505 | 2.0 |
| Poland | 71 | 110 | 2.0 |
| South Korea | 27 | 70 | 1.9 |
| Andorra | 5 | 115 | 1.5 |
| New Zealand | 26 | 64 | 1.1 |
| Russia | 104 | 32 | .9 |
| Chile | 14 | 84 | .8 |
| Argentina | 22 | 72 | .7 |
| Bulgaria | 4 | 50 | .6 |
| Iran | 20 | 45 | .5 |
| Greece | 17 | 40 | .4 |
| Turkey | 12 | 25 | .3 |
| Lebanon | 7 | 18 | .2 |
| Slovakia | 322 | * | * |
| Slovenia | 55 | * | * |
| Serbia | 19 | * | * |
| China | 100 | * | * |
| Rest of the World | 900 (Approximately) | * | * |
| Total | 6,000 | 25,664 | 380.6 |

*Source:* Based on Snow24, 2000, and Lazard, 1996.
* = unknown

days skied is up, the actual number of skiers is down. The fear is that vacation skiers (e.g., skiers from Northern European countries such as Germany, the Benelux countries, the United Kingdom, and Scandinavia, which represent half the skier market for European alpine countries), are skiing less often.

It is difficult to gauge how much the ski industry is worth worldwide. Statistics provided by the National Ski Areas Association (NSAA, 2000) indicate average total gross revenues of US$17.1 million for each American resort, split between sales of lift tickets, accommodations, food and beverage, ski shops, and real estate. In the United States, snow sports participants generate more than $12 billion (Packer, 1998). Taking the summer months into consideration, total economic contributions jump to well over the $15 billion mark. Total skiing equipment expenditures alone amounted to $649 million in 2000 ("Off the Map," 2000).

## DESTINATIONS

Today, there are approximately 6,000 ski areas in seventy-eight countries, although data exist for only 5,665 of these areas (Thorne, 2000b). Of the recorded ski areas, about 4,000 are in Europe, nearly 800 are in North America, and almost 500 can be found in Asia. The remaining ski centers are divided between Australia, South America, and Africa. The four largest resort groups in North America account for approximately 18 million skier visits annually, broken down in Table 4.2. America's biggest ski resort chains have been buying many smaller resorts, and investing in new hotels, ski lifts, and snow making equipment. Three chains have even listed themselves on stock exchanges in the past few years—something previously unheard of ("Winter Wonderlands," 1998).

The big resorts have several advantages. They can afford to invest in all the latest technology. Their lifts are warm and spacious, and the guaranteed snow is neatly groomed. By broadening into accommodation, skiing lessons, and other activities, the big chains can also capture more of the industry's profits. Historically, ski companies have been content to be little more than lift operators (as they still are in Europe), allowing local businesses to glean most of the potential income. Even in the United States, the typical skier still hands less than

TABLE 4.2. Breakdown of Top Four Ski Centers in North America

| Ski Operator | No. of Facilities | Total Visits 2001 |
|---|---|---|
| Intrawest | 11 | 6.2 |
| American Ski Company | 7 | 5.0 |
| Vail Resorts Inc. | 5 | 4.6 |
| Booth Creek Inc. | 8 | 2.1 |

20 percent of his holiday cash to resort owners. Vail, by contrast, earns so much money from secondary activities that it can afford to not charge for use of its lifts in the evening. It manages six hotels, seventy-two restaurants, forty shops, and over 13,000 condominiums.

Resort operators still earn a large portion of their profits on the slopes selling lift tickets, food, and equipment. Property development and management has become an important part of the ski business. For resort operators, the most desirable visitors are those whom the trade calls destination skiers, the longer-stay tourists. Resort operators are increasingly banking on these visitors to fill hotels, townhouses, and condominiums in the valleys below the slopes. The operators benefit not only from selling townhouses and condos but also by helping the new owners rent their properties to other visitors. Typically, they charge a management fee equal to half the rent.

The biggest risk to such development remains the weather and global warming. To thrive without snow, some operators have invested heavily in snowmaking equipment. They have also added nonski activities such as conference centers and golf courses for summer visitors. The aim is to provide improved year-round facilities to help attract property buyers, no matter what the weather.

Skiing in North America is in many ways different from skiing in Europe (Hudson, 1998). Many of these differences are positive. Traditionally there is an abundance of snow, and nearly all U.S. resorts have extensive snowmaking facilities. Snow grooming is immaculate; the service is friendly and efficient; and most resorts have free guided tours of the mountain. Lift queues are rare and well organized; the tree line often goes right to the top of the mountain; and the accommodation is much more spacious and luxurious than the European equivalent. However, some find the scenery less attractive than the Alps, with resorts lacking the European charm and atmosphere. Most of the mountain restaurants are huge self-service eateries with little character or culinary pretensions, despite representing better value for the money.

Generally higher standards in North American destinations result from each resort and lift system being owned by one company. Everyone from the ski shop attendant to the ski instructor works for the same organization under a single corporate identity. By contrast, ownership of the slopes in traditional European resorts may be split between a dozen small farmers. This means a wide range of lift companies, ski schools, ski buses, and other services all coexisting in the same village, usually spiced by generations of interfamily rivalry. By contrast, the world's largest resort operating business, Compagnie des Alpes, a French company, operates a dozen of France's famous ski resorts. Unlike the popular finance model of the leading North American chains, which raise revenue from real estate, Compagnie des Alpes still gains more than 90 percent of its revenue from lift ticket sales, and sells more lift tickets than anyone else in Europe (Thorne, 2000a).

The European winter sports market divides clearly in two (Spring, 1996a). Southern European countries of Austria, Switzerland, southern Germany and France, and northern Italy represent about one-half of the skier population (14 million). Skiers from these countries have relatively easy access to the Alps, and buses from Vienna, Salzburg, Munich, and Geneva take ski clubs and students to mountain resorts with regularity. The remaining half of the European market lives in the north. The bulk of this market is a vacation market. Depending on the country, skiers from the north spend an average of six to fifteen days on a ski holiday. Most skiers from the north drive to the Alps, a trip that can take up to twelve hours for the British and seven hours for Parisians.

The major developed ski areas of Europe shared by the five nations of the Alpine are: France, Italy, Austria, Switzerland, and Germany. Together they provide an area of approximately 5,800 square kilometers of posted and managed skiing (Lewis and Wild, 1995). Recall that Table 4.1 indicates that Japan represents over 19 percent of the world's ski area activity with some 460 resorts and 3,600 lifts. Shiga Kogen is Japan's biggest single-ticket resort, consisting of twenty-one ski areas, incorporating seventy-four lifts over six mountains. In

Japan there are only lift queues at peak times. Each time a new lift is built, the old one is left in place. So instead of lift queues there are crowded pistes full of corporate travelers, identically dressed and emblazoned with their company logos. They ski in tight groups, even though they have widely differing abilities. The resorts are geared toward weekend skiers from cities, and the slopes are fairly empty during the week. Japanese resorts were slow to accept snowboarders, but the most successful resorts now pursue them aggressively.

As for the rest of the world, many of the resorts in Chile, Argentina, New Zealand, and even Australia have a strong curiosity value and compelling scenery, but sometimes offer surprisingly little in the way of challenging skiing (Wilson, 1996). It is relatively easy to book skiing holidays to these countries, and some operators offer ski trips to unusual destinations such as India and Alaska. Japanese skiers who try the slopes at the Japanese-owned resort of Alyeska, the main ski area in Alaska, are astonished by how much space there is. India on the other hand boasts kilometers of untracked pistes in its resorts of Gulmarg in Kashmir; Auli in Uttar Pradesh; and Kufri, Narkanda, Manali, and Rohtang in Himachal Pradesh. Skiing is also increasingly popular in South Korea where the main resorts, Dragon Valley and Muju, are only one hour from Seoul. There are also plans to build the first ski resort in North Korea. However, between them, these destinations comprise a very small percentage of the total skiing market.

In the first decade of the new millennium, it looks certain that China will be the world's leading growth area for winter sports, with the number of resorts in the country expanding rapidly. Environmental issues, and in some cases the lack of space which has slowed development in Europe and North America, are rarely significant factors in Chinese ski area development. The increasing disposable income for China's growing wealthier class is the main driving force behind this growth. Recently established resorts are using "Western" ski lifts, skis, and other infrastructure in a bid to attract the some 15 million skiers residing in neighboring Asian nations such as Japan and Korea.

## SKI FIELD LOCATION AND DEVELOPMENT

Ski field location, perhaps more than any other type of tourism, is heavily dependent on appropriate physical conditions, namely a good snow cover and suitable slopes. Research has shown that lack of snow is a major concern for skiers and nonskiers alike (Gilbert and Hudson, 2000; Carmichael, 1992). Martinelli (1976) stresses the need for early season snow cover as this is when demand is often the greatest (over the New Year holiday season in particular) and when the financial success or failure of many ski areas is decided. If the temperature is low enough, many resorts use the snowmaking equipment to put down a base at the start of the season if natural snow has not yet accumulated.

Resort ski fields must offer a range of slopes to attract a variety of skiers. Sibley (1982) suggests that novice slopes should be less than 20 degrees, intermediate slopes 20 to 45 degrees, and advanced slopes 45 degrees or steeper. Experienced skiers will also look at the variety of runs available and at the total vertical drop. A certain amount of flat, stable land must also be available near the slopes to provide adequate building sites. Considerable care must be taken in locating both base and uphill facilities to avoid avalanche paths. Many of the more modern resort developments (in France, for example) offer a variety of pistes in terms of aspect and difficulty. These pistes converge on a single reception area where the accommodation and other facilities are built. Such a design gives skiers immediate access to all parts of the ski field.

A ski field will also have an advantage if it links with other ski fields, although this does have economic consequences in terms of revenue distribution. Proximity to summer resorts or attractions is another advantage, as the summer season becomes ever more important to ski resorts. Proximity to the market is another key factor in influencing visitor numbers. Accessibility to urban areas is especially important for resorts catering to day and weekend skiers, which is the case for many North American resorts.

Ski field development depends on the exploitation of natural resources and a significant investment is required to provide necessary uphill facilities. This, coupled with difficulties of access and sparse populations in many alpine areas, has led to much outside participation in the development process (Pearce, 1995). Barker (1982) identifies differences in scale, intensity, and form of tourism development between the western Alps (France and western Switzerland) and the eastern Alps (eastern Switzerland, northern Italy, Austria, and Bavaria). In Western Europe, large integrated ski resorts have been built in the subalpine zone long after the local population retreated to the main valley where agriculture, forestry, and manufacturing provided employment. In these resorts, the main thrust for development came from distant urban capital. By contrast, tourism in the eastern Alps coexists with a strong pastoral economy, and the impetus for development has come from strong rural communities with a tradition of local autonomy in planning, which has favored community-based investment initiatives. An example of such a resort is Verbier in Switzerland (see Figure 4.2).

## THE CONSUMER

According to the National Ski Areas Association (2000), alpine skiers in America are predominantly male (60 percent), are thirty-five years old on average, are college educated, and tend to have managerial or professional jobs. Besides skiing they participate in tennis, cycling, sailing, and racquetball, and are twice as likely to buy wine, invest in real estate, and travel overseas than the average person. The majority of snowboarders are male (73 percent) and young (more than 89 percent are under twenty-five) with the average age being twenty-one years old. Many snowboarders are students, and they also like to mountain bike, hike, skateboard, surf, and play video games.

European skiing consumers are different from those in North America (Spring, 1996a). European skiers tend to be younger, and incomes and self-ranked skier ability levels are lower. One significant difference is that European resorts draw a more cosmopolitan cast of skiers from around the world. They attract a greater number of Asians, South Americans, and skiers from Arabic countries than do North American resorts. Terrain, so important to American skiers, is less important to northern Europeans (except the Germans who tend to rank themselves as better skiers). European skiers take ski holidays on average three out of every five seasons. The notion of skilled consumption suggests that frequent participation in order to increase skill levels should be a prominent feature of activities such as skiing. Richards (1995), from a survey of 1,415 U.K. skiers, discovered that advanced skiers take more skiing holidays than do intermediate-level skiers.

There have been several interesting studies of skiing behavior (Mills, 1985; Boon, 1984; Mills, Couturier, and Snepenger, 1986; Goeldner, 1978; Tikalsky and Lahren, 1988; Spring, 1995) and desti-

FIGURE 4.2. Skiers above the Swiss resort of Verbier. (Photo used with permission of Office du Tourisme Verbier.)

nation choice (Hudson and Shephard, 1998; Carmichael, 1992, 1996; Dilley and Pozihun, 1986; Ewing and Kulka, 1979; Keogh, 1980; Klenosky, Gengler, and Mulvey, 1993; Richards, 1995). Past market research in the skiing field has focused on existing skiers, and parallel research concerning skiing's latent demand markets has been less evident. However, as concerns for a falling ski market have surfaced, so has interest in identifying potential markets that may be persuaded to try skiing. Williams and Basford (1992) examined the nonskier population and found that the two major deterrents preventing respondents from participating in skiing were perceptions of the activity's dangers and costs. Gilbert and Hudson (2000) investigated the constraints facing both skiers and nonskiers and found that economic factors were major constraints for nonskiers, but they also faced a number of intrapersonal constraints. They perceived skiing to be harder to learn than other sports and suggested that they would feel self-conscious or embarrassed when learning to ski. Nonskiers also thought the activity would make them cold and wet, and that it would be dangerous, expensive, and too stressful. There was the feeling that skiing is an elitist sport, and that they were not chic and glamorous enough to go. Skiers, on the other hand, were constrained by time, family, or economic factors.

## FUTURE PROSPECTS

In North America, Japan, and Europe, insofar as one can tell, skiing has decreased in popularity. Results of two recent surveys suggest that the number of skiers and snowboarders have declined, with women skiers in particular falling off at a double digit pace ("Breaking News," 2000). However, North America continues to lead the world in investment in resort real estate, and the trend to use winter sports as an attraction to bring in revenue for base operations continues to be the dominant financial model for more and more resorts. This concept is mirrored by many of the world's new snow-dome developments, which use indoor snow as a novelty attraction to crown state-of-the-art but basically conventional twenty-first-century retail and leisure developments (Thorne, 2000a).

Despite the fall in skier numbers, there are still major investments taking place in many parts of the world. One interesting development is that Intrawest, one of the largest North American ski resort owners, will be partnering with French conglomerate Compagnie des Alpes in building a new resort village at Les Arcs, France. French resorts have always been criticized for being ugly, cramped, and boring with poor service standards. This new partnership could be a huge boost for European skiing. Canada's skiing industry also continues to grow with many new resort development projects in the pipeline. There has also been considerable ski resort investment in the southern hemisphere, especially in Australia.

The continuing popularity of snowboarding bodes well for the future of ski resorts, and it has helped to reverse the decline of skiing after the boom years of the 1970s and early 1980s. Over the past decade most ski resorts have adapted to the demand for specially designed snowboard runs and parks; they have their eye on future profits that would be generated by snowboarders switching to more traditional forms of skiing later in life.

## Environmental Issues

Environmental awareness, however perceived, will have the greatest impact on skiing in the next few decades. Skiing, in both practice and infrastructure, is causing numerous environmental problems that consequently give rise to serious challenges for the industry. In fact, a major deterrent to the further development of the ski market comes in the form of growing environmental concerns about human pollution and traffic congestion in the mountains and the intensive use of natural resources by skiers (Hudson, 1995). The continual use of the same location and the same runs, together with the pressure to expand skiing areas, has brought skiers and conservationists into conflict. Environmental lobbies have already succeeded in imposing restrictions on heliskiing, off-piste skiing in woods, and on new lift installations. As a result, there will be no new lifts built in the Alps, apart from replacements, and some resorts in France, Switzerland, Austria, and even Scotland, have introduced underground funicular systems to avoid confrontation with environmental issues. Developers in North America are also fighting ongoing battles with powerful environmentalist groups.

Although ski resorts acknowledge that mistakes have been made over the past forty years, a new management style and a new commitment to have skiing coexist with the environment has emerged (Castle, 1999). The Aspen Skiing Company in Colorado, Heavenly Ski Resort at Lake Tahoe, Whistler in Canada, and Sundance in Utah have all taken a lead in showing ski destinations how to be environmentally friendly. Finding common ground between ski resorts and environmentalists is a matter of communication. Ski areas seeking local support for new projects are realizing that early talks with all stakeholders help to establish positive relationships. By working through their differences, the parties can often reach a consensus before a plan is formalized and submitted to public agencies for review. Ski resorts of the future will have to view environmental problems as business issues. They should make environmental investments for the same reasons they make other investments: because they expect them to deliver positive returns or reduce risks.

There is even the possibility of gaining competitive advantage by being environmentally friendly (Hudson, 1996), and resorts are now ranked according to their environmental commitment. In June 2000, about 160 U.S. ski areas, including the twenty biggest, signed the Sustainable Slopes charter. The charter was developed with input from a variety of ski industry leaders; environmental groups; federal, state, county, and local agencies; outdoor recreation groups; ski industry suppliers; and other stakeholders. The charter is a voluntary set of guiding principles and tools that assist ski resorts in effectively integrating environmental protection concepts into all aspects of design, maintenance, and operation of ski resorts. There is also a new scorecard report produced by a coalition of conservation groups that grades ski areas on environmental criteria. According to this scorecard, Sundance is the most environmentally friendly ski area in the western United States (Hansen, 2000). The scorecard is based on ski resorts' performance against criteria such as expansion into undisturbed land and environmental efficiency.

### The Impact of Global Warming

Another major challenge to future development is global warming. The Royal Geographical Society indicated in their last conference that many of Europe's famous ski resorts are at increasing risk of landslides as global warming melts the permafrost that holds many mountain surfaces together ("Warming Permafrost," 2001). Temperatures in many ski resorts have risen by 1$^C$ over the past fifteen years, and with a predicted continuation of rising global and regional temperatures, skiing destinations will experience less snowfall and shorter skiing seasons. These impacts will be especially pronounced in low-lying ski resorts where commercial ventures are already marginal (Viner and Agnew, 1999). There are some scientists, however, who suggest that warmer winters could lead to increased precipitation levels in some resorts, but they tend to agree that winter will begin later and spring will begin sooner (Rosa, 2001).

To thrive without snow, some operators have invested heavily in snowmaking equipment. In the United States the average snowmaking system covers approximately 67 percent of terrain (Bender, 2000), and most U.S. ski resorts now have snowmaking equipment. Intrawest believes that snowmaking is an economic necessity. The company has invested $113 million in snowmaking equipment for its resorts and has an annual operating budget of $9 million just for making snow (Schreiner, 2000). At its eleven resorts, Intrawest turns an average of 1.5 billion gallons of water per season into enough snow to cover 39,000 football fields to a depth of one foot.

## The Impact of Technology

Technological advancements will continue to affect many areas of the ski industry. These include bigger and faster ski lifts (see Figure 4.3) and even centrally heated cabins already in use in Vermont. Information will become more readily available to skiers, with a trend for placing touch-screen terminals throughout mountain areas. New computer technology has revolutionized how multiple resorts offer combined lift tickets. The most innovative of these is a smart card kept in a pocket or glove that opens the lift access gate automatically. Equipment is improving all the time with shaped skis proving to be a great success, and designs are being developed for computerized bindings. Titanium is now being used to ensure lightweight skis, and advances in lightweight, waterproof, and breathable fabrics are improving the performance of ski clothing. There are continuing technological breakthroughs in attempts to make artificial snow in temperatures up to 30$^C$. In fact, snowmaking technology has advanced to such an extent that indoor ski centers could become a big trend in the new millennium (Thorne, 2000b).

Internet sites for choosing and booking holidays are transforming the operations of travel agents and tour operators. An increasing number of bookings are made via the Internet as skilled consumers are assembling their own ski holidays using their own extensive product knowledge. A recent survey found that 94 percent of skiers have access to the Internet and that 52 percent have used it to research or book a ski or snowboard vacation (Potter, 2000). Of the 7.4 million downhill skiers in the United States, 60.5 percent use the Internet, giving skiing one of three highest Web usage rates for sports ("Travel Hit," 2000). In another survey of skiers, of those with Internet access, 66 percent accessed the Web site of the resort they were visiting, and 68 percent accessed another area's Web site (Spring, 2000).

Most destinations have created their own sites on the Internet, and the larger resorts offer online booking. All Vail-owned resorts, American Skiing Company resorts, Booth Creek resorts, and some others

FIGURE 4.3. Lift technology is becoming increasingly sophisticated: This new "funite" lift in Verbier carries 2,000 people an hour. (Photo used with permission of Office Tourisme Verbier.)

such as Aspen Snowmass, Jackson Hole, Big Sky, and Snowbird, have partnered with WorldRes, an online booking distributor, to handle Web reservations (Hirschfeld, 2000). In California, 20 percent of Heavenly's guests use the Internet to book at least part of their ski vacation—half of them through Heavenly's own online booking system (Potter, 2000). Of that 20 percent, 59 percent booked airfare, 50 percent lodging, and 26 percent car rentals.

In fact, many resorts in the United States are finding that the Internet is working well for them. A ski area's Web site now ranks above the area's brochure as an influential source of information. For many resorts, the venture online has been highly cost-effective, as it carries a far lower cost impression than other media and can be aimed at a much more targeted audience. In addition, the Internet is providing new and powerful ways for resorts and consumers to communicate. As technology advances and Internet usage expands, the power and versatility of this medium as a marketing and communications tool is sure to grow.

## *The Ski Market of the Future*

Currently, communication is predominately directed toward those who are already skiing converts, with too narrow a focus on those that visit ski resorts or read the few skiing publications in circulation. If the sport is to be revitalized, then the audience cannot be only skiers. In North America, efforts have been made to tap into the 35 million persons whose demographic profiles make them potential skiers. However, for many reasons, such as insufficient funding, flawed research, merger complications, recession, and poor staffing, efforts have been unsuccessful.

For the nonskier, changing preconceived attitudes about the sport requires education. This has been cited as one of the most powerful influences of travel behavior (Zimmer, Brayley, and Searle, 1995), and this includes information disseminated through advertising. It may not be possible to overcome people's fear of heights, lack of desire for physical challenge, or fears of learning a new sport. However, it is clear that the decision to ski or not to ski is income sensitive, and creative marketers can influence travel behavior by increasing the perceived income of the market, or by reducing its influence through the establishment of a sense of value and purchasing power in the minds of potential consumers. It is also clear that nonskiers perceive skiing to be dangerous, so marketing messages must counter this argument. In fact, research has shown that skiing is about as dangerous as table tennis, with just 2.6 injuries per 1,000 participant (Bosely, 1998).

The value of skiing is centered around the excitement that it generates, but the ski industry appears to have a problem marketing this excitement. The question for marketers is how to recapture and sell the essence of skiing—the exhilaration, fascination, sense of independence and freedom, the beauty of the mountains, rush of adrenaline, the sore muscles, and the incredible high that skiers feel at the end of a day of skiing. The consumer passion and emotional commitment that accounted for skiing's tremendous popularity and growth in the time after World War II needs to be regenerated. Somehow, ski marketers need to capture the magic and think creatively about how to put this magic into images and language that the information age demands.

The ski industry also needs to address the dramatic decrease in the number of female skiers and snowboarders. In North America between 1997 and 2000, the dropout rate among females was between 20 and 30 percent (Korobanik, 2000). One reason for this could be the new image skiing and snowboarding have that is intimidating to women. For example, virtually every advertising campaign for snowboarding shows the extreme side of the sport. Thus, a future challenge for the industry will be to lure females back to the slopes (Hudson, 2000).

## The Future for Destinations

### The Ski Slopes

Most ski destinations must satisfy an increasingly fragmenting and demanding market with more specialized facilities and services. They must do so while bringing these customer segments together to share the limited number of ski slopes. Demographic fragmentation means formulating multiple marketing messages that address such targets as the increasing number of older customers, families, and the youth market which has taken to snowboarding, a new and special market segment in itself. If one adds to this mix the higher demands, new values, tastes, lifestyles, and changes in leisure time and finances of each of these segments, then resorts and operators will have to be even more flexible and diverse in their services and communications. Most ski resorts will have to assimilate these groups on the mountain, creating an atmosphere where no one is alienated or made uncomfortable by the presence of others. Of all the people who take an introductory ski lesson, only 8 to 10 percent come back to the slopes. Ski schools must therefore make it their priority to convert more beginners into avid skiers (see Figure 4.4).

For existing skiers, one of the main constraints to participation is the problem of overcrowding (Carmichael, 1992; Hudson, 1998). It was suggested previously that the industry was mature and that skiers are skiing fewer hours every day. This, coupled with the rapid increase in alternative activities, could alleviate some of the overcrowding problems. One area in which American ski resorts have invested is lift queues. Ski lift queues remain (with the exception of accidents) the biggest obstacle to the enjoyment of skiing in Europe (Scott,

FIGURE 4.4. Ski schools need to make more effort converting beginners into regular skiers. (Photo used with permission of Office du Tourisme Verbier.)

1994). Many European ski resorts do not offer the same quality of service in their ski lifts as do their American competitors (Hudson and Shephard, 1998).

Despite huge investments resorts have made in snowmaking equipment, and some relatively good snow conditions over the past few years, lack of snow is still a major constraint to skiing participation, especially for those who have skied before. With global warming starting to have an effect on the snow cover at many ski destinations, all resorts will have to make the investment in snowmaking eventually, and a budget needs to be set aside to communicate this investment and its benefits to consumers.

*Provide Alternative Winter Sports*

Successful resorts of the future should treat skiing as a form of entertainment by establishing more off-slope diversions. The larger ski chains in North America are expanding the range of activities they offer, such as ice-skating, sledding and dogsledding, snowmobiling, and tubing—the increasingly popular activity of sliding down the slope on the inner tube of a truck tire. The idea is to turn big resorts into full-fledged winter theme parks, attracting more beginners and families to the slopes. *The Economist* ("Winter Wonderlands,"1998) believes that this "Disneyfication" of America's winter sports is unstoppable.

Ski destinations cannot afford to ignore the active nonskier who still travels to the mountains in the winter. An analysis of market trends in North America and Europe suggests that an increasing proportion of those who take winter sports holidays on a regular basis do not ski at all (see Figure 4.5). Among the French, for example, it is estimated that as high as 40 percent do not ski while on winter holidays (Cockerell, 1994).

FIGURE 4.5. Visitors to Jasper in Canada enjoy an ice canyon tour in the winter.

*Counteract Seasonality*

The trend toward nonskiers visiting ski resorts supports the premise that more resorts in which skiing is not the only activity need to be developed, and they must include sporting and entertainment facilities that remain open throughout the year, rather than just the winter months. A key reason that ski destinations attract limited visitors at certain times of the year is that skiing is perceived as a strictly seasonal business. Most ski resorts depend on winter activities to make or break their year financially. Few other industries exist solely from late autumn until spring. Many alpine ski resorts have started to attract summer tourists by developing a wide range of sports and other activities, but more investment is required by many destinations, along with aggressive marketing to communicate the availability of these facilities. Chair lifts and cable cars are operating for walking holidays—a growing summer activity. Many resorts already have swimming pools, skating rinks, tennis courts, guided walks, bike trails, and in some cases glacier skiing. Others have started to advertise rock-climbing, white-water rafting, paragliding (parachuting off a mountainside), canyoning (abseiling down waterfalls and hiking), and hydrospeeding (swimming down white-water rapids on a specially designed surf board).

## *CASE STUDY: WHISTLER RESORT IN CANADA*

Nestled in Canada's spectacular Coast Mountains, Whistler Resort is 120 kilometers north of Vancouver, British Columbia (see Figure 4.6). From its early days as a little known summer fishing retreat, Whistler Resort has become the country's most acclaimed recreational destination. Without the millions of dollars of marketing clout that some of the big U.S. ski destinations wield, the resort is prospering through vision, tenacity, and marketing savvy that is unequalled in the Canadian hospitality sector. Led by Tourism Whistler (formerly Whistler Resort Association)—the worldwide destination marketing representative of the hotels, restaurants, and shops at the foot of the Whistler and Blackcomb mountains—the resort has positioned itself for continued success.

FIGURE 4.6. Whistler Village. (Photo courtesy of Tourism Whistler, Leanna Rathkelly, photographer.)

Whistler boasted a 124 percent jump in revenues in 1999-2000, and its affluence is evident in the increasing number of million-dollar-plus ski homes and luxury condos being built, and in rising hotel prices. A modest room cost $150 (Canadian) per night, and the lift ticket was $59 Canadian per day in 1999-2000. Studies show that the majority of winter visitors are single males, aged between twenty-two and forty-four, with annual earnings (in 1999) of $50,000 to $75,000 (Canadian). They stay an average of five nights and make full use of the new business communications center at the top of Whistler Mountain. The center is one of the few things on the mountain that is free, but it more than pays for itself in terms of public relations value and in providing more business for the mountain.

Whistler Mountain (formerly known as London Mountain) first opened for skiers in 1966. Lift tickets at that time were five dollars per day, and the resort recorded 15,000 skier visits that first year. Before Whistler became famous for skiing, the area was known as Alta Lake and visitors came in the summer months to fish. In the 1940s Rainbow Lodge on Alta Lake was the most popular lodge west of Jasper, and people came from as far away as Winnipeg to spend their honeymoons there. Highway 99 was completed in 1965, paving the way for development at Whistler. Over the past decade, Whistler has experienced unprecedented growth and rising stature as a world-class, year-round destination. Strong growth in visitor numbers has consistently been achieved in both summer and winter, year after year. In response to this success, the resort has undergone many changes. Huge increases in the number of accommodation properties (the resort has attracted investments totaling $550 million in construction between 1995 and 2000), retail shops, and restaurants, along with extensive on-mountain improvements and expansions, have followed on the heels of the growth in overall visitor and skier numbers. These changes have improved the product offerings at Whistler, but they have also resulted in a temporary excess of supply over demand. Accelerated growth in visitor numbers is therefore vital so that these new businesses will be viable in both the short and long term.

Whistler has a world-class reputation for skiing and heliskiing, but it is also known for being friendly to snowboarders. At a time when other resorts were slow to acknowledge the snowboarding culture, Whistler greeted snowboarders with open arms, and the relationship has paid off. The World Ski and Snowboard Festival held each April attracts thousands of young enthusiasts from all over the world. Hotel rooms are fully booked during the event, which spans two weekends to maximize occupancy rates. Events at the 2001 festival included a filmmaker's showdown, an action sport fashion show, an interactive adventure village, and the World Alpine Ski Schools Championships, which tests the skills of ski and snowboard instructors.

The staging of major events at Whistler is not a new undertaking, and although they lost the Skiing World Cup to Lake Louise, they are anxiously awaiting 2003, when the International Olympic Committee decides the host city for the 2010 Winter Games. A successful bid is expected to generate $1 billion in revenue from ticket sales, sponsorships, and television rights.

Whistler Village itself has a European influence, with gabled roofs and cobblestone pathways, and at the base of North America's largest ski area (7,071 acres of skiable terrain), retail mingles with hotels, condominium developments, and services. Since its establishment as a municipality in 1975, building investment has exceeded $2 billion (Canadian). Now, with more than 20,000 hotel beds, and 15,000 of those within 500 meters of the lifts, Whistler boasts the most ski-in/ski-out accommodations of any mountain recreation resort in North America. In the 1999-2000 season, total skier visits reached a North American record of 2.19 million visits—up 35 percent from 1998-1999. The same winter, the number of room nights generated increased to 616,201. Origins of visitors in 2000-2001 can be seen in Appendix A at the end of this chapter.

For the first time, in the summer of 1996, the number of summer visitors exceeded the number of winter visitors. This trend has continued but, the value of the winter market continues to exceed that of the summer market. Winter visitors stay longer, spend more, and come from further abroad. When evaluating performance based on the number of room nights generated, winter accounts for 60 percent of the total, while summer accounts for 40 percent. This discrepancy is further amplified by an average winter room rate that is approximately 60 percent higher than the average summer rate.

Over the years, Whistler and Blackcomb have each strived to match the other in size, services, and facilities. This rivalry has resulted in excellent lift systems and visitor facilities. There is fast access to the slopes from six separate mountain bases with high-speed lifts. Indeed, out of a total of thirty-two lifts, there are ten high-speed quad chairs and three gondolas. Both mountains are similar in size, offering a variety of terrain for skiing and snowboarding enthusiasts all covered by the price of one lift ticket. In 1997, when Whistler and Blackcomb merged under the ownership of industry giant Intrawest, the rivalry between the two resorts disappeared. The company invested more than $24 million on a capital plan for the 1998-1999 season, which included a new quad chairlift for the peak, remodeling the summit restaurants on Whistler Mountain, and a renaissance of the Creekside base area. Expansion is planned through 2004 at Creekside. A mountain neighborhood will be established at the base of the gondola. Plans have been drawn up of a carefully landscaped village with buildings of traditional architectural style. This is intended to preserve the spirit of the community and its history.

Along with its reputation of being one of the top ski resorts in the world, comes a level of responsibility. Intrawest has always taken this responsibility seriously when planning on-mountain development. Environmental stewardship is an important part of the process. Arthur DeJong, Whistler/Blackcomb's mountain planning and environmental manager, has the job of ensuring that the environment is impacted in the least possible way by all projects. He has created the Habitat Improvement Team, a corps of managers and employees who help local conservation groups restore habitats for fish, wildlife, and plant species in Whistler Valley. Whistler is also spending $1.5 million (Canadian) over a five-year period for watershed restoration on its lands in a program called Operation Green-Up.

Tourism Whistler, the destination marketing representative, is a nonprofit association. It was formed in 1980 and is unique in that it is a legislated membership organization empowered to market Whistler. It is responsible for developing coordinated strategies in the areas of sales, advertising, media relations, and promotion of the entire resort. This includes the operation of a central reservations booking service as well as an activity and information center. Tourism Whistler is also responsible for the operation of the Whistler Conference Center and the Whistler Golf Club. The association comprises three sector groups—accommodations, commercial business, and ski operators on the two mountains—and representatives from each serve on the board of directors. A member's meeting takes place annually to review both long- and short-term visions. Involving Whistler's 9,000 full-time residents in the marketing process has been vital in achieving community cohesion and effective operations, and residents play significant roles staging such annual events as diverse as the Winter Start Festival, World Ski and Snowboard Festival, and the Whistler Summit Concert Series.

The mission statement for Tourism Whistler's marketing department is "to work closely with key strategic partners and take a leadership role in developing targeted and effective marketing programs that increase tourism to Whistler for the benefit of all members" (Whistler Resort Association, 1999, p. I). Building partnerships has been an essential component of the marketing objectives, and working with organizations such as the Canadian Tourism Commission and the Ottawa-based Tourism Industry Association of Canada (TIAC), the group has helped to maximize efficiencies. In some overseas markets, for example, Whistler is promoted as part of British Columbia's Golden Triangle, along with Vancouver and Victoria. A North American free phone line and direct-dial service from Vancouver help position the destination as accessible and world class. The association also cooperates with Canadian Pacific Hotels and Delta Hotels to produce joint promotional material, especially for its growing conference business.

The importance of strategic partnerships is clearly demonstrated in Whistler's 1999 business plan. Each department had a number of partnership activities planned, which involved external partners, industry partners, and in-resort partners. For example, the research department worked with the accommodations sector to produce monthly business performance reports. Key statistics generated by this project included year-to-year comparisons of room nights generated, average daily rates, revenue per available room, booking sources, travel type, area of guest origin, and house and paid occupancy rates. Demographic profiles of Whistler's seasonal visitors can be seen at the end of the chapter in Appendix B. There are also some new and innovative partnership activities planned within the Whistler Resort Association (WRA) that include integrated participation between departments.

Tourism Whistler's marketing team of twenty-five people produces most of its advertising and promotional material in house to give them greater control over their image and costs. The group also regularly conducts customer surveys to gauge satisfaction levels, identify areas that need improvement, and formulate strategies. One area the group is attempting to improve is Whistler's appeal as a summer destination. Currently, average occupancy for summer runs at about 43 percent, which is relatively high for what is predominantly a ski destination. However, the marketing team is determined to increase this figure, and many of their promotions focus on the destination's soft-adventure appeal, with particular emphasis on attracting vacationers from the United States and Germany.

Tourism Whistler's new name, adopted in 2000 (after nineteen years as Whistler Resort Association), was accompanied by a new logo. The new symbol is intended to represent Whistler's signature side-by-side mountains, featured in handpainted brush strokes that evoke a carefree, youthful, yet classic and timeless image. The graphic is underscored by the word "Whistler" in purple and silver. A newly revised Web site completes the trio of changes. The site has been redesigned as a more informative and consumer-friendly system while simultaneously offering a more sophisticated navigation scheme. Their Director of Marketing, Jill Greenwood, says they designed the new site specifically for consumers planning a trip to Whistler: they simplified and streamlined the process of online bookings of vacation packages. Tourism Whistler's new Web site address is listed at the end of this chapter.

Tourism Whistler's strategies and tactics for the new millennium are to build upon successful campaigns and patterns from the past, and to incorporate new initiatives and directions. These strategies focus on building upon the year-round success of the resort by smoothing the peaks and valleys through targeted, timely programs. Their three main marketing objectives are (1) to achieve growth of 10 percent in overnight stays for both winter and summer; (2) to continue to diversify the market base by developing new market opportunities; and (3) to attract high-yield customers with longer lengths of stay and higher daily spending.

However, the future presents both opportunities and challenges for the marketing of Whistler Resort. Some of these challenges include the economic situation in Asia; the poor British Columbia economy; continued competition for a limited skier base; and achieving growth rates to offset the increase in available accommodations. Yet, the biggest challenge could be hosting the 2010 Olympic Winter Games. Whistler, along with Vancouver, is pulling together the Canadian bid for these Games and, despite all the planning and control, if the Games do come to the Fraser Valley, they will bring unprecedented challenges. The two-way highway from Vancouver is already strained and there have been suggestions of building a new road in from the east. This could trigger exactly the sort of sprawl and loss of community that Whistler has tried to avoid.

## *APPENDIX A:*
## *HOTEL MARKETS AREA OF ORIGIN*

| | Summer 2000 Room Nights (Percent) | Winter 2000/2001 Room Nights (Percent) |
|---|---|---|
| British Columbia | 45.9 | 21.9 |
| Ontario | 6.7 | 7.8 |
| Alberta | 2.0 | 1.5 |
| Quebec | 1.3 | 1.3 |
| Other Canada | 3.2 | 3.7 |
| **Total Canada** | **59.1** | **36.2** |
| Washington | 9.7 | 9.2 |
| California | 6.9 | 7.3 |
| Oregon | 0.9 | 0.9 |
| New England | 0.8 | 2.2 |
| Middle Atlantic | 2.0 | 3.7 |
| South Atlantic | 2.4 | 4.1 |
| Midwest | 3.9 | 3.5 |
| Other Mtn | 1.6 | 3.8 |
| Texas | 2.4 | 1.6 |
| Other United States | 1.2 | 1.8 |
| **Total United States** | **31.8** | **38.1** |
| United Kingdom | 2.3 | 9.4 |
| Germany | 1.6 | 1.2 |
| Other Europe | 1.4 | 1.8 |
| **Total Europe** | **5.3** | **12.4** |
| Japan | 1.1 | 5.8 |
| Australia/New Zealand | 0.8 | 5.0 |
| Other International | 1.9 | 2.8 |
| **Total Other International** | **3.8** | **13.6** |
| **Total, All Markets** | **100** | **100** |

# APPENDIX B:
# DEMOGRAPHIC PROFILES
# OF WHISTLER'S SEASONAL VISITORS

|  | Summer 1998 | Winter 1997-1998 |
|---|---|---|
| **Base** | 1,036 | 1,704 |
| **Gender** | | |
| Male | 56% | 58% |
| Female | 44% | 42% |
| **Age*** | | |
| Under 25 | 5% | 14% |
| 25-34 | 14% | 27% |
| 35-44 | 27% | 30% |
| 45-54 | 35% | 22% |
| 55+ | 20% | 8% |
| **Household Income** | | |
| <$50,000 | 19% | 20% |
| $50,000-$74,999 | 17% | 12% |
| $75,000-$99,999 | 21% | 13% |
| $100,000-$149,999 | 22% | 20% |
| $150,000+ | 20% | 35% |
| **Previous Visitation** | | |
| First time | 50% | 43% |
| Repeat | 50% | 57% |
| **Household Composition** | | |
| Married with no children | 40% | 26% |
| Married with children | 38% | 35% |
| Single with no children | 20% | 35% |
| Single with children | 2% | 4% |
| **Length of Stay** | | |
| Average no. of nights | 3.4 | 6.1 |

*Age reflects survey respondents

### RELEVANT WEB SITES

Database of winter sports resorts: snow24.com

Ski Area Management: saminfo.com

Canadian Ski Council: skicanada.org

Ski Club of Great Britain: skiclub.co.uk

Ski-Trac International: ski-trac.com

Whistler Resort: whistler.com

Ski Magazine: skimag.com

Ski and Snowboard Directory: skipages.com

Listings for UK skiers: ski.co.uk

Snowboarding search engine: idsnobord.com

Guide to worldwide skiing: goski.com

Information on resorts worldwide: 1ski.com

Intrawest: intrwest.com

Online ski magazine: firsttracksonline.com

Japanese ski guide: skijapanguide.com

Ski Area Citizen's Coalition report card: skiareacitizens.com

National Ski Areas Association: nsaa.org

Trail maps of United States and other resorts: skimaps.com

Snowsports Industries America (SIA): snowlink.com

Tourism Whistler: www.tourismwhistler.com

# REFERENCES

Barker, M.L. (1982). Traditional Landscape and Mass Tourism in the Alps. *Geographical Review,* 72(4): 395-415.

Bender, C. (2000). Snowmaking Survey. *Ski Area Management,* 39(6): 52.

Beyrouti, M. (2000). More Skiers and Snowboarders are Visiting Canadian Ski Areas. *Travel-log,* Winter, pp. 1-8.

Boon, M.A. (1984). Understanding Skiing Behaviour. *Society and Leisure,* 7(2): 397-406.

Bosely, S. (1998). Medipack: Injuries. *The Guardian,* London, November 7, Travel section, p. 11.

Bray, R. (1995). Difficult Market That Could Be on a Slippery Slope. *Travel Weekly,* February 1.

"Breaking News" (1999). *Ski Area Management.* Accessed online <http://www.saminfo.com/news.htm>. November 8.

"Breaking News" (2000). *Ski Area Management.* Accessed online <http://www.saminfo.com/news.htm>. May 2.

Carmichael, B. (1992). Using Conjoint Modelling to Measure Tourist Image and Analyse Ski Resort Choice. In Johnson, P. and Thomas, B. (Eds.), *Choice and Demand in Tourism* (pp. 93-106). London: Mansell.

Carmichael, B. (1996). Conjoint Analysis of Downhill Skiers Used to Improve Data Collection for Market Segmentation. *Journal of Travel and Tourism Marketing,* 5(3): 187-206.

Castle, K. (1999). Mitigation Over Litigation. *Ski,* 64(4): 134-142.

Cockerell, N. (1988). Skiing in Europe—Potential and Problems. *EIU Travel and Tourism Analyst,* 5, 66-81.

Cockerell, N. (1994). Market Segments: The International Ski Market in Europe. *EIU Travel and Tourism Analyst,* 3: 34-55.

Dilley, R.S. and Pozihun, P. (1986). Skiers in Thunder Bay, Ontario: Perceptions and Behaviour. *Recreation Research Review,* 12(4): 27-32.

Ewing, G.O. and Kulka, T. (1979). Revealed and Stated Preference Analysis of Ski Resort Attractiveness. *Leisure Sciences,* 2 (3/4): 249-275.

Gilbert, D. and Hudson, S. (2000). Tourism Demand Constraints: A Skiing Participation. *Annals of Tourism Research,* 27(4): 906-925.

Goeldner, C.R. (1978). *The Colorado Skier: 1977-78 Season.* Business Research Division, Graduate School of Business, University of Colorado.

Hansen, B. (2000). Ski Areas Graded on Environmental Practices. *Environment News Service.* Accessed online <http://ens.lycos.com/ens/nov2000>. December 1.

Hirschfeld, C. (2000). Cyber Planning. *Skiing,* 53(4): 149-150.

Hudson, S. (1995). Responsible Tourism: A Model for the Greening of Alpine Ski Resorts. In Fleming, S., Talbot, M., and Tomlinson, A. (Eds.), *Policy and Politics in Sport, Education and Leisure,* (pp. 239-255). Brighton: England LSA Publications.

Hudson, S. (1996). The "Greening" of Ski Resorts: A Necessity for Sustainable Tourism, or a Marketing Opportunity for Skiing Communities? *Journal of Vacation Marketing*, 2(2): 176-185.

Hudson, S. (1998). There's No Business Like Snow Business!: Marketing Skiing into the 21st Century. *Journal of Vacation Marketing*, 4(4): 393-407.

Hudson, S. (2000). The Segmentation of Potential Tourists: Constraint Differences Between Men and Women. *Journal of Travel Research*, 38 (4): 363-368.

Hudson, S. and Shephard, G.W. (1998). Measuring Service Quality at Tourist Destinations: An Application of Importance-Performance Analysis to an Alpine Ski Resort. *Journal of Travel and Tourism Marketing*, 7(3): 61-77.

Keogh, B. (1980). Motivations and The Choice Decision of Skiers. *Tourist Review*, 35(1): 18-22.

Klenosky, D.B., Gengler, C.E., and Mulvey, M.S. (1993). Understanding the Factors Influencing Ski Destination Choice: A Means-End Analytical Approach. *Journal of Leisure Research*, 25(4): 326-379.

Korobanik, J. (2000). What's Happened to the Women on the Nation's Ski Hills? *Calgary Herald*, December 21, p. D7.

Kottke, M. (1990). Growth Trends: Going Both Ways at Once. *Ski Area Management*, 29(1): 63-64, 96-97.

Lazard, A.J. (1996). Gathering Stats Worldwide. *Ski Area Management*, 35(5): 60-73.

Lewis, R. and Wild, M. (1995). *French Ski Resorts and UK Ski Tour Operators*. The Centre for Tourism Occasional Papers, Sheffield Hallam University.

Liebers, A. (1963). *The Complete Book of Winter Sports*. New York: Coward-McCann.

Loverseed, H. (2000). Winter Sports in North America. *Travel and Tourism Intelligence*, 6: 45-62.

Martinelli, M. (1976). Meteorology and Ski Area Development and Operation. In *Proceedings Fourth National Conference on Fire and Forest Meteorology*. United States Department of Agriculture/Forest Services Technical Report Number, RM-32.

McLennan, M. (2000). The Untold History. *Ski Canada*, 29(3): 74-81.

Mills, A.S. (1985). Participation Motivations for Outdoor Recreation: A Test of Maslow's Theory. *Journal of Leisure Research*, 17(3): 184-199.

Mills, A.S., Couturier, H., and Snepenger, D.J. (1986). Segmenting Texas Snow Skiers. *Journal of Travel Research*, 25(2): 19-23.

National Ski Areas Association (NSAA) (2000). *1998/99 Economic Analysis of United States Ski Areas*. Lakewood, Colorado.

National Ski Areas Association (NSAA) (2001). Media Center. Accessed online <http:// www.nsaa.org/media>, October 31.

"Off the Map: Snow Days" (2000). *American Demographics*, December, p. 72.

Packer, J. (1998). Everything You Ever Wanted to Know About Ski and Snowboard Tourists But Were Afraid to Ask. *Journal of Vacation Marketing*, 4(2): 186-192.

Pearce, D.G. (1995). *Tourism Development*. Harlow: Longman.

Potter, E. (2000). The Well-Wired Skier. *Ski,* 65(4): 79-81.

Richards, G. (1995). Retailing Travel Products: Bridging the Information Gap. *Progress in Tourism and Hospitality Research,* 1(1): 17-29.

Rosa, B. (2001). Skiing's End? *Skiing Winter Adventure,* 53(6): 32.

Schreiner, J. (2000). Snowmakers Hold Key to "Core" Business. *National Post,* December 4, pp. C1, C7.

Scott, A. (1994). We Have Lift-Off. *The Sunday Times,* London, Travel section, June 3.

Sibley, R.G. (1982). *Ski Resort Planning and Development.* Foundation for the Technical Advancement of Local Government Engineering in Victoria, Melbourne.

Spring, J. (1995). Are We on the Brink of a Boom? *Ski Area Management,* 34(4): 39-68.

Spring, J. (1996a). European Skiers: Not So Different. *Ski Area Management,* 35(5): 61-80.

Spring, J. (1996b). More Days/More Fun But Shrinking Numbers. *Ski Area Management,* 35(4): 44-45.

Spring, J. (1997). Crossovers Fuel Boarding. *Ski Area Management,* 36(3): 55-56.

Spring, J. (2000). Who Visited This Season? *Ski Area Management,* 39(3): 54-59.

Tanler, B. (1966). A Decade of Growth. *Ski Area Management,* 5(4): 10-14.

Thorne, P. (2000a). 2001—A Global Ski Odyssey. *Ski Area Management,* 40(6): 47-49.

Thorne, P. (2000b). *Y2K Ski Hemispheres Magazine,* January, pp. 84-89.

Tikalsky, F.T. and Lahren, S.L. (1988). Why People Ski. *Ski Area Management,* 27(3): 68-114.

"Travel Hit" (2000). *Ski,* 65(4): 82.

Viner, D. and Agnew, M. (1999). *Climate Change and Its Impacts on Tourism.* Report prepared for WWF-UK by the Climate Research Unit, University of East Anglia, Norwich.

"Warming Permafrost Puts Resorts in Alps at Risk" (2001). *National Post,* January 5, p. A10.

Whistler Resort Association (1999). 1999 Marketing Summary. Whistler Resort Association, Whistler, B.C.

Wickers, D. (1994). Snow Alternative. *The Sunday Times,* London, Travel section, November 27, p. 9.

Williams, P. (1993). The Evolution of the Skiing Industry. In Khan, M.A., Olsen, M.D., and Var, T. Van (Eds.), *VNR's Encyclopaedia of Hospitality and Tourism* (pp. 926-933). New York: Nostrand Reinhold.

Williams, P.W. and Basford, R. (1992). Segmenting Downhill Skiing's Latent Demand Markets. *American Behavioral Scientist,* 36(2): 222-235.

Wilson, A. (1996). Where the Wild Things Are. *The Sunday Times,* London, Travel section, October 20, p. 15.

"Winter Wonderlands" (1998). *The Economist,* January 31, p. 86.

Zimmer, Z., Brayley, R.E., and Searle, M. (1995). Whether to Go and Where to Go: Identification of Important Influences on Seniors' Decisions to Travel. *Journal of Travel Research,* 33(3): 3-10.

# Chapter 5

# Marine Tourism

## Gayle Jennings

## *INTRODUCTION*

Marine tourism is a burgeoning sector of the tourism industry at a global, national, state, and local level. A number of marine sports comprise the marine tourism product, sports such as boating, sailing, fishing, diving, snorkeling, surfing, windsurfing, parasailing, water-skiing, canoeing, kayaking, jet skiing (see Figure 5.1), and jet boat riding. Each type of marine tourism attracts both different and similar types of tourists; involves individuals in varying periods of participation depending on skills and experience levels; accesses different and the same locations for the pursuit of the activity; and uses equipment, which requires either minimal or substantial financial outlay depending on the skill level of the participant(s) and the type of sport tourism pursued.

In general, marine tourism participation rates are difficult to ascertain (Wilks and Atherton, 1994a) as a number of sports and participants do not report activities. This is due to several reasons including the more independent nature of marine sports activities, the absence of legislation requiring registration to either conduct the activity or use equipment (for example, boats are registered, surfboards are not), or the add-on nature of marine tourism activities in the overall tourism experience. Moreover, the study of marine tourism is difficult because differences exist between recreationalists and tourists, although both use the same sites and locations for their activities (Miller, 1993). Data sets are thus sporadic and dependent on the individual interests of researchers, the collective interest of management agencies, and trends or fads. This will be evident when you read through

FIGURE 5.1. Jet skier takes flight. (Courtesy of the Great Barrier Reef Marine Park Authority. Photograph by J. Jones.)

this chapter and consider the participation rates and the dates that these rates were obtained.

The historical roots of marine tourism are founded in the pursuit of the three Ss—sun, sea, and sand. This means that marine tourism has been and will continue to be a significant sector of overall tourism. Furthermore, the economic benefits of marine tourism are substantial. For example, in Australia, the economic contribution of marine tourism is approximately 2 percent of gross domestic product (Driml, 1996). Although the economic impact is significant, it is important to note that the diffusion of marine tourism throughout economies makes it difficult to determine who is a tourism operator and who is not (Miller, 1993), which results in making the determination of economic impact a complex task. For example, would a windsurfing shop that supplies local recreationalists and tourists with equipment be classified as a local supplier or a tourism operator? Such ambiguities pervade both sports tourism and tourism products in general, at generating, intermediary, and destination locations.

As the number of marine tourism sports is manifold, concentrating on all of them within this chapter would result in presenting minimal information on each. Consequently, this chapter will focus on five: boating, fishing, sea kayaking, diving, and surfing. Each of these will be outlined in turn (background, participation rates, motivations, locations, impacts) before addressing generic marketing issues, management issues, and future directions regarding marine tourism. A global perspective will be provided and specific examples will be drawn from the Australian context. The chapter concludes with a case study that examines usage of the Great Barrier Reef in Australia for marine tourism. Remember, this chapter concentrates on participants rather than spectators and organizers, although the latter two are markets worthy of investigation in their own right.

## TYPES OF MARINE TOURISM

### Boating

Boating activities in a marine environment include use of boats that are primarily powered by motors or by sails. Within the motorboat category a variety of types can be subclassified: power boats, motor cruisers (see Figure 5.2), and the associated activities of waterskiing, jet skiing, and racing. Within the sailboat category, there are a variety of options such as sailing, cruising, and racing. There are also four other types of vessels that facilitate marine tourism activities such as: sea kayaks and canoes, windsurfers, and surfboards.

The number of boats (motor and sail powered) in the world is estimated to be over 20 million, with approximately half of those located in the United States and Canada ("Pleasure Boating," 1987). There are approximately 500,000 registered vessels in Australia (Driml, 1996). The number of pleasure boats in Japan has been increasing over time from some 80,000 in 1970 to about 280,000 in 1990 (Kotani, 1991). However, Japan has become involved in the use of boats for leisure activities only toward the end of the twentieth century compared with other Western nations such as England and the United States (Kotani, 1991), which have a longer history of boating as a leisure activity. The increase in boating participation in Japan is directly attributable to increases in leisure time over the same period ("Plea-

FIGURE 5.2. Motor cruiser on a mooring buoy. (Courtesy of the Great Barrier Reef Marine Park Authority. Photograph Anonymous.)

sure Boating," 1987). However, further increase is limited by the number of marine facilities available for marine-based activities such as marinas and limited production of marine equipment such as boats (Okubo, 1989).

Within each boating category, various subcategories exist with which boaters identify. These subcategories are determined based on boat design (for example, material of construction, number of hulls; and, for sail-powered vessels, the number of masts and mast location and configurations). Other means of differentiating is by the number of people allowed aboard the vessel (solo or single handed; double handed, two people or crewed); the duration of the voyage (short term, three months; long term, eighteen months or more); or by the geographical location of the voyage (coastal, off-shore, also known as blue-water cruising and around the world cruising, that is, circumnavigating). Boating may also be undertaken as part of cruising races in defined geographical areas such as the Sydney to Noumea Yacht Race, or as part of competitive racing events such as the BOC Round the World Challenge.

## Sailing

Sailing attracts a variety of marine tourists. It can be differentiated into a typology of sailing experiences, e.g., recreational racing, cruising, and recreational chartering. This chapter will not address recreational racing tourism experiences.

*Cruising.* Cruising by individuals (yachties or cruisers)[1] who sail and live aboard their own yachts/vessels has been increasingly popular since the late twentieth century. This is due to:

- Improvements in yacht design, especially with regard to sailing efficiency and comfort
- Increased affordability of navigation equipment
- Developments in telecommunications equipment, particularly wider ranging satellite coverage which provides greater contact with home bases and search-and-rescue facilities
- Greater freedom and finances to travel resulting from early retirement packages, investments, and improved income bases of the middle class
- A change in values regarding work and leisure relationships and the notions of active retirement and early retirement (Jennings, 1999, p. 65)

Cruisers tend to be of mature age, well educated, from professional or semiprofessional backgrounds of middle class incomes or above, and financially secure. More couples than family groups participate, and there are more male solo sailors than female. Cruising is pursued for a variety of reasons, which include the inherent challenges and adventure it provides, a desire to see the world or the fulfillment of a lifelong dream, or because of a sense of belonging—wanting to be with a partner who wants to go cruising (Jennings, 1999; Macbeth, 1985).

*Cruising Locations.* The cruising waters of the world are located in the South Pacific, Indian Ocean, Red Sea, Mediterranean Sea, North Atlantic, North Pacific, and Far East. The most popular cruising location is the Mediterranean Sea. The second most popular location is the Caribbean. Table 5.1 overviews the key cruising regions of the world, as well as specific sites within those regions, and the estimated number of vessels that cruise in those regions when the weather is optimal for cruising (e.g., no expected cyclones, hurricanes, tsunamis).

TABLE 5.1. Overview of Cruising Regions and Specific Sites and Estimated Numbers of Cruising Vessels

| Cruising Region | Examples of Specific Sites | Estimated Numbers in Cruising Season |
|---|---|---|
| North Pacific | Line Islands, Marshall Islands, Galapagos, Alaska, Canadian coastline, United States coastline especially California, Mexico's Baja California | Approximately 1,000 U.S. yachts to Hawaii, and approximately 200 international (non-U.S.) yachts to Hawaii |
| South Pacific | Fiji, Tonga, Tahiti, Marquesas, Hawaii, New Zealand, New Caledonia, Vanuatu, Australia, French Polynesia, American Samoa, Western Samoa, Cook Islands | Approximately 1,000 yachts |
| Indian Ocean | Sri Lanka, Bali, Melaka, Thailand, Christmas Island, Cocos, Keeling, Mauritius, Chagos Archipelago, Seychelles, Cape of Good Hope | Approximately 100 yachts |
| Red Sea | Bab el Mandeb, Aden, Djibouti, Sudan, Egypt | No data available |
| Mediterranean Sea | Gibraltar, Madeira, Spain's Costa del Sol (Gibraltar, Malaga), Balearic Islands, French coastline, Corsica, Sardinia, Italy, Greece, Turkey | 2,000 yachts. But, 5,000 yachts either entered or left the Mediterranean via Gibraltar during 1987 |
| North Atlantic | Azores, Bermuda, Canary Islands | No data available |
| Far East | Singapore, Philippines, Hong Kong, Japan | Approximately 20 yachts |
| Caribbean | Barbados, St. Lucia, Antigua, Martinique, Guadaloupe, Virgin Islands | No data available |
| Canal Cruising | French waterways, English waterways, German waterways, United States waterways | No data available |

Among cruisers, all of the previously described boater categories and subcategories may be found. It is worth further differentiating types of cruisers by drawing on the Pacific region for analogy. Three categories of yachties can be identified as market segments within the Pacific Rim: the "milkrun" segment,[2] the fly-cruise segment, and the circumnavigation segment. The "milkrun" segment describes those yachties who undertake a circular navigation of the Pacific, usually originating in North America. It may also apply to yachties whose travel originates in Australia or New Zealand and who engage in circular navigations of Pacific waters. These circular navigations may be of varying lengths, such as North America to Hawaii and back, or from New Zealand to Fiji to Tonga and return. The second segment, the fly-cruisers, fly to various locations and then board their own vessels for extended cruising in Pacific waters, returning home by air travel at the conclusion of their holiday period. The third segment, those undertaking world circumnavigations, may travel across the tropical waters of the Pacific Ocean or via the lower latitudes around Cape Horn or through the tropics and lower latitudes. Within the Pacific, circumnavigators may travel from Panama to the Marquesas, to the Society Islands to Samoa, Fiji, Australia, and on into the Indian Ocean. An alternative route may be via Cape Horn to Juan Fernandez, St. Felix, the Marquesas, Samoa, Fiji, and New Zealand. Some yachties include the Galapagos Islands, Easter Island, and Pitcarn Island in their itineraries. Each of the three types produces various social, economic, and environmental impacts because of the nature of their overall cruising experience.

*Chartering.* Sailing can also be defined in terms of its management through the tourism industry such as in the case of yachting charters. Specific examples include bareboat charters (see Figure 5.3), skippered yacht charters, crewed yacht charters, and flotilla yachting holidays (Richens, 1992). Table 5.2 provides an overview of the difference between each of these and the market segment to which each appeals.

Charter locations are concentrated in the Mediterranean and Caribbean, however, yacht chartering is available to varying degrees within each of the cruising locations noted in Table 5.1.

*Impacts.* The impacts of cruising and chartering are similar. There are social impacts (positive and negative host-guest interactions: increased understanding, friendship, cultural exchange, social pathologies, demonstration effects, and cultural commodification), environmental impacts (negative impacts such as pollution, coral damage, anchor damage, souveniring of shells and coral, congestion, exceeding carrying capacity, and conflict between user groups), and economic impacts (increased income generation in host communities, positive income and employment multiplier effects, economic leakages when supplies and equipment are bought from other

FIGURE 5.3. Bareboat charter under sail. (Courtesy of the Great Barrier Reef Marine Park Authority. Photograph by B. Barnett.)

regions). The degree to which impacts occur varies between cruisers and yacht charter groups. For example, the impacts of charter activities tend to concentrate in one geographic area (due to insurance regulations, safety, and support strategies) whereas cruisers tend to disperse over a greater geographic area. Therefore, social, environmental, and economic impacts are distributed over a wider area in the case of cruisers than in the case of charterers.

### Fishing

Recreational fishing is a popular leisure time activity in national parks and wilderness areas (Borschmann, 1987), and in marine parks and areas. As an activity, fishing is also strongly aligned with the pursuit of recreational boating (see Figures 5.4 and 5.5). In Australia, according to the National Recreational Fisheries Working Group, approximately 4.5 million people participate in recreational fishing, the

TABLE 5.2. Overview of Types of Charters, Sociodemographics of Charterers, and Their Motivations

| Type of Charter | Sociodemographics | Motivations |
|---|---|---|
| Bareboat: tourists rent a boat and sail it themselves. One renter must demonstrate rudimentary sailing skills. | • 35-50 years old<br>• Middle to higher income brackets<br>• Some sailing experience | • Experience some adventure<br>• Spend time with family and friends |
| Skippered yacht charter: tourists rent the boat and the services of a skipper (captain). | • 35-50 years old<br>• Middle to higher income brackets<br>• Couples and families<br>• Some sailing experience | • Learn sailing skills<br>• Experience some adventure<br>• Spend time with family and friends |
| Crewed yacht charter: tourists rent the boat and the services of a skipper and crew (cook, deckhands, engineer). | • Higher income brackets<br>• Little if any sailing experience | • Experience some adventure<br>• Personalized service |
| Flotilla yachting holiday: tourists may either rent a bareboat, a skippered yacht, or cruise in company with other boats. One experienced sailor organizes the sailing itinerary and manages the flotilla on a day-to-day basis. | • Couples and families<br>• Middle to higher income brackets | • Safety with a leader in charge of the overall experience of the group<br>• Social dimensions of group activities<br>• Experience some adventure<br>• Develop sailing skills |

*Source:* Based on Richens (1992) and author's personal observations.

majority (70 percent) are men (Dovers, 1994). Recreational fishing is also included in most on-site activities at sun, sea, and sand locations and during the travel to and from phases of the overall travel experience of tourists.

*Motivation*

Although the desire to catch fish is the primary goal of recreational fishers, there are noncatch-related motivations associated with the experience (Dovers, 1994; Fedler and Ditton, 1994). Noncatch-related motivations include "escape, freedom, relaxation and personal liberty" as well as the desire to experience a "frontier spirit" (Johnson and

FIGURE 5.4. Fishers and their catch. (Courtesy of the Great Barrier Reef Marine Park Authority. Photograph by N. Collins.)

FIGURE 5.5. Game fishing boat looking for catch. (Courtesy of the Great Barrier Reef Marine Park Authority. Photograph by L. Zell.)

Orbach, 1986, p. 326). Other noncatch-related motivations include to "relax and unwind, to be outdoors," to enjoy the company of others, to experience the "thrill/contest of catching fish," and to obtain a source of food (PA Management Consultants, 1984b, p. 38). Gartside (1986) reported similar motivations: a sense of "escapism" from daily life and work and "enjoyment of the environment" (p. 15), and Kenchington (1993) identified personal challenge as yet another motivating factor. A social aspect of recreational fishing was also reported by PA Management Consultants (1984a) who stated that men favored fishing with friends over fishing with their families. Conversely, women favored fishing with their families more than with their friends (PA Management Consultants, 1984a). More recently, Jennings (1998) also found that marine fishers used particular areas due to:

- The quality of the fish stocks
- The amenity of the setting
- Provision of safe anchorages
- Ease of access from port of departure

Marine fishers also chose to fish in the company of family and friends, although more men tended to pursue the activity than women (Jennings, 1998). The sociodemographics of fishers who participated in the study indicated that the average age of fishers was forty-five to forty-nine years, and occupations included skilled workers, service industry workers, and professionals (Jennings, 1998).

## Locations

As previously noted, fishers tend to pursue their activities at sun, sea, and sand locations. Tourists who fish, similar to recreational fishers, fish from the beach, near offshore reefs and sites, in estuarine areas, and from offshore locations. They also engage in sport fishing for marlin and swordfish.

## Impacts

Social impacts related to fishing are generally associated with behaviors exhibited at fishing sites and nearby locations. These include, for example, conflicts between fishers and other location users, congestion at sites, loss of amenities due to carrying capacity being ex-

FIGURE 5.4. Sea kayakers underway. (Courtesy of the Great Barrier Reef Marine Park Authority. Photograph by J. Jones.)

ceeded, and unsocial behavior such as shouting, drinking, and rowdiness. Environmental impacts include overfishing, undersized fishing, fishing out of season, anchor damage, noise pollution from generators, mega fauna hits by motorboat propellers, indiscriminate catch waste if nets are used, and vandalism. Economic impacts of recreational fishing are significant. Money is spent on fishing equipment, bait, ice, drinks, and food supplies possibly, and also fuel, oil, engine parts, boat hire, charter tickets, and environmental management charges to access specific sites. Fishing in tourism locations generates employment, multiplier effects derived from income and employment, as well as revenue leakages if goods and services are purchased outside the destination region.

## Sea Kayaking

The sport of sea kayaking (see Figure 5.4) has its roots in the traditional form of travel used for movement around the Arctic Sea and Greenland waters developed by the Inuit peoples (Effeney, 1999). The word *kayak* has its origins rooted in the description of a "hunter's boat" (Effeney, 1999). Global-level participation rates are not available. However, sea kayakers are smaller in number than, for example, boaters and fishers. Sea kayakers may be classified according to four groups (Morgan, 1998):

- Fearless thrill seekers (These kayakers engage in a high level of adventure for a short duration.)
- Daring thrill seekers (These kayakers are not fully confident that their skills will meet the challenges of a sea kayaking adventure. They are, therefore, dependent on equipment and instructors/guides to manage the perceived risk of their adventure. The experience, consequently, has a low level of adventure for a short duration.)
- Ecotourists (These kayakers engage in low-level adventure for a long duration. Subsequently, for these kayakers, the equipment is considered adequate as is the perception of their skills to manage the risks of the expedition in order to enjoy the setting.)
- Competence testers (These kayakers seek a high-level challenge in an expedition, one that tests their skills. The primary motivation of this group is a low level of adventure for a long duration). (Morgan, 1998)

Safety, the natural setting, and perceptions of risk can conflict (Jones and Ellis, 1996) depending on the type of kayaker. Table 5.3 presents a suggested checklist to determine risk for any expedition. It is useful for kayakers and operators of kayaking expeditions.

An example of sea kayaking as an extreme sport was organized independently of the tourism system, although dependent on sponsors for support (eighty sponsors in all). Called the 1999 Greenland kayak and dog expedition, conducted by Lonnie Dupre and John Hoelschre, the expedition covered 2,000 miles traveling halfway around Greenland. The budget for the expedition was US$400,000 (Dupre, 2000). The planning of the expedition took twenty-six months. The risks as recognized by Dupre (2000, p. 13) were "physical, emotional and financial."

*Motivation*

What motivates a person to undertake such an extreme adventure?

So what motivates me to live with the Inuit and travel by kayak and dog sledge in the High Arctic for 15 months? As long as I can remember, I've always been interested in what was around the next corner. I was raised on a Minnesota country farm and, as a child, roamed freely, exploring the nearby woods and swamp. We lived a lot on what we grew or raised on the farm, or what my father brought home from hunting and fishing. I soon learned to hunt and fish as well. Our modest means and farm lifestyle dictated a self-sufficiency that I embraced early. I also became fascinated with the wildlife I encountered while exploring the countryside. I often wondered if there were still people that subsisted on hunting, fishing, and gathering. Later in life, these experiences helped me to understand and admire the ways of the Inuit. Being raised in Minnesota, I also became accustomed to the cold at a young age. . . .

As a family we would always go "up north" to a Minnesota lake for holiday vacations, usually relaxing and fishing. On our way, I wondered just how far "north" went. Were there people who lived up there? How did they handle the cold? I eventually started reading all the material I could get my hands on pertaining to the Inuit (Eskimos) and the Arctic. With my first trip to the Arctic of Alaska in 1983 at the age of twenty-two, I was hooked. I wondered then how I could see and experience the whole Arctic—the environment and its people; not just the villages, but the vast lands of the caribou, polar bear, and muskox. I concluded that the best way was by traditional methods of dog sledging and kayaking.

I confess that the spirit of adventure is strong in me. I easily become bored with everyday life. I often long to step back in time, back to the Arctic where life is a bit less complicated and the basic necessities do not include a late-model car. I love to travel silently with only the sound of dogs' feet hitting the snow and the sliding of the sledge runners. For me, the adventure is in a kayak paddle breaking the surface of glass-flat water on a majestic fjord that has rarely been visited. Seeing new things around each cape, over each hill, or beyond each piece of pack ice keeps me going forward and interested. This is the adventure. After all, isn't life's process supposed to be an adventure?

The expedition around Greenland by dog sledge and kayak epitomizes the human spirit of adventure, and represents an incredible test of individual will. When combined with other objectives of the project, the expedition became much more than a saga of humans pitted against nature and the elements. It offered opportunities to learn about our planet, our fellow inhabitants, and ourselves. (Dupre, 2000, p. 13)

## *Impacts*

The impacts of sea kayaking are minimal due to the small size of expeditions. Social impacts between hosts and guests are relatively small as most expeditions venture into unpopulated areas. Invariably, there can be entries into cultural and indigenous locations that require prior approval. Environmental impacts are associated with loss of gear, rubbish and other human waste products, damage at campsites, and unsettling of local species. Economic impacts can also vary as demonstrated in the previous example. The costs of an expedition can be enormous or they can be small. Economic impacts are generated via equipment

TABLE 5.3. Checklist for Determining the Risk Associated with Sea Kayaking Expeditions

| Low risk | 1 | 2 | 3 | 4 | 5 | High risk |
|---|---|---|---|---|---|---|
| Landings in safe and surf locations | | | | | | Exit into water (no sloping shore) |
| Skilled and adept from practice | | | | | | Novice kayaker |
| Careful, alert, and circumspect | | | | | | Naive and careless |
| Protected waters with others | | | | | | Single journey in unprotected waters |
| Fair-weather conditions | | | | | | Storm conditions |
| Flat sea without currents | | | | | | Confused sea with running currents |

*Source:* Based on Alderson (1996) <http://www.wavelengthmagazine.com/1996/apr96risk.php>.

purchases and repairs, employment of local expedition leaders, fee entry to locations, supplies, and travel to and from expedition locations.

## Diving

Diving, that is, scuba (self-contained underwater breathing apparatus) diving (see Figure 5.5), as an activity, has developed from the 1950s and 1960s when the focus was on spearfishing and raiding wrecked ships (Driml, 1996). Today, the focus is on underwater photography and natural history (Driml, 1996). In Australia, approximately 700,000 people dive per year (Driml, 1996). An estimated 55,000 divers are trained each year with half of those being tourists (Driml, 1996). It is estimated that some 85,000 resort divers pay tuition each year (Wilks, 1993). The contribution of diving to the tourism industry is approximately $350 million per year (Driml, 1996).

FIGURE 5.5. Scuba diver searching for quality coral and fish. (Courtesy of the Great Barrier Reef Marine Park Authority. Photograph by B. Cropp.)

Essentially, dive travel is the one of the fastest-growing sectors in tourism (Dignam, 1990; Tabata, 1992; Hamdi, 1995; Davis, Banks, and Davey, 1996).

On a global level, 85 percent of diving travelers reside in the United States (PATA, in Tabata, 1992). The Caribbean is a renowned diving location and the dive industry is particularly concentrated in the Bahamas, Cayman Islands, and Bonaire (Weaver, 1994). For each of these locations respectively, divers generated in excess of US$80-90 million, US$30 million, and US$52.3 million during 1985 (Dixon and Sherman, 1990, cited in Weaver 1994). Interest in scuba diving by Asian populations has increased significantly over the past three decades (Hamdi, 1995), with approximately 220,000 divers in Asia and around 40,000 divers in Singapore and Hong Kong. Japan has some 500,000 divers making the total for Asia approximately 740,000 to 760,000 divers. The sociodemographic profile of divers leans toward young, well-educated, financially secure people in managerial, professional, or sales positions. They are predominantly male (Tabata, 1992).

Courses provide participants with opportunities to acquire the necessary scuba diving knowledge and skills regarding equipment, underwater science, effects of depth on the body, the diving environment, planning dive times, diving skills, and safe diving (NAUI, 1990). There are a number of internationally accredited agencies:

- PADI, Professional Association of Dive Instructors
- NAUI, National Association of Underwater Dive Instructors
- BSAC, British Sub-Aqua Club (reports training 100,000 divers per year)
- CMAS, Confederation Mondiale des Activities Subaquatique (World Underwater Federation)
- NASDS, National Association of Scuba Diving Schools
- SSI, Scuba Schools International (merged with NASDS in 1999)

Courses range from four-hour resort dive courses, which enable participants to dive with an instructor, to five-day internationally recognized certificate courses (Hill, 1993) offered by the internationally accredited agencies listed previously.

## Locations

Diving destinations around the world are noted in Table 5.4. The primary determinants of dive site selection are water clarity, quality and variety of coral and fish, price, access, and underwater aesthetics (O'Reilley, 1982, 1992; Dixon and Sherman, 1990). With regard to site selection, divers were surveyed to determine their willingness to pay for their dive experience. Findings indicate that divers "are willing to pay a premium for environmental quality and good diving" (Dixon and Shermon, 1990, p. 182).

## Motivation

Divers may be clustered into three types: hard core, tourist, and potential (Rice, 1987). Each group has different motivations. The first, the hard-core diver, seeks diving experiences that provide challenge and have substantial drawing power based on exotic or interesting flora and fauna. Tourist divers include diving as a vacation activity, though it is not the sole focus of the holiday. The potential diver may engage in resort diving to determine if he or she wants to continue the pursuit. Overall, diving motivations are related to:

- A desire for a wilderness experience
- An interest in the marine sciences
- The unique image of the sport
- An interest in the underwater environment: underwater formations, historical wrecks, pelagic fish, mega fauna, and corals
- The engagement in a hobby such as underwater photography
- The experience or trial of the sport
- The experience of adventure due to perceived risks (Davis and Tisdell, 1994)

## Impacts

Impacts of scuba diving will be viewed only from an environmental perspective in this section. Scuba's social and economic impacts mirror those of the previous types of marine tourism. Impacts from divers include coral damage from fin hits, holding on to coral, rubbish from vessels, spearfishing, and overcollecting (Driml, 1996). Environmental impacts associated with fin damage suggest that con-

TABLE 5.4. Some Destinations for Dive Travel

| Asia-Pacific | South and Central America | Caribbean | Africa, Indian Ocean, and Red Sea |
|---|---|---|---|
| Australia | Belize | Bahamas | Egypt |
| Indonesia | Galapagos | Curacao | Kenya |
| Papua New Guinea | Venezeula | Jamaica | Maldives |
| Hawaii | Cabo San Lucas | St. Vincent | South Africa |
| | | U.S. Virgin Islands | |

*Note:* Based on <http://www.naui.org/index-side.html>

trol of buoyancy is an issue for some divers. However, the Great Barrier Reef Marine Park Authority (GBRMPA) reports that "results from recent studies on the impact of diving activities on the Reef, indicate that the majority of divers cause little detectable damage to corals" (GBRMPA, 2000). Additional impacts arise from the interactions of the various types of divers who use each site, which can cause, for example, conflicts between users and congestion at dive sites (Davis and Tisdell, 1994; Hawkins and Roberts, 1992, 1993; Scura and van't Hof, 1992; Phillips, 1992).

## *Surfing*

Surfing has its origins in Pacific Ocean cultures (Orams, 1999) and is thought to have been around since the tenth century (Brasch, 1995, cited in Orams, 1999). Today, surfing constitutes a subcultural lifestyle (Pearson, 1979), a recreational activity, and a form of tourism. Using Pearson's (1979) classification, surfing can be described as a play sport or an athletic sport (that is, either amateur or professional respectively). As a subculture and way of life, surfing has its own mores and codes of conduct (Pearson, 1979). However, currently, in Australia, there is a breakdown in the observance of these mores and codes of conduct, as more nonsubcultural participants engage in surfing. Conflicts between marine users results. As Gerard (2000) comments, "Surfing has strong cultural traditions in Australia, but recent incidents of violent surf rage caused by the dangerous overcrowding of popular beaches has put the sport under the microscope" (pp. 2-3).

An estimated 2 million Australians regularly surf using boards according to surfing associations (Driml, 1996). During the 1990s in Australia there was a call by surfing associations for the establishment of surfing reserves at premium sites such as Bells Beach, Victoria, and Margaret River, Western Australia (Driml, 1996), in an attempt to reduce such conflicts.

## Locations

Globally, surfing destinations are located in a number of regions. Table 5.5 lists some of these locations.

## Impacts

Surfers often complain about water quality at surfing sites. Surfing impacts are mainly due to trampling on the tracks to surf sites and in-

TABLE 5.5. Surfers and Destinations

| Location | Specific Nations | Primary Generating Nations for Surfers at These Sites |
|---|---|---|
| Europe to Morocco | Ireland, France, Spain, Portugal, Morocco | Australia, New Zealand, United States, and Germany |
| West Coast South America | Ecuador, Peru to Chile | Australia, United States, Brazil, and European nations |
| Indonesia | Sumatra to Timor | Mainly Australia and some European nations |
| Australia | Southern Queensland, south, and around to Port Headland | Australia (Japan for Sydney and England most other places) |
| Mexico, Central America | Mexico, Guatemala, El Salvador, Nicaragua, Costa Rica, and Panama | United States |
| South Africa | Durban to Jeffreys Bay | Australia |

*Source:* Sanders (1999, pp. 87-91).

sufficient parking (Driml, 1996). Gerard (2000), who reported on a law of the surf forum held in Byron Bay, Australia, commented that surfers were still considering the need to introduce user fees to surf sites as the number of surfers now exceeds the number of surf breaks available. This suggestion was made in an attempt to reduce over-crowding on beaches (Gerard, 2000). There are beaches in Hawaii where surfers pay to surf, and there are already sites along the South Australian coastline that are accessed only by paying an entry fee (Gerard, 2000). The forum also discussed the need to introduce formal legislation in an effort to ensure that more surfers adhere to the moral code of conduct of the sport.

## MARKETING ISSUES

> The travel market of the future will exhibit a growing sophistication (Weiler and Hall 1992); will be more aware of choices available to them and will come from more diverse lifestyles (Martin and Mason 1987); will have a desire for new experiences with a substantial adventure component, and a desire to be a part of the decision making (Fay, McCure and Begin 1987); will have a preference for active participation in favor of traditionally passive involvements in travel packages that reflect custom tailoring to specific market segments (Schwaninger 1987). They will be experienced and value conscious, and intent on travel experiences that facilitate self development, learning and unique individual experiences. (Lipscombe, 1996, p. 39)

Although Lipscombe's comments focus on aged adventure tourists, his comments are also applicable to the adventure tourist or sports tourist of any age. Such tourists are more discerning and more demanding based on individualized travel expectations than tourists of yore. Further, the perception that adventure travel is for the youth market is incorrect (Berno et al., 1996). The baby boom generations of developed nations are pushing the tourism industry to cater to their needs as they age, have disposable income and more education, and want more value for their money in their travel experiences. Marketing issues are associated with:

- Providing diversity of choice
- Providing multiplicity and flexibility in products

- Customizing travel experiences
- Including learning components
- Accessing competencies of operators and sports tourists
- Understanding legal responsibilities. (Jennings, 2001)

With regard to the first three points on this list, the complementing of dive experiences, for example, with cultural experiences and shopping will add to the overall experience of dive tourists from Asia (Hamdi, 1995). Alternatively, the diversity in dive sites throughout the 340 Palau Islands provides for quality diving (Hng, 1993) and adds to the attractiveness of the destination. With regard to the latter two points, another challenge is the matching of competencies and knowledge of the marine activity safety standards. Sometimes concerns run contrary to customer expectations and this is linked to common law responsibilities of tourism operators (Wilks and Atherton, 1994b). All operators have a "duty of care" to their clients, a responsibility to morally and legally look out for their clients to prevent mishaps and/or accidents from occurring (Ardlie, 1990), and participants have a duty of care to each other (Wodak and Gatehouse, 1993). It is also interesting to note that "[e]xemption clauses on tickets and even publicly displayed notices announcing that the occupier takes no responsibility for accidents or injuries to patrons will not provide reliable legal protection. For this reason it is essential that all tourism operators carry full liability insurance" (Wilks and Atherton 1994b, pp. 7-8). Although such exemption clauses and liability release forms are effective in the United States (Wilks and Atherton, 1994b), in other countries such as Australia, for example, they are not. Furthermore, advertising and promotional materials require careful consideration. Mrs. Dillon, a passenger aboard the *Mikhail Lermontov* which sank ten days into a cruise, was awarded compensation not only for injuries and loss of possessions, but also for loss of enjoyment (Wilks and Atherton, 1994b). Consequently, as marine tourism grows, there is a complementary growth in lawsuits by tourists. Therefore it is imperative that operators gain information with regard to health and safety issues associated with each and every client to ensure that duty of care is responsibly given (Wilks and Atherton, 1994b). Moreover, with regard to employees, there is a strong need for operators to understand occupational health and safety regulations, and some employers do not (Wilks and Atherton, 1994b).

To reiterate, today's sports tourists are more educated, more experienced with regard to travel, have access to information technology and increased travel knowledge, are more discerning with regard to product selection, and want to engage in learning opportunities and skill development during travel experiences (Cleverdon, 1993; Poon, 1992; Urry, 1990; Moscardo, 1996; Lipscombe, 1996).

## MANAGEMENT ISSUES

To manage multiple use, conservation, and preservation efforts in marine areas, a variety of management tools may be used. Such tools include generation of resource inventories, application of the precautionary principle, research, public participation, development of tourism and recreational opportunity spectra, zoning maps, management plans, issuing of permits, education, development and adoption of best practice codes, and the use of enforcement strategies. These tools are drawn from the repertoire used by the Great Barrier Marine Park Authority in Australia (Jennings, 1997).

### Resource Inventories

Resource inventories list assets of specific locations or sections of marine areas and identify their subsequent values. These assets may be important in terms of their natural, cultural, historical, aesthetic, and/or use value. Resource inventories assist marine managers in zoning based on use values, help in the development of management plans of specific sites, and aid in long-term monitoring of usage and its impacts.

### The Precautionary Principle

When little or no scientific data are available to make informed decisions regarding management, the precautionary principle is applied. This principle means that management decisions are predicated on very conservative and precautionary management practices until relevant scientific data become available. Once the latter is available, management practices are then reviewed and modified if necessary.

## Research

The role of research for managers of marine areas is threefold: to gather information on the state of marine areas; to gather information on the effects of usage within the area; and to evaluate the quality of management practices. The information gathered provides data and subsequently leads to informed management recommendations regarding overall management as well as site-specific management.

## Public Participation

Public participation is a process whereby individuals, interested parties, and stakeholders are involved in the determination of management practices developed for marine areas. It can be incorporated in the development of management plans as well as when considering changes in zoning practices.

## Tourism and Recreational Opportunity Spectra

Recreational opportunity spectra (ROS) enable managers to provide marine users with a variety of recreational experiences in a variety of natural settings (Stankey and Wood, 1982). These settings range from urban to wilderness settings and feature activities appropriate to each, as well as to the overall recreation or tourism experience sought by the park user (Driver, 1989, cited in Watson, 1989). The tourism opportunity spectrum (TOS) is an adaptation of the recreation opportunity spectra for tourism planning (Butler and Waldbrook, 1991). The TOS and ROS enable managers to reduce conflict between users and to provide variety in recreation and tourism experiences in marine areas.

## Zoning Maps

Marine areas are broken up into a number of sections. In each of these sections, zoning plans are developed. For the Great Barrier Reef Marine Park Authority, zoning plans have been the cornerstone of park management (McGinnity, 1992). Zoning plans specify the activity or range of activities that are considered appropriate for various locations within each section. Usage in each of the zones ranges from

general use, where most activities are allowed, to nonuse areas classified as preservation zones. Zoning attempts to separate conflicting
uses and activities, and ensures the protection of the environment.
Public consultation is part of the zoning process and may take some
years to complete. Theoretically, zoning plans should be reviewed on
a regular basis, perhaps every five years. Alternatively, management
of zones and areas can be based on three types of usage, such as in
1986 in the Pitons National Park, St. Lucia, Caribbean, where marine
reserve areas (MRAs), fisheries priority areas (FPAs), and undesignated
usage areas were established (Meganck, 1991).

## Management Plans

Once zoning plans are established for each section, management
plans may be developed for various areas within each section. The development of the management plan involves public participation so
that final plans contain management frameworks, principles, and strategies that reflect public interest and commitment. While zoning plans
organize users and activities at a macro level, management plans organize users and activities at the micro level.

## Permits

The use of permits serves to regulate the type and number of users in
specific areas (Adler, 1993; see Claridge, 1994, for a discussion of this
in the Great Barrier Reef Marine Park). Permits are generally required
for research, tourist operations, and extractive activities. The granting
of a permit provides recipients permission to conduct a specific activity
or activities in specified areas or locations for a specific period of time.
The establishment of a permit system enables managers to monitor and
manage environmental impacts of various activities within a park or
area, including management of carrying capacities.

## Education

Education is used by managers to facilitate the adoption of ecologically sustainable practices by marine users. Education strategies include public meetings, lectures, workshops, interpretive signage, in-

formation pamphlets and brochures, multimedia productions, ranger-guided tours, and self-guided tours. Education aims to generate voluntary compliance to sustainable use of marine areas by increasing the knowledge and awareness of user groups and individuals.

### *Best Practice Codes*

The development of best practice codes regarding marine area usage supplements and extends education. Best practice codes are developed in conjunction with various stakeholder, industry, and user groups. These codes identify the best way to experience and operate within marine areas to ensure minimal environmental damage and user conflict. Consequently, codes have several aims: to raise users' awareness, to educate users, and to complement other sustainable management practices (Mason, 1996). As with education, codes are founded on voluntary compliance.

### *Enforcement*

Some marine managers are able to apply legal measures to ensure conformity with regulations and guidelines derived from legislation. Users who do not conform to the rules and regulations may be fined, have their equipment confiscated, or in some cases face imprisonment. Of all the management practices, this is the least preferred option of the Great Barrier Reef Marine Park Authority, which prefers to move users to voluntary compliance regarding ecologically sustainable practices rather than statutory conformance.

## *FUTURE PROSPECTS*

Marine tourism is a growing component of the overall global tourism product. As developments in technology increase, further modifications to marine sports equipment will occur, which may result in increased participation rates and a broadening of activities among users. The potential for user conflicts, congestion, crowding, and exceeding carrying capacity is a certainty unless managers can do their jobs effectively. This may mean that previously unregulated activities become more regulated, and user-pay systems become more widespread to provide the types of marine tourism experiences desired while maintaining the sustainability of the resource base of the marine setting being used. Profiles of marine tourists emphasize a more discerning tourist, which means that providers need to be flexible, and offer individualized or tailored experiences if they are to remain competitive, otherwise marine tourists may choose to broker their own travel experiences outside the tourism industry network. Another challenge for the industry is providing challenging and adventurous marine tourism experiences within an environment where tourists are becoming more litigation minded in evaluating their travel experiences and satisfaction levels. Furthermore, duty of care has significant consequences for participants, providers, and employees—in being informed and aware of their rights—and this again has litigious implications in most developed nations.

## *SUMMARY*

A variety of marine tourism experiences are available to people who wish to engage in them. The motivations of participants range from the pursuit of challenge and adventure to the development of skill prowess and self-actualization. The sociodemographics of marine tourists categorize them as people drawn from developed nations with excess leisure time, and middle-class salary ranges. They are well educated and range in age from teenagers through persons in their seventies. Mostly, people from Western countries predominate in these activities. The degree of reliance on the tourism industry for provision of such experiences ranges from fully guided and arranged experiences to completely independently organized and arranged experiences. The impacts of marine tourism are primarily related to conflicts between user groups, overcrowding, loss of amenity, increased regulations, and environmental impacts. Management tools used in marine tourism include resource inventories, precautionary principles, public participation, tourism and recreation opportunity spectra, zoning maps, management plans, permits, education, best practice codes, and enforcement.

## CASE STUDY:
## SHOALWATER BAY IN THE GREAT
## BARRIER REEF, AUSTRALIA

### *The Great Barrier Reef, Australia*

The Great Barrier Reef extends approximately 2,000 kilometers along the coastline of the state of Queensland, Australia. The Reef contains around "2900 individual reefs and 900 islands" (Great Barrier Reef Marine Park Authority, 1996a, p. 1) as well as 1,500 fish species, 400 hard and soft coral species, 4,000 types of molluscs, 240 bird species, and 6 turtle species (Geen and Lal, 1991). Spatially, the Great Barrier Reef is the largest coral reef system in the world (Great Barrier Reef Marine Park Authority, 1994a). As a system, it is primarily used by Aboriginal and Torres Strait Islanders, commercial fishers, recreational boaters and fishers, and commercially organized tourists (McPhail, 1996). In order to protect, conserve, and manage use of the Great Barrier Reef, the Great Barrier Reef Marine Park Act, 1975, was enacted. The Act established the Great Barrier Reef area as a national marine park, specifically, the Great Barrier Reef Marine Park (GBRMP). The enactment also nominated key managers of the Park, calling them the Great Barrier Reef Marine Park Authority (a Commonwealth statutory agency) and the Queensland Department of Environment (a state government department). The latter is responsible for the day-to-day management of the marine park while the Great Barrier Reef Marine Park Authority (GBRMPA) is responsible for the overall management and care of the park. The authority's main aim is: "To provide for the protection, wise use, understanding and enjoyment of the Great Barrier Reef in perpetuity through the care and development of the Great Barrier Reef Marine Park" (GBRMPA, 1996a, p. 4).

Charged with this aim, the GBRMPA has managed the Great Barrier Reef according to principles of ecologically sustainable development since its inception (Kelleher, 1994). The adoption of an ecologically sustainable management style was further reinforced with the addition of the Great Barrier Reef on UNESCO's World Heritage list in 1981.[3] Although World Heritage listing obliges the authority to protect, conserve, and present the Great Barrier Reef World Heritage Area and to ensure its appreciation by future generations (GBRMPA,

1996c), it has not meant a change in approach to the overall management style, since management has always been predicated on ecological sustainability.

## Great Barrier Reef Marine Park Users

There are over 1.5 million visitors per annum (Driml and Common, 1996) who come as commercially organized tourists to the Great Barrier Reef. These tourists access the reef via day-trip vessels (the primary means of access), overnight charters, and multiday charters involving sailing, fishing, and/or diving (Aiello, 1998). Vessels range in size from small (less than forty people) to large, high-speed catamarans carrying in excess of 400 passengers (Aiello, 1998). User numbers have increased 30 percent. In addition to commercially organized tourists, a diverse range of other users visit the Great Barrier Reef Marine Park. These include traditional indigenous users (Aboriginal and Torres Strait Islanders); nonindigenous local users; commercial extractive users; commercial tourism operators and noncommercially based tourists (independent tourists); and vicarious users.

In managing the marine park and the World Heritage Area for conservation and preservation purposes, as well as for multiple use as required by the Great Barrier Reef Marine Park Act and other obligations under the Great Barrier Reef World Heritage Area (GBRWHA) listing, a diversity of management practices are utilized by the Great Barrier Reef Marine Park Authority: resource inventories, precautionary principles, public participation, tourism and recreation opportunity spectra, zoning maps, management plans, permits, education, best practice codes, and enforcement procedures.

When considering the overall management of the marine park, the authority takes user perspectives into consideration during public participation processes associated with the development of zoning and management plans. It also considers user feedback from advisory committees to formulate general management practices related to voluntary compliance (for example, development of codes of practice). The GBRMPA must also consider the growing number of users and their impact on the reef, and the best means to manage their usage levels based on sustainable practices. Management is assisted by data recorded in the permit system though research and monitoring of usage and impacts, and by periodic reviews of zoning and management plans.

One area in the Mackay/Capricorn section of the marine park is the Shoalwater Bay area, located between the latitudes of 22° 08'S to 23° 00'S and longitudes of 150° 02'E to 151° 02'E.

Primary users of the Shoalwater Bay are recreational fishers, boaters, some local kayakers, and organized mass tourists. In a GBRMPA-funded study by Jennings (1998) to determine the recreational marine usage of the Shoalwater Bay area, a variety of research methods were used to gather data on primary users. Research was conducted utilizing mail surveys, self-selection surveys, secondary data analysis, and a modified delphi technique. Secondary sources held by the GBRMPA and the Queensland Department of Environment provided data on vessel visitation over the period from 1988 to 1995. A modified delphi technique (Moeller and Shafer, 1994) was used to determine the drawing area for the study and the proportionate sampling sizes for the mail survey of registered boat owners, and to determine user groups and usage patterns.

Three sociocultural issues identified in the study regarding user groups and their usage patterns were associated with changes in Western leisure patterns, recreational motivations of nonindigenous local users, and the potential for user conflicts.

### Changes in Leisure Patterns

An increase in the standard of living in Western countries has increased leisure time and discretionary income availability for pursuing leisure activities. This can be attributed to a number of social changes, particularly the establishment of a minimum basic wage and working day length, increases in holiday period entitlements (and the associated payment for such holidays), increases in income levels, and increases in leisure time including forced leisure through early retirements (Parker and Paddick, 1990) and unemployment (Lynch and Veal, 1996).

The consequences of changing leisure patterns suggests a need for the GBRMPA to commission research into the leisure patterns of residents adjacent to the marine park and World Heritage Area. Such a need was reiterated by Dr. Ian McPhail, then chair of the GBRMPA, who stated, "It is difficult to understand the marine use associated with adjacent residential development" (McPhail, 1996). Since resident use of the GBRMP and the GBRWHA has been growing at a rate of 11 percent per annum (the same rate as tourism overall) such research seems imperative. This research might be conducted under the auspices of the GBRMPA as the lead agency or in conjunction with other government agencies at state and local levels.

### Recreational Motivations

Reasons for using Shoalwater Bay and adjacent waters include the quality of the fish stocks, the amenity of the area (particularly its wilderness values), the area's proximity to user residences, the provision of safe anchorages, and the appropriateness of the area for recreational and tourist activities.

Motivations of nonindigenous local users need to be considered by management when developing zoning and management plans and when organizing recreation and tourism opportunity spectra for the study area. In particular, preserving the quality of the fish stocks and maintaining the wilderness environment need to be planning priorities. Subsequently, social carrying capacity considerations (Nielsen, Shelby, and Haas, 1977) and limits of acceptable change (Stankey, McCool, and Stokes, 1984; McCool, 1989; Knopf, 1989) need to be determined and monitored over time. Commercial tourism permits may also need to be capped to ensure that amenity and wilderness values in particular are maintained.

### Conflict

Jaakson (1988), when writing about recreational boating, noted that "[f]reedom is a central tenet in recreation. The sharing of an area with other users, however, often detracts from the freedom that users may perceive to be important for their recreation satisfaction" (p. 96). A number of other writers (Gartside, 1986; Kenchington, 1993; Dovers, 1994) have discussed conflicts.[4] The major conflict appears to focus on the continuous debate between recreational and commercial fishers regarding who is responsible for diminishing fishing stocks. Given that the number and types of recreational fishers have increased along with leisure time (Dovers, 1994; Kenchington, 1993), incomes (Kenchington, 1993), and technology, recreational fishers have become more sophisticated in their fishing practices and wider ranging in their fishing activities.[5] This brings them into greater direct competition with commercial operators for fish stocks and fishing grounds (Gartside, 1986). Dovers (1994) also mentions the reluctance of recreational fishers to consider the contribution their individual catches make in the overall recreational catch effort. The impacts of recreational and commercial fishers on each other's catches, argues Dovers (1994), is difficut to perceive, particularly in cases where each group targets different species. A lack of data on the proportions of the catches taken in shared target species. Further, Kenchington (1993) states that commercial fishers tend to move on to other sites when fish stocks decline, while local recreational fishers continue to fish the same area. It is important to add that both groups are interested in protecting the marine environment and fishing stocks (Gartside, 1986).

Dovers (1994) suggests that potential for conflict exists among the various types of recreational fishers whether they are occasional fishers; affiliated, committed fishers; unaffiliated fishers; domestic tourist/fishers; or international tourist/fishers. Graefe and Fedler (1986) state that satisfaction associated with recreational fishing experiences is affected by crowding and congestion. The mixing of various fisher types at locations can cause dissatisfaction through a sense of crowding especially when the location is considered a wilderness area. In the study of Shoalwater Bay and adjacent waters, a conflict was particularly evidenced with regard to recreational fishers' attribution of declining fish stock to commercial fishers. Alternatively, recreational fishers considered commercial fishing and other commercially based extractive activities to be inappropriate for most areas included in the study.

Continued and further research needs to be undertaken regarding catch efforts, and information needs to be disseminated to commercial operators and recreational fishers. With scientific information in hand, informed debate may be undertaken and strategies can be developed through consultation with stakeholders regarding fishing practices and controls, which need to be affected to maintain quality fish stock.

Development of a tourism and recreational opportunity spectrum would need to incorporate wilderness areas which were both easily accessible and more difficult to access due to the geographic distance to be traveled and availability of transportation. Management plans might also dictate an acceptable number of site users for issuing permits. Limits of acceptable change and social carrying capacity might also be a consideration in zoning to reduce conflicts between user groups. Further, education based on research might have to be undertaken to inform users of the impacts of their individual and total group activities.

## Conclusion

This case study has examined the sociocultural issues associated with recreational and tourism management in Shoalwater Bay within the Mackay/Capricorn section of the Great Barrier Reef, Australia. The main issues—changing leisure patterns, recreational motivations of nonindigenous local users, and the potential for user conflicts—highlight the need to maintain the natural, aesthetic, cultural, and use values of the study area, particularly, the environmental setting and quality of its resources for local nonindigenous users. However, this case study notes that managers must also consider the perspectives of indigenous and commercial extractive users and commercial tourism users. The application of the recreational and tourism opportunity spectra would appear to be able to achieve this end. Coupled with public participation in its creation, research and monitoring of usage over time must be supplemented with other management tools such as permits and the involvement of advisory groups and committees.

## RELEVANT WEB SITES

### Cruising Sites

Cruising Association: http://www.cruising.org.uk/
Seven Seas Cruising Association: http://www.ssca.org

### Diving Sites

NAUI, National Association of Underwater Divers: http://www.naui.org

PADI, Professional Association of Dive Instructors: http://www.padi.com

BSAC, British Sub-Aqua Club: http://www.bsac.com

### General Diving Site with Links to Other Sites

http://www.divernet.com

### General Scuba Diving Location Maps

http://www.scubadiving.com/travel/

### Surfing (Contains Links to Other Sites)

http://surfing.about.com

### Fishing

http://www.sunfish.org.au
http://www.fishnet.com.au
http://www.the-fishing-network.com

### Sea Kayaking

http://www.seekayak.com

### General Sites

Great Barrier Reef Marine Park Authority: http://www.gbrmpa.gov.au

CSIRO Marine Research: http://www.marine.csiro.au

### Adventure Travel Site

http://www.zulusports.com

International Union for Conservation of Nature and Natural Resources (IUCN); The World Conservation Union: www.iucn. org

# NOTES

1. The terms *cruiser* and *cruising yachtie* are used by members of the subculture to describe themselves.

2. The "milkrun" is also known as the "California Highway" since most vessels depart from and return to North America from California (Macbeth, 1985).

3. The Great Barrier Reef World Heritage Area covers 348,700 square kilometers. Of this area, 93 percent constitutes the Great Barrier Reef Marine Park and the other 7 percent contains Queensland waters and islands not included in the Great Barrier Reef Marine Park (GBRMPA, 1994a)

4. "Conflict is defined as goal interference attributed to another's behaviour" (Jacob and Schreyer, 1980, p. 369).

5. Merrick (1993) noted that "recreational angling has traditionally been conducted in estuarine areas or immediate coastal areas" (p. 45). Dovers' (1994) expands traditional fishing areas to include distant offshore areas. Dovers' entire classification includes (1) inland native species; (2) inland exotic species; (3) beach, rock, estuary, and jetty and wharf; (4) near offshore; and (5) distant offshore (p. 108).

# REFERENCES

Aiello, R. (1998). Interpretation and the marine tourism industry, who needs it?: A case study of Great Adventures, Australia. *Journal of Tourism Studies,* 9(1): 51-61.

Alder, J. (1993). Permits, an evolving tool for the day-to-day management of the Cairns section of the Great Barrier Reef Marine Park. *Coastal Management,* 21: 25-36.

Alderson, D. (1996). From calamity to control, Trip risk assessment. Wave-length paddling Magazine. Accessed online <http://www.wavelengthmagazine.com/1996/apr96risk.php>.

Ardlie, M. (1990). Civil claims arising out of sporting incidents. *Law Society Bulletin,* 12(5): 137-138.

Berno, T., Moore, K., Simmons, D., and Hart, V. (1996). The nature of the adventure tourism experience in Queenstown, New Zealand. *Australian Leisure,* 7(2): 21-25.

Borschmann, R. (1987). *Recreational fishing in national parks and wilderness areas.* Conference paper presented at the Twenty-Second Assembly of the Australian Fresh Water Fisherman's Assembly, Khancoban.

Butler, R.W. and Waldbrook, L.A. (1991). A new planning tool: the tourism opportunity spectrum. *The Journal of Tourism Studies,* 2(1): 2-14.

Claridge, G. (1994). *Managing roving tourist program operations, a review of approaches in the Great Barrier Reef Marine Park.* October, Townsville: Great Barrier Reef Marine Park Authority.

Cleverdon, R. (1993). Global tourism trends: influences, determinants and directional flows. *World Travel and Tourism Review,* 3: 81–89.

Cornell, J. (1989). *World cruising survey.* London: Adlard Coles.

Davis, D. (1999). Tourist levies and willingness to pay for a whale shark experience, *Tourism Economics,* 5(2): 161-174.

Davis, D., Banks, S.A., and Davey, G. (1996). Aspects of recreational scuba diving in Australia. In Prosser, Gary (Ed.), *Tourism and Hospitality Research: Australian and international perspectives: Proceedings from the Australian Tourism and Hospitality Research Conference, 1996* (pp. 455-465). Canberra: Bureau of Tourism Research.

Davis, D.C. and Tisdell, C.A. (1994). Recreational scuba-diving and carrying capacity in marine protected areas. Discussion Paper No. 153 (University of Queensland, Department of Economics). St. Lucia: University of Queensland, Department of Economics.

Dignam, D. (1990). Scuba diving among mainstream travellers. *Tour and Travel News,* March 26.

Dixon, J. and Sherman, P. (1990). *Economics of protected areas: A new look at benefits and costs.* London: Earthscan Publications.

Dovers, S. (1994). Recreational fishing in Australia: Review and policy issues. *Australian Geographical Studies,* 32(1): 102-114.

Driml, S. (1996). Coastal and marine tourism and recreation. In Zann, L. (Ed.), *The state of the marine environment report for Australia: Technical report* (pp. 159-165). Townsville: Great Barrier Reef Marine Park Authority.

Driml, S. and M. Common (1996). Ecological economics criteria for sustainable tourism: Application to the Great Barrier Reef and the wet tropics World Heritage Areas, Australia *Journal of Sustainable Tourism,* 4: 3-16.

Dupre, L. (2000). *Greenland expedition: Where the ice is born.* Minnetonka, MN: NorthWood Press.

Effeney, G. (1999). *An introduction to sea-kayaking in Queensland.* Ashgrove West, Australia: Gerard Effeney.

Fedler, A.J. and Ditton, R.B. (1994). Understanding angler motivations in fisheries management. *Fisheries,* 19(4): 6ff.

Gartside, D.F. (1986). Recreational fishing. Paper presented to National Coastal Management Conference, Coffs Harbour, Australia, in *Safish,* 11(2): 15-17.

Geen, G. and Lal, P. (1991). *Charging users of the Great Barrier Reef Marine Park: A report to the Great Barrier Reef Marine Park Authority.* Canberra: Australian Bureau of Agricultural and Resource Economics.

Gerard, I. (2000). Overcrowding rules the waves. *Orbit, The Weekend Australian,* December 30-31, pp. 2-3.

Graefe, A.R. and Fedler, A.J. (1986). Situational and subjective determinants of satisfaction in marine recreational fishing. *Leisure Sciences,* 8(3): 275-295.

Great Barrier Reef Marine Park Authority. (1994a). *The Great Barrier Reef, keeping it great, a 25 year strategic plan for the Great Barrier Reef World Heritage Area, 1994-2019.* Townsville: Great Barrier Reef Marine Park Authority.

Great Barrier Reef Marine Park Authority. (1994b). *Great Barrier Reef: World Heritage Area and Great Barrier Reef Marine Park, BRA Q188 Map.* Townsville: Great Barrier Reef Marine Park Authority.

Great Barrier Reef Marine Park Authority. (1996a). *Annual report of the Great Barrier Reef Marine Park Authority 1995-1996.* Townsville: Great Barrier Reef Marine Park Authority.

Great Barrier Reef Marine Park Authority. (1996b). *Draft corporate plan 1997-2001: Version 26 November, 1996.* Townsville: Great Barrier Reef Marine Park Authority.

Great Barrier Reef Marine Park Authority. (1996c). *Relevant international conventions.* Accessed online <http://www.gbrmpa.gov.au/general/almanac/conventions.html>, April, 19.

Great Barrier Reef Marine Park Authority. (2000). Tourism and recreation: diving and snorkeling. Accessed online <http://www.gbrmpa.gov.au/corp_site/key_issues/tourism/best_environmental_practice.html>, August 16.

Hamdi, H. (1995). Take the plunge! *PATA travel news: Asia/Pacific edition,* July, pp. 6-8.

Hawkins, J. and Roberts, C. (1992). Effects of recreational scuba diving on fore-reef slope communities of coral reefs. *Biological Conservation,* 62: 171-178.

Hawkins, J. and Roberts, C. (1993). Effects of recreational scuba diving on coral reefs: trampling on reef-flat communities. *Journal of Applied Ecology,* 30: 25–30.

Hill, A. (1993). Travel: Lizard's no place for loungers, *BRW.* October, 3(9): 74-75.

Hng, L. (1993). Diver's paradise, *PATA travel news: Asia/Pacific edition,* August, pp. 20-21.

Jaakson, R. (1988). Recreation boating and spatial patterns: Theory and management. *Leisure Sciences,* 11: 85-98.

Jacob, G.R. and Schreyer, R. (1980). Conflict in outdoor recreation: A theoretical perspective. *Journal of Leisure Research,* 12: 368-380.

Jennings, G. (1997). Non-indigenous sociocultural issues associated with recreational and tourism management in Shoalwater Bay within the MacKay/Capricorn Section of the Great Barrier Reef Marine Park. Proceedings of the International conference on Sustainable Tourism Development in Vietnam, Hue, May 22-23, pp. 284-289.

Jennings, G. (1998). *Recreational usage patterns of Shoalwater Bay and adjacent waters.* Research publication No. 50. Townsville: Great Barrier Reef Marine Park Authority.

Jennings, G. (1999). From the center to the margins: An ethnography of long term ocean cruisers. Unpublished Ph.D. thesis. Murdoch: Murdoch University.

Jennings, G. (2001). Flow: Having the right skills for the challenge. Proceedings of 32nd Annual Conference of the Travel and Tourism Association, 2001: A Tourism Odyssey, June 10-13, Fort Meyers, Florida, p. 236-246.

Johnson. J.C. and Orbach, M.K. (1986). The role of cultural context in the development of low-capital ocean leisure activities. *Leisure Sciences,* 8(3): 319-339.

Jones, R.A. and Ellis, G.D. (1996). Effects of variation in perceived risk on the secretion of β-endorphine. *Leisure sciences,*18(3): 277-291.

Kelleher, G. (1994). In Great Barrier Reef Marine Park Authority, *Corporate Plan, 1994-1999 with specific objectives for 1994-1995* (1994). Townsville: Great Barrier Reef Marine Park Authority.

Kenchington, R. (1993). Tourism in coastal and marine environments—a recreational perspective, *Ocean and Coastal Management,* 19: 1-16.

Knopf, R.C. (1989). The limits of acceptable change (LAC) planning process: potentials and pitfalls. In Graham, R. and Lawrence, R. (Eds.), *Towards serving visitors and managing our resources, Proceedings of workshop on visitor management* (pp. 201-211). Ontario, Canada: University of Waterloo.

Kotani, K. (1991). Promoting the use of pleasure boats in Japan. *Japan 21st,* 36(11): 123-125.

Lipscombe, N. (1996). The aged and adventure: a perfect match. *Australian Leisure,* 7(3): 38-41.

Lynch, R. and Veal, A.J. (1996). *Australian leisure.* Longman: Melbourne.

Macbeth, J. (1985). *Ocean cruising: A study of affirmative deviance.* Unpublished doctoral thesis. Murdoch: Murdoch University.

Mason, P. (1996). Codes of conduct in tourism. *Progress in Tourism and Hospitality Research,* 2: 151-167.

McCool, S.F. (1989). Limits of acceptable change some principles. In Graham, R. and Lawrence, R. (Eds.), *Towards serving visitors and managing our resources, Proceedings of workshop on visitor management* (pp. 195-200). Ontario, Canada: University of Waterloo.

McGinnity, P. (1992). Zoning the Cairns Section, *Reflections,* 27: 5-13.

McPhail, I. (1996) *Managing the Great Barrier Reef Marine Park.* Accessed online <http://www.gbrmpa.gov.au/chair/chair.html>, April, 19, 1997.

Meganck, R. (1991). Coastal parks as development catalysts: a Caribbean example. *Ocean and Shoreline Management,* 15: 25-36.

Merrick, J. (1993). Inland water resources, *Australian Planner,* March pp. 45-48.

Miller, M.L. (1993). The rise of coastal and marine tourism. *Ocean And Coastal Management,* 20: 181-199.

Moeller, G.H. and Shafer, E.L. (1994). The delphi technique: A tool for long-range travel and tourism forecasting. In Ritchie, J.R. and Goeldner, C.R. (Eds.), *Travel and tourism and hospitality research,* second edition (pp. 473-480). New York: John Wiley and Sons.

Morgan, D. (1998). Adventure tourists on water: Linking expectations, affect, achievement and enjoyment to the adventure. Working paper number 1960/ 1998. Caulfield East, Australia: Monash University.

Moscardo, G. (1996). Using tourism research to develop new tourism products. Proceedings from *It's showtime for tourism* (pp. 57-65). Lexington, Kentucky: Travel and Tourism Research Association annual conference.

National Association of Underwater Instructors (NAUI). (1990). *The NAUI textbook,* Second edition. Capalaba, Australia: NAUI Australia.

Nielsen, J., Shelby, B., and Haas, J.E. (1977). Sociological carrying capacity and the last settler syndrome. *Pacific Sociological Review,* 20(4): 568-581.

Okubo, T. (1989). Growth seen in marine sports facilities. *Business Japan,* 34(11): 69- 71.

Orams, M. (1999). *Marine tourism: Development, impacts and management.* London: Routledge.

O'Reilley, M.B. (1982). Sport diving in Texas: A study of participants, their activity, and means of introduction. Unpublished master's thesis. College Station, TX: Texas A & M University.

PA Management Consultants. (1984a). *National survey of participation in recreational fishing, Report No. 1 for the Australian Recreational Fishing Confederation.* Melbourne: PA Management Consultants.

PA Management Consultants. (1984b). *National survey on recreational fishing, Report No. 2 for the Australian Recreational Fishing Confederation.* Melbourne: PA Management Consultants.

Parker, S. and Paddick, R. (1990). *Leisure in Australia.* Melbourne: Longman Cheshire.

Pearson, K. (1979). *Surfing subcultures of Australia and New Zealand.* St. Lucia: University of Queensland Press.

Phillips, S. (1992). The dive tourism industry of Byron Bay: A management strategy for the future. Unpublished integrated project dissertation, Faculty of Resource Science and Management. Northern Rivers, Australia: University of New England.

"Pleasure boating to grow with increase in leisure time" (1987). *Business Japan.* 32(11-12): 63-64.

Poon, A. (1992). *Tourism, technology, and competitive strategies.* Wallingford, Oxon: CAB International.

Rice, K. (1987). Special report: Scuba diving—dive market requires specialized skill, information. *Tour and Travel News,* February 9, pp. 24-7.

Richens, H. (1992). Case study. Yachting holidays, an experience with island adventures. In Weiler, B. and Hall, M.C. (Eds.), *Special interest tourism* (pp. 185-197). London: Belhaven Press.

Sanders, M. (1999). Six by six, six epic six month surf trips. *Australia's Surfing Life,* August, pp. 87-91.

Scura, L. and van't Hof, T. (1992). Economic feasibility and ecological sustainability of the Bonaire Marine Park. Draft divisional working paper, environment department. Washington DC: The World Bank.

Stankey, G.H., McCool, S.F., and Stokes, G.L. (1984). Limits of acceptable change: A new framework for managing the Bob Marshall Wilderness Complex. *Western Midlands,* Fall: 3-7.

Stankey, G.H. and Wood, J. (1982). The recreation opportunity spectrum: An introduction. *Australian Parks and Recreation,* February, pp. 6-14.

Tabata, R. (1992). Case study. Scuba diving holidays. In Weiler, B. and Hall, M.C. (Eds.), *Special interest tourism* (pp. 171-184). London: Belhaven Press.

Urry, J. (1990). *The tourists gaze, leisure and travel in contemporary society.* London: Sage.

Watson, M. (1989). *Recreation planning: A seminar summary and discussion of the ROS and LAC models.* A report submitted to the Great Barrier Reef Marine Park Authority, Townsville.

Weaver, D. (1994). Ecotourism in the Caribbean basin. In Cater, E. and Lowman, G. (Eds), *Ecotourism: A sustainable option?* (pp. 159-176). Chichester: John Wiley.

Wilks, J. (1993). Calculating diver numbers: Critical information for scuba safety and marketing programs. *SPUMS Journal,* 23(1): 11-14.

Wilks, J. and Atherton T. (1994a). Fitness to participate in adventure activities: Medical and legal considerations arising from recreational scuba diving. *South Pacific Underwater Medicine Society Journal,* 24(3): 137.

Wilks, J. and Atherton, T. (1994b). Health and safety in Australian marine tourism: A social, medical and legal appraisal. *Journal of Tourism Studies,* 5 (2): 2-16.

Wodak, T. and Gatehouse, M. (1993). The law and diving. In Wilks, J., Knight, J., and Lippmann, J. (Eds.), *Scuba safety in Australia* (pp. 153-165). Melbourne: JL Publications.

Zann, L. (Ed.). (1996). *State of the marine environment report for Australia: Technical summary.* Townsville, Queensland, Australia. Great Barrier Reef Marine Park Authority for Ocean Rescue 2000 Program: Department of Environment, Sport and Territories, Canberra.

Chapter 6

# Golf Tourism

Mark Readman

Golf is a curious sport whose object is to put a very small ball in a very small hole with implements ill-designed for the purpose.

Sir Winston Churchill

## INTRODUCTION

It is estimated that there are over 60 million golfers worldwide. Almost 44 percent of this market is located in the United States, 25 percent in Japan, and 12 percent in Europe. These golfers play on over 30,000 golf courses of which 16,000 are situated in the United States. In the past fifteen years the popularity of golf has grown enormously and the influx of foreign visitors to international destinations has grown with it. The value of golf tourism grew by 8 percent in 1998-1999 alone and is currently worth an estimated $10 billion annually (not including earnings in the Far East). Golf therefore represents the largest sports-related travel market. This market is served by its own trade association, the International Association of Golf Tour Operators (IAGTO). IAGTO's mission is "to represent the interests of its members and the global golf tourism industry; to create business opportunities for operators and industry partners; to generate and improve access to valuable market information; to raise awareness of its members' golf tourism products and services; to promote the implementation of best practices in the golf tourism industry and to further the development of golf travel worldwide" (IAGTO, 2002).

It is recognized that a study of golf tourism could encapsulate virtually any form of golf participation including active domestic participation, business or incentive golf, or travel simply to observe golf. For the purpose of this chapter golf tourism is defined as travel for noncommercial reasons to participate in golf activities away from the traveler's local environment. This chapter is concerned with the reasons for the growth and diversity of the golf tourism market. It also presents some descriptors of the global marketplace and some repercussions resulting from the phenomenon that is golf tourism. Finally, case studies are presented on Pinehurst Resort in the United States and Tobs Kenya Golf Safari.

## GOLF HISTORY
## AND DEVELOPMENT OF GOLF TOURISM

### Misty Origins

The origins of golf have been the subject of numerous debates. Frequently, the Dutch are credited with being the originators of the game (Van Hengel, 1985). Their game, *kolven,* which dates back to 1297, had some of golf's characteristics with contestants trying to hit, with a minimum of strokes, two wooden objects placed at opposite ends of a court. Similar was the Belgian game of *chole,* which involved a ball being hit by a team toward a distant target—sometimes several miles away. The earliest record of this game, still played occasionally in southern Belgium, dates back to 1353 (Green, 1993). Even back as far as 1338, German shepherds were granted permission to define their territories by striking pebbles with their crooks— the distance the shot covered made the boundaries of their grazing rights. *Paganica,* a Roman game involving someone standing beside a ball and striking it, was probably the forerunner of the ancient Flemish game of *chole* and its French equivalent *jeu de mail.*

### A Scottish Game

Golf is unique and is no doubt the result of a natural evolution of some of these early sports. To suggest that the game may not be Scottish would be inaccurate, however, for it is the invention of the hole which swings the origins of the golf debate in Scotland's favour. Despite the earlier versions it was the Scots who created the concept that the game of golf starts with the ball situated at a point just above the ground and ends with it disappearing below ground level into the cup (Campbell, 1994). The first reference to the game in Scotland dates back to 1457 when the Scottish parliament declared that the game of golf was interfering with the practice of archery, and thus the defense of the realm, declaring golf to be "utterly cryit doun and nocht usit" (Brasch, 1972, p. 98). Despite this proclamation golf was popular with Scottish and English royalty (Mary, Queen of Scots, was the first woman golfer) and common people, which resulted in golf courses appearing all over Scotland—the most famous of these being St. Andrews in approximately 1552 (Brasch, 1972).

Once the English aristocracy had commandeered the sport for themselves and seen to it that ordinary people could not interfere with their sport, the spread of golf was inevitable. English aristocrats ensured their privacy by creating private clubs, exclusive membership systems, dress codes, etiquette standards, and a strict adherence to the first rules created by the Honorary Company of Edinburgh Golfers in 1744 (Green, 1993). The Royal and Ancient (R and A) golf club of St. Andrews assumed the responsibility of formulating the rules of golf in 1897.

## *Golf Expansion*

During the nineteenth century, Great Britain was extending its empire in all directions. Wherever the British army went it took the game of golf with it. Thus the first golf club outside Britain was in India, with the opening of the Bangalore Club in 1820 and another club established in Calcutta, later to become Royal Calcutta in 1829 (Davies and Davies, 1999). Asia followed as courses were built between 1888 and 1890 in such places as Taiping in Malaya, Bangkok in Thailand, and the first Japanese course in 1901 on the slopes of Mount Rokko near Kobe (Green, 1993). As the influence of the British, particularly the British Army, spread, so did the game of golf. Courses opened in Australia and New Zealand in 1871, the most famous of which, was Royal Melbourne. Royal Cape Town was founded in 1885 in South Africa, and a course that later became known as Royal Montreal (Canada) opened in 1873 (Davies and Davies, 1999). Elsewhere around the globe, groups of British workers built golf courses in their spare time, as was seen when engineers laying railway lines in South America founded Buenos Aires Golf

Club in 1878. Other groups of British workers introduced the sport to France, Germany, Sweden, Denmark, and Holland, where it received differing levels of support.

Golf was well established around the world by 1885, although not in the country that was to refine and define it during the twentieth century. Although golf is generally acknowledged (Green, 1993; Campbell, 1994) to have been founded in the United States only just over a 100 years ago, in actuality the game of *colf* was mentioned in the court records of the justices at Fort Orange in New York state in 1650. In addition, other documents indicate that golf clubs existed in the southeastern states prior to the American Civil War. These clubs subsequently disappeared during that war.

### Golf Reaches America

John Reid is acknowledged as the founding father of golf in the United States (Barrett, 1994; Green, 1993). Reid, a Scottish expatriate businessman, imported clubs and balls from Scotland and in 1888 set up a rudimentary three-hole golf course near his house in Yonkers, New York. The players of this first course formed a club called St. Andrew's (its name copied from its famous Scottish predecessor—complete with an apostrophe to differentiate it). Very soon this club was forced to expand, doing so by building a course on land studded by apple trees close to the Hudson River. These early club pioneers henceforth became known as the Apple Tree Gang. Golf caught on very quickly, and "in 1890, Reid's cow pasture was the country's only golf course. By 1896, the figure had risen to over 80. Four years later, there were 892 . . . meaning that by 1900 there were more American courses than British ones" (Green, 1993, p. 21). This huge growth was fueled by the arrival of hundreds of Scotsmen in the professions of architects, greenkeepers, and teaching professionals.

### Golf Booms

The United States Golf Association (USGA) was formed in 1894 and, boosted by economic booms in the 1890s and 1920s, golf continued to blossom. By the end of this period there were over 5,600 golf facilities in the United States (Beditz, 1994). This situation remained relatively unchanged until the 1960s, when golf in the United States experienced a second growth period. This was due to two factors. First, the U.S. government provided financing for the development of public golf facilities, changing a largely private, club-organized sport into one that allowed mass participation for the first time. Second, media exposure of the developing professional tours affected its growth. "Television exposed the World and the United States to such golfing personalities as Arnold Palmer, Gary Player and Jack Nicklaus" (Beditz, 1994, p. 548). A third growth period followed a period of economic recession due to spiraling oil prices and inflation in the 1970s. This final expansion was spectacular, the participation rate rising by 2.1 percent to 10.2 percent of the population, especially among the middle and older age groups, and the number of golf courses increasing to over 13,000 (Beditz, 1994). At one point in the early 1990s, golf courses were opening at a rate of one per day (see Table 6.1). This growth was largely due to an increase in available funding (due to deregulation of the banking industry and new banking institutions aggressively funding new development). In addition, golf courses became a major part of real estate and new resort developments and for the first time began to attract real estate buyers to particular locations.

Worldwide during the twentieth century, golf experienced similar patterns of growth. In Japan, the number of golf courses increased from approximately thirty prior to the World War II to 116 in 1957, and 1,700 in 1992—with land running out for suitable new sights (Zaitsu et al., 1994). In France, the number of golfers doubled between 1981 and 1985; Spain experienced similar growth, and in the 1980s the numbers of golfers increased by 60 percent in the Federal Republic of Germany, 57 percent in Italy, 42 percent in Sweden, and 41 percent in Switzerland (Priestley and Ashworth, 1995). In Britain, the Royal and Ancient Golf Club of St. Andrews famously predicted a "need to increase the numbers of golf courses by nearly 700 by the year 2000" (1990).

## *Golf Tours and the Spread of Golf Tourism*

As previously stated, one of the determining factors in golf's increase in worldwide popularity was the development of media interest, in particular television coverage of golf tournaments. According to Green (1993), the U.S. Professional Golfers' Association (PGA) Tour started in the 1920s with a nucleus of tournaments including the

TABLE 6.1. U.S. Golf Course Development in the 1990s

|  | 1990 | 1991 | 1992 | 1993 | 1994 | 1995 | 1996 | 1997 | 1998 | 1999 |
|---|---|---|---|---|---|---|---|---|---|---|
| Course openings | 289 | 351 | 354 | 358 | 381 | 468 | 442 | 429 | 448 | 509 |
| Courses under construction | 560 | 583 | 616 | 671 | 769 | 820 | 850 | 932 | 1,069 | 936 |
| Courses in planning | 781 | 681 | 580 | 543 | 541 | 562 | 808 | 720 | 708 | 903 |

*Source:* NGF (2000). *Golf Facilities in the U.S.,* 2000 Edition (used with permission).

U.S. Open (founded in 1895), the Canadian Open (1904), and the Texas Open (1922). Very quickly new events were added to the tour which broadly followed the sun. Spring events were held in Florida and the southern states, moving northward as summer advanced, returning south in the autumn. The tour produced many great players, such as Walter Hagen, Gene Sarazen, Ben Hogan, and Sam Snead, but it was the media coverage of duels between the likes of Arnold Palmer, Jack Nicklaus, and Gary Player that helped produce the golf-playing boom of the 1960s. Today the designation of a course as a "championship course" improves its appeal to the golf tourist. These three greats, together with others, played events on both the U.S. PGA Tour and the PGA European Tour, thus spreading interest in foreign golf courses to the American public.

The PGA European Tour comprises myriad events spread around Europe and includes places such as Dubai, Singapore, and Morocco. Originally, European tour players were banned from competing outside Europe, but as these barriers have been dismantled European stars have achieved success on American soil. The achievements of players such as Ballesteros and Olazabal (Spain), Langer (Germany), Johansson and Parnevik (Sweden), Rocca (Italy), and Van de Velde (France) have been inspirations to the development of the game in their respective countries and have added to the desire of Europeans to emulate their heroes and travel to play courses in other parts of the world.

The game in Japan was given a huge boost in 1957 when, in a complete surprise, Japan won the World Cup. Since then Japan has taken to the game with great enthusiasm. Today the Japanese PGA Tour is a hugely popular and rich tour, domestically covering over thirty-nine events. The wealth of Japanese golf is such that professional Japanese golfers do not have to leave Japan and endure foreign languages, foods, and customs to achieve economic success. The exceptions to this rule are the likes of Isao Aoki, Masashi (Jumbo) Ozaki, and Tsuneyuki (Tommy) Nakajima. Their success, combined with the huge cost of playing golf in Japan and extensive media coverage of foreign events, has led to large numbers of Japanese golfers traveling to golf destinations in the United States, Europe, and Asia.

Other PGA tours include the Australian Tour comprising a group of the national Opens of Eastern countries such as Hong Kong, Malaysia, India, China, the Philippines, Thailand, and eight to twelve events in Australia and New Zealand. The Sunshine Tour meanders through southern Africa during the winter months from November to March. These tours have produced the likes of Greg Norman (Australia) and Ernie Els (South Africa), and have raised the profile of golf destinations in various countries, especially in winter months. Add to these tours the Ladies Professional Golf Association (LPGA) tours of Europe and the United States, the hugely popular senior tours, and myriad smaller tours, and the result is a continually dynamic worldwide golf tournament. This traveling entourage attracts a large media circus fueling interest and development of golf in all areas of the globe.

## THE DEVELOPMENT AND USE OF GOLF
## AS A DESTINATION MARKETING TOOL

As has been illustrated, combinations of factors have led to the expansion of the game of golf worldwide and, consequently, to an increase in the desire to travel for the purpose of playing the sport. These factors include greater visibility of the game via mass media and the televising of increasing numbers of international golf championships. These determinants, added to the success and media coverage of national representatives, have led to explosions of interest in terms of golf course development and golf participation in different countries (see Table 6.1). In countries with higher standards of living and harsher climates during much of the year (northern Europe), or a shortage of facilities (Japan), this explosion in golf interest has led to a dramatic increase in golf tourism.

Combined with this greater desire for golf travel has been the use of golf by different tourist destinations to develop and diversify their product. It has been well established (Storey, 1994; Maguire, 1999; Mintel, 1999; NGF, 2000) that golfers around the world come mainly from a narrow demographic grouping (those from AB social groups, i.e., higher economic status, better off financially, and better educated; male; and over fifty years old).

There has been a drift toward golf participation among the female and youth segments of society; for example, the number of women playing golf in the United States has grown by 23.9 percent to 5.7 million in the past ten years, while the number of young people playing golf has risen by 46 percent to 2 million in the same time period (Maguire, 1999). Despite this, the game of golf is still male dominated in terms of participation, and it is this section of the traveling population that tourist destinations have attempted to attract (see Tables 6.2 and 6.3).

## REASONS FOR THE DEVELOPMENT
## OF THE GOLF TOURISM PRODUCT

### Reduction of Seasonality

Tourist destinations have attempted over the past ten years to achieve a number of goals. First, reduction of seasonality: destinations that have traditionally attracted tourists for the reasons of hot climate and sandy beaches have attempted to extend their vacation season by adding products that do not necessarily require these attributes. For example, in Spain, the Costa del Sol is now marketed as the "Costa del Golf" with over thirty golf developments lined up along the 50-kilometer strip of sand. There are also many examples of winter destinations building courses to attract tourists to the mountains in the summer (see Figure 6.1).

TABLE 6. 2. Characteristics of U.K. Regular Golfers (Playing Monthly)

| Social Group | Golf Population (Percent) |
|---|---|
| All | 100 |
| Men | 78 |
| Women | 22 |
| 16-19 | 6 |
| 20-24 | 10 |
| 25-29 | 9 |
| 30-44 | 34 |
| 45-59 | 28 |
| 60-69 | 10 |
| 70+ | 3 |
| AB | 42 |
| C1 | 22 |
| C2 | 23 |
| D | 11 |
| E | 2 |

*Based on:* Haywood et al., 1993, p. 158.
*Note:* Letters refer to social class membership. roups A/B—professional and managerial; C—technical; D/E—semi- and unskilled manual workers.

## *Improvement in Quality of Destination Product*

By targeting individuals who stay longer, spend more, and in some cases demand a higher quality product, an improvement in quality of destination product can be achieved. Such developments have occurred in Cyprus, Sicily, and Portugal. By the same token, the attraction of this type of visitor can help destinations achieve an additional aim of image improvement. Some traditional destinations at the cheaper end of the market have been blighted by a poor international image resulting from the mass tourism of the younger, lower-spending segment of the population. The building of higher quality hotels and infrastructure can help change the type, spending patterns, and, in time, the image of a destination. The Costa del Sol region of Spain, mentioned previously, is such an example.

TABLE 6.3. 1998 U.S. Golf Trips by Socioeconomic Group

| | All Golf Travelers (in thousands) | Average No. of Trips | Total No. of Trips |
|---|---|---|---|
| All Golf Travelers | 11,803 | 6.0 | 63,246 |
| *Gender* | | | |
| Male | 9,100 | 7.1 | 64,610 |
| Female | 2,703 | 4.9 | 13,245 |
| *Age* | | | |
| 18-29 | 2,219 | 6.8 | 15,089 |
| 30-39 | 3,258 | 6.4 | 20,851 |
| 40-49 | 2,845 | 7.1 | 20,200 |
| 50-59 | 1,888 | 7.6 | 14,349 |
| 60 and over | 1,593 | 4.7 | 7,487 |
| *Household Income* | | | |
| Less than $30,000 | 1,711 | 4.9 | 8,384 |
| $30,000 - $39,999 | 1,275 | 3.2 | 4,080 |
| $40,000 - $49,999 | 1,251 | 5.9 | 7,381 |
| $50,000 - $74,999 | 3,317 | 6.3 | 20,897 |
| $75,000+ | 4,249 | 8.9 | 37,816 |

*Source:* NGF, *The U.S. Golf Travel Market,* 1998 Edition (used with permission).

### Product Diversification and Improved Destination Profitability

Improvement in length of stay and increased tourist spending, and hence enhanced profitability, can be achieved through product diversification. The addition of new facilities to a resort can also have the effect of seasonality reduction and attraction of different sections of the population. Developments in Tunisia and Morocco fit this description; golf courses have been built to complement their seaside resorts, often with capital from Middle Eastern oil states, thus adding to the countries' winter sun attraction. As a result of this type of development, Morocco has increased the number of golf courses from

FIGURE 6.1. Golf tourists in the mountain resort of Verbier, Switzerland. (Used with permission of Office du Tourisme Verbier.)

fourteen to thirty in the period 1990 through 2000 (<http://www. tatfilalet.com/tourism/golf>, 2002).

### Economic Growth

Economic growth and the attraction of strong foreign currency are other reasons for golf tourism's development. By allowing the building of infrastructure and bringing in quality resort builders and operators, countries have been able to achieve economic growth by attracting foreign tourists. Good examples of this practice exist in East Asia, where countries such as Malaysia, Thailand, the Philippines, and Indonesia have all built golf infrastructures to attract international guests. This is particularly so for the Japanese who have a reputation for being highly enthusiastic golfers and travelers. In Japan it is not unusual to pay several hundred U.S. dollars to play a round of golf. Land for development of new courses is limited, hence golf is often one of those activities sought by the Japanese on their travels.

Courses have been built in Cuba, Puerto Rico, Mexico, and South America for the same reason. In these cases the sought-after reward is the U.S. dollar. In Puerto Rico, new courses endorsed by such names as Greg Norman, Jack Nicklaus, and Arnold Palmer have been developed, and were due for opening early in the twenty-first century. These developments include five-star private resorts and a championship course at Rio Mar (Puerto Rico), constructed with private-sector investors and government money from the Puerto Rico Tourism Company (Strickland, 1997).

Thus, through the development of golf, it is expected that economies can be kick started, or speeded up as a result of resorts becoming more profitable, tourism destinations better developed, and infrastructures improved. The attraction of the golf tourist has become a key target in the tourism development strategies of regions around the world. Tables 6.2 and 6.3 illustrate that in different countries the golfer or golf traveler is older and from higher socioeconomic groupings, and thus fits perfectly into the image of the higher-quality tourist. In addition, surveys have shown that this tourist stays longer and spends an average of 2.5 to 4 times the amount of other tourists.

## THE GOLF MARKET PRODUCT

As golf continues to spread around the globe, developers, whether Government organizations or private institutions, have to make hard choices as to how to finance their projects. Such decisions have an enormous impact on the size of golf tourism development, how a new course is marketed, the type of tourist a destination will attract, and the likelihood of interaction with the surrounding community. Priestley and Ashworth (1995) identify four types of golf tourism products: famous championship courses, single integrated resorts, golf courses associated with property developments, and networks of courses forming golf regions. The next section of this chapter looks at each type of golf development and assesses their differences and the impact on the type of tourist the product will attract. In this instance the designation *famous championship course* is replaced by a wider designation, the *trophy course.*

### Trophy Courses

Once a golf course has held a championship of note (one of the four majors or at least an international tournament) it immediately becomes the target of golf tourists. These individuals represent modern-day trophy hunters wishing to play golf in the footsteps of their heroes. Carnoustie Golf Course is a good example, the scene of the 1999 British Open; it has seen a large increase in American golfers keen to tame the course Tiger Woods found so difficult. Wealthy Japanese and American golfers, in particular, are well known for taking international trips to fulfill their ambitions and play on the world's most famous courses. St. Andrews and other Open venues in Scotland, England, and Ireland are particular targets of avid golfers' wish lists. In some cases the trophy to be gained may be the experience of courses created by famous designers such as Robert Trent Jones, Dan Maples, or, more recently, Jack Nicklaus.

Courses holding championship tournaments have the effect of ensuring their long-term popularity among golf tourists and may also serve the purpose of attracting golfers to their regions. In this instance a round of golf on a championship course will form the highlight of a longer tour of the other courses in the area. To this end tourism authorities, regional development agencies, and tourism operators sponsor events or seek private sponsorship and television coverage to attract new events or raise the profile of events in their areas. In the late 1990s, Turespaña undertook this task and sought out sponsorship of players, events, and courses to improve the recognition of golf in Spain. This initiative, combined with the awarding of the Ryder Cup to Valderama in 1997, generated golf tourism, increased hotel room occupancy rates, increased tourism spending, and reduced seasonality in the Costa del Sol region of Spain. As a result, Spain now attracts 600,000 golf tourists per year (58.8 percent to the Costa del Sol) worth 214,000 million pesetas. In 2001, Spain will increase the number of courses to 235—four times the 1980 number (Turespaña, 2000).

Undoubtedly the success of an event can put a destination on the map and raise its status to that of "golf trophy course" in the eyes of the golf tourist. Courses such as Montecastillo (Spain) and Sun City (South Africa) illustrate this. In an attempt to attract golf tourists in recent years a whole host of championship courses have sprung up. However, this can sometimes be a mistake, as a newly developed course may be too long or too difficult to provide a pleasant experience for the average golfer. In the long run, this may discourage tourists and local members from playing a course, especially if it fails to attract a well-known event. Alternatively, championship-designated new courses built alongside existing ones as part of a complex may only have the effect of transferring attention from the old course to the new one, rather than attracting new customers.

### Single Integrated Resorts

"Golf resorts may be defined as self-contained leisure complexes, which include (as minimum requirements) accommodation facilities and one golf-course, to which other golf courses and facilities may be added" (Priestley and Ashworth, 1995, p. 209). These resorts are normally associated with exclusive developments and will often disassociate themselves from their host communities through the erection of perimeter walls and security systems. The development of this type of golf tourism product thus requires a larger area than a single golf course, as infrastructure in the form of accommodations, restaurants, and other facilities is necessary. These exclusive areas or "islands within islands" as Sulaiman (1996) referred to them, have been developed in the United States (especially Florida and California), Australia, the Caribbean, and other nations and regions wishing to diversify their tourism product. In addition, the recent development of golf in Asia has often followed this model, and in some cases large-scale golf "leisurescapes" have been created, such as in Malaysia, Indonesia, and Thailand. Examples of these "megadevelopments" (Cartier, 1998) include the Golden Valley Golf Resort in Melaka (Malaysia), which was envisioned as three eighteen-hole courses on 400 acres of land in 1992 but ended up as only twenty-seven holes of golf. In addition, a karaoke lounge, Japanese hot bath, and residential bungalows and chalets were added (Cartier, 1998). Pleumarom (1992) identified similar new developments in Thailand including Kaeng Krachan Country Club in Phetchaburi province. This resort now comprises three championship courses, 700 residential plots, a five-star deluxe hotel, retail outlets, and numerous other sports facilities (Pleumarom, 1992). This type of destination typically attracts affluent golf visitors who stay within the resort and rarely venture out or spend money beyond the walls of these secure estates, preferring instead to buy inclusive packages of activities that occur within the confines of the resort. In Japan, memberships at these new resorts in surrounding countries are traded like items in a stock exchange and given as rewards in business incentive schemes.

## *Golf Courses Associated with Property Developments*

This category of golf development is an extremely popular method of financing property development, especially in the southern United States, e.g., North Carolina, South Carolina, and Florida. There the practice is to build the golf course first and then sell off plots of land for property development. This type of development, also prevalent in Languedoc-Roussillon (France) and Catalonia (Spain) (Priestley and Ashworth, 1995), attracts the golf tourist who is likely to buy a second home or a time-share property. This type of tourist typically stays longer, adventures into the local area, and therefore contributes more fully to the economic well-being of the host community. At the same time this type of development requires much more land. While the typical golf course in Europe takes up about 64 hectares, golf courses associated with property developments can cover much larger areas, up to 5,000 hectares in some cases (Pleumarom, 1992).

As in Europe and the United States, this type of development is becoming more visible in the Far East where foreign investment in golf courses has led to Japanese expatriate communities building luxury second homes on golf courses as a retreat from congested and polluted cities.

## *Networks of Courses Forming Golf Regions*

Golf regions may be formed by grouping destinations that, although developed separately at first, are now marketed jointly. This marketing strategy has the effect of persuading the golf tourist to buy a package that may include a combination of accommodations and golf courses in one area, which results in an extension of the tourist's stay and a spreading of the resultant economic benefit throughout the region. A good example of this type of development exists in Alabama where a group of courses all built by the same designer, Robert Trent Jones, are marketed together as the Robert Trent Jones Trail. Elsewhere, the Costa del Sol (Spain) is now marketed as the Costa del Golf, and in Myrtle Beach, South Carolina, the South Carolina Tourist Board will tailor packages of the area's many golf courses to the needs of the visitor.

## THE WORLD GOLF TOURISM MARKET

### General Destinations

Golf is certainly one of the major growth areas within the tourism industry. Estimating its total size and value is difficult due to the highly disparate nature of the industry as a whole. According to Sports Marketing Surveys (2000), the worldwide golf tourism market (excluding the Far East) is estimated at $10 billion with the U.S. market alone worth $8 billion and Europe $2 billion. Golf, having gone through its many growth periods, can now be played anywhere in the world. Golf courses exist in the mountain ranges of the Himalayas and in the deserts of Arabia where the Emirates Golf Course is watered by desalinated water from the Arabian Gulf. Golf can be included as part of safari travel in Africa (see case study of Mount Kenya Golf Club) or played in the searing heat of Death Valley where an aptly named Furnace Creek golf course exists. Course types range from full eighteen-hole championship and nine-hole courses to pitch-and-putt practice facilities, which are currently being built in large numbers around the world. More facilities including driving ranges and putting courses of both the juvenile (miniature golf in the United States) and practice green variety also exist in increasing numbers. In the United States alone, the World Pitch and Putt Corporation will have opened a total of 224 courses by 2001 (Golf Developments, 1997). There is even a well established World Putting Championship in which international competitors qualify in their own countries for the finals, which are held at the Walt Disney World Resort every November for a purse of $500,000. In an infamous moment in history, the game of golf experienced its first extraterrestrial golf tourist when, in 1971, Alan Shepard smuggled a six iron onto the Apollo 14 mission and, upon landing on the moon, hit a shot with it sending it miles and miles into space.

Overall there are some 30,000 golf courses in the world covering an area greater than the total size of Belgium. In Europe alone there are over 5,000 courses (Table 6.4) and in the United States there are over 16,500 courses, of which 500 new courses opened in 1999 alone

TABLE 6.4. Members of Golf Clubs and Numbers of Courses in Europe 1985-2000

| Country | No. of Players 1985 | No. of Players 2000 | Percent Increase 1985-1992 | Percent Increase 1992-2000 | No. of Courses 1985 | No. of Courses 2000 |
|---|---|---|---|---|---|---|
| United Kingdom | 815,015 | 1,178,795 | 12 | 18 | 1,859 | 2,612 |
| Sweden | 107,000 | 439,653 | 176 | 49 | 181 | 393 |
| Germany | 67,332 | 345,206 | 141 | 114 | 190 | 583 |
| France | 63,724 | 277,459 | 205 | 43 | 156 | 511 |
| Ireland | 125,000 | 215,834 | 6 | 63 | 257 | 388 |
| Spain | 29,521 | 151,080 | 121 | 133 | 84 | 201 |
| Netherlands | 16,055 | 140,000 | 267 | 137 | 32 | 116 |
| Denmark | 25,000 | 91,350 | 76 | 208 | 51 | 130 |
| Finland | 6,011 | 66,558 | 482 | 90 | 18 | 96 |
| Italy | 18,000 | 56,140 | 103 | 54 | 61 | 216 |
| Norway | 5,600 | 65,000 | 195 | 294 | 9 | 90 |
| Austria | 5,024 | 54,703 | 245 | 216 | 23 | 108 |
| Belgium | 9,300 | 36,648 | 137 | 67 | 18 | 76 |
| Switzerland | 11,000 | 34,153 | 78 | 75 | 30 | 70 |
| Portugal | 3,000 | 7,500 | 37 | 83 | 24 | 59 |
| Iceland | 2,600 | 7,200 | 92 | 44 | 24 | 61 |
| Czech Rep. | 1,300 | 7,124 | 15 | 375 | 7 | 19 |
| Luxembourg | 800 | 3,200 | 5.6 | 279 | 1 | 6 |
| Slovenia | 150 (1986)* | 2,948 | N/A | 883 | 2 (1986) | 10 |
| Hungary | 295 (1991) | 1,152 | | | 1 (1991) | 6 |
| Turkey | 480 (1997) | 1,500 | N/A | N/A | 6 (1997) | 13 |
| Greece | 750 | 1,230 | 0 | 64 | 5 | 5 |
| Poland | 500 (1993) | 900 | N/A | N/A | 4 (1993) | 6 |
| Croatia | 106 (1993) | 168 | N/A | N/A | 2 (1993) | 1 |
| Slovakia | 193 (1996) | 921 | N/A | N/A | 1 (1996) | 2 |

TABLE 6.4 *(continued)*

| Estonia | 200 (1995) | 200 | N/A | N/A | 1 (1995) | 1 |
| Russia | 100 (1993) | 1,000 | N/A | N/A | 2 (1993) | 3 |
| Israel | N/A | 900 | N/A | N/A | — | 2 |

*Source:* European Golf Association, list of member federations, unions, and associations 2000 (used with permission of the EGA).
*Denotes figures available from this date

(Table 6.1). These courses serve an estimated worldwide golf population of 60 million.

This next section identifies the main golf destinations around the world and provides a description of the profile for each, wherever possible statistics for the size and value of each destination are given.

### United States

There are 26.7 million golfers ages twelve years and over in the United States playing on a total of 17,108 golf courses. The five states with the highest number of courses are Florida (1,261), California (1,007), Michigan (971), Texas (906), and New York (886) (National Golf Foundation, 2002).

The market for golf in the United States has grown dramatically since the mid-1980s with the number of players rising 33 percent from 19.9 million in 1986 to 26.7 million, the present figure. During the same period the number of courses in the United States increased 25 percent from 13,353 to 16,743 (NGF, 2000). The rate of new course construction has increased significantly over the past ten years from an average of about 150 per year to more than 400 openings per year (Table 6.1). In addition, the golf travel market has grown to "almost 12 million golfers aged 18 or older in 1998, compared with 10.5 million four years ago. These 12 million travelling golfers played 72 million rounds of golf, or just over 14 percent of all rounds played in the US during 1998" (NGF, 1998, p. 5). One out of every two adult golfers today plays at least one round of golf while traveling for business or pleasure, and nearly 65 percent of all golf travelers have annual household incomes of more than $50,000 (see Table 6.3).

Only 8 percent of Americans hold a passport (NGF, 2000), so the vast majority of American golf tourism is domestic travel. The majority of these trips are short, organized trips of four to six days and include three or four rounds of golf. The five main destinations are Myrtle Beach (South Carolina), Orlando (Florida), South Florida, Phoenix (Arizona), and northeastern states (see Table 6.5).

In the United States, the total golf population in 1998 was 24.1 million (see Table 6.6). Americans who travel abroad for golf do so in relatively small numbers to destinations such as Mexico, Canada, the Bahamas, Aruba, the United Kingdom, Australia, and Japan. The reason for travel is most often a "once in a lifetime" trip to well-known championship courses in these countries. One of the most

TABLE 6.5. Top U.S. Golf Destinations

| State | Percent of Golf Travelers |
| --- | --- |
| Florida | 30 |
| South Carolina | 15 |
| California | 15 |
| Texas | 15 |
| North Carolina | 12 |
| Arizona | 11 |
| Nevada | 10 |
| Michigan | 9 |
| Pennsylvania | 5 |
| Illinois | 4 |
| Ohio | 4 |
| Wisconsin | 4 |

*Source:* NGF, *Golf Travel in the U.S.,*1998 Edition (used with permission of the NGF).

TABLE 6.6. U.S. Golf Travelers (Age Eighteen and Older) 1989-1998

|  | 1989 | 1994 | 1998 |
|---|---|---|---|
| Golf travelers as a percentage of all golfers | 35.0 percent | 46.6 percent | 48.6 percent |
| Estimated number of golf travelers | 7.9 million | 10.5 million | 11.8 million |
| Male | 82.6 percent | 79.4 percent | 77.1 percent |
| Female | 17.4 percent | 20.6 percent | 22.9 percent |
| Number of nontraveling golfers | 14.8 million | 12.1 million | 12.3 million |
| Total golf population | 22.7 million | 22.6 million | 24.1 million |

Source: NGF U.S. Golf Travel Market, 1998 Edition (used with the permission of the NGF).

sought-after destinations of the overseas golf traveler is St. Andrews, Scotland, the "home of golf."

## Europe

In Europe, all countries have experienced growth in both the numbers of players and golf courses (see Table 6.4). Established golf destinations have seen steady increases over the past fifteen years, but the most spectacular growth can be seen in the rest of Europe where golf course development shot up by as much as 500 percent in some cases. For example, in Germany, the number of courses trebled between 1985 (190) and 2000 (583), and in Austria, courses rose nearly fivefold in the same period (23 in 1985 to 108 in 2000). Even in lesser-known European golf destinations, growth has been significant, with Iceland increasing the number of courses from thirteen (1985) to fifty-nine (2000). Countries who until recently formed part of the Soviet Union are also developing golf, for example Slovenia (two courses in 1986 to ten courses in 2000).

Many of these courses have been developed to serve the demands of rapidly growing golf populations within individual countries (see Table 6.6). Overall the total number of players affiliated with a golf club has increased from 1,312,032 (1985) to 3,187,841 (2000). This figure does not include the estimated 1.25 million to 1.75 million players (EGA Statistics, 2000) that are not members of a club in Europe. However, in a large number of cases the increase in courses has been undertaken to achieve tourism development. A good example is Spain where golf is being used to open up the interior of the country to tourism. Eighteen courses, a mixture of older and newly designed, are being marketed together in the Valencia region to attract golf tourists.

According to Sports Marketing Surveys (2000), the value of golf tourism in Europe is estimated at £2 billion. Principal tourism flows within Europe are twofold. First, golfers from northern countries traveling to warmer countries to play golf, and second, golfers from all over Europe traveling to the famous courses in Britain and Ireland for the same purpose are the principal contributors. In 1998, 476,000 British golfers took golf holidays either at home or abroad, thus representing an annual expenditure of £480million (IAGTO, 2002). The principal destinations for British and German tourists in search of golfing holidays are England, Spain, and Portugal, with 74 percent of all golf tourists to Spain coming from these two countries (Turespaña, 2000).

### Asia and the Far East

In Asia, golf has become a symbol of status and influence. Enthusiasm for the game is growing at an incredible rate among the region's growing middle- and upper-class citizens, particularly in the industrializing nations of Indonesia, Malaysia, Thailand, and the Philippines. However, it is in Japan that "golf fever" has hit the hardest. In Japan over 20 million golfers squeeze onto approximately 2,000 golf courses with potentially another 1,000 courses in various stages of development (Takeda, 1996). Each course has to accommodate an average of 10,000 players. As a result, memberships to the more exclusive clubs can run several million yen, and rounds of golf have to be booked several months ahead. To accommodate the practice needs of the Japanese golfer, multistory driving ranges are a feature throughout the country, and it is quite possible for a Japanese golfer never to set foot on a Japanese golf course. Instead, the success of the Japanese economy has pushed its golfers overseas and, in particular, to its near neighbors. Entrepreneurs in nearby countries, eager to lure these affluent golf-playing visitors, became the driving force behind frantic construction of golf courses in the late 1980s. As a result the Philippines, for instance, now has eighty golf courses with twenty more in construction and dozens more in the planning stages (Gluckman, 1997). Similarly, Thailand now has 160 courses, Malaysia, 155, and Indonesia, 90, with all eyes on Korea and China for the next golf explosion. Golf tourism in the Far East is no longer targeted solely at the Japanese. Tourism facilitators such as airlines, travel agents, and hotel chains are increasingly marketing the area as an inexpensive golfing destination to the rest of the world. The golf course and tourism lobby in Thailand alone claims that Thailand needs at least 300 courses to cope with expected demands (Pleumarom, 1992).

## *Africa*

Figures for golf tourism and golf development in Africa in general are extremely hard to summarize due to the disparate nature of this continent. Many of the countries within it have their own golf associations, but reliable figures from these associations are hard to collect, with the exception of Morocco, Kenya and, most notably, South Africa (see the earlier discussion of Morocco). In an attempt to diversify the tourism product and increase destination profitability in Kenya, golf has been offered alongside the attraction of safari. Ten golf courses in the highlands region around Mount Kenya are marketed jointly with safari activities (see case study). The other twenty-eight courses in Kenya stretch from the capital of Nairobi to the Indian Ocean and have been advertised together as a packaged chain by travel agents (Olmstead, 1997). South Africa is busy marketing its 400 golf courses to the British, Dutch, and Australasian business incentive markets combining economy, climate, wildlife, and scenery in its advertising campaigns. Furthermore, specialist golf tour operators have helped open up the golf market to international golfers, mainly from Britain, with packages tailored to their demands. Central to some of these packages are the golf resorts at Sun City (North West Province), such as Lost City and the Gary Player Country Club, which hosts the annual Million Dollar Challenge, one of the world's richest tournaments.

## *Australia*

Golf is Australia's largest participant sport with over 500,000 registered golfers belonging to 1,559 clubs and an additional estimated 1.2 million social golfers (AGU, 2000). The majority of golf courses are concentrated in the southeast corner between Melbourne and Sydney, but it is the courses on Queensland's Gold and Sunshine Coasts that benefit from international golf tourism. According to the Australian Tourist Commission (ATC), 10 percent of all Japanese visitors to the country played golf (Sullivan, 1996), and a significant number of additional visitors came from South Korea and Singapore. These golf tourists mainly represented trophy hunters who visited to play on courses made famous by televised tournaments such as the Australian Open at Huntingdale, Victoria. New Zealand's 399 golf courses, serving 125,000 registered club members (NZGA, 2000), also benefit from an influx of golfers from Japan. Courses on New Zealand's North Island gain the most visitors.

### *South America*

If figures for Africa are difficult to find, course numbers and golf tourist information for South America are almost impossible to gather. Golf tourism is developing slowly in this part of the world with small numbers of Americans traveling to destinations including Palmilla (Mexico) and Cartagena (Colombia). Here, American golf course architects such as Jack Nicklaus are involved in a number of new developments. Elsewhere on the continent golf is beginning to thrive; for instance, in Argentina there are now 210 golf clubs serving 39,000 players (Associacion Argentina De Golf, 2000).

## *GOLF TOURISM EFFECTS*

To reiterate, the benefits of developing golf for tourism reasons include improvement in the profitability of tourism by attracting tourists from higher socioeconomic groupings. Another reason involves assisting tourism product diversity and creation of employment (it is estimated that up to 125 full-time jobs can be created as a result of a golf course's development) (Llewelyn-Davies, 1997). In addition, it is presumed that associated golf infrastructures also create additional employment. Seasonality can be reduced as golf tourists will visit and play golf in traditional low periods.

Although golf can bring many economic advantages to tourism destinations, many instances in which the practice of using golf to solve tourist destination problems have led to controversy. So strong is opposition to the game that an organization dedicated to its elimination, the Global Anti-Golf Movement (GAGM), under the guidance of Japanese professor Gen Morita, was launched on World No Golf Day, April 29, 1993 (Takeda, 1996).

The negative impacts of the game can vary according to location, size, and design. Indeed, where golf courses have been built using the land's natural contours and vegetation, as in the links courses of England and Scotland, there is very little impact. Elsewhere, when courses have been built in environmentally sensitive areas or there has been some disruption to the local community, criticisms abound.

### Sociocultural Impacts

Pleumarom (1992) has noted that the golf course business has been a major cause of large-scale land acquisition and landlessness in Thailand among rural people. Golf developers cheaply buy small pieces of agricultural land around villages. Speculation among foreign investors causes the prices of these pieces of land to rise and to quickly become financially out of reach of the local population. In the meantime, access to the land is denied, making it more difficult for the local population to carry out farming practices. Eventually, those who manage to hold onto their land are forced to sell. This experience has been repeated in other parts of the Far East.

In areas where large golf developments have been built, other impacts can be felt. Segregation is often achieved through the erection of walls or security systems creating a separate, exclusive enclave that has little contact with the local population, causing a fragmentation of that community. However, segregation can also be achieved by differentiating the new development from its surrounding environment. A golf course can have the effect of doing this on its own, being different by its very design and maintenance, but if foreign infrastructure is added such as condominiums, clubhouses, additional sports facilities including basketball courts, and other additions such as restaurants and retail outlets, then separation is complete. At the most prestigious developments this globalization is a crucial theme. Connell (1999) highlighted this impact in Manila (Philippines), but it can be illustrated all over the world with American-designed golf courses being surrounded by Spanish-style residential properties, Italian restaurants, French boutiques, and English bars selling Irish ales.

The golf industry can directly impact the native population, particularly in the area of employment. Far from creating employment as proponents of golf advocate, golf development can actually create unemployment, especially in labor-intensive agricultural regions. Golf courses create many construction jobs during the development phase, but once the course is operating, only thirty to forty people are needed as greens keepers, caddies, and clubhouse staff—all low-paid positions (Plumarom, 1992). With the advent of new technologies, such as water sprinkler systems, golf carts, and mowing machines, personnel needs are further reduced. In addition, in some countries such as Thailand and the Philippines it is customary for caddies to be female, with the most employable caddies being the most attractive women. These women are vulnerable to sexual exploitation which has led to the perception that the golf tourism industry is somehow linked to the sex tourism industry. All of the previous contribute "further to the impoverishment of the local people," including the "sharp rise in living costs as a consequence of the tourism invasion" (Plumarom, 1992, p. 108).

### Environmental Impacts

In contrast to traditional Scottish courses where natural features dictate course conditions, modern golf course design requires a consistency of landscape to eliminate unfair lies and unpredictable bounces. Thus the landscape of modern golf design is a highly manicured, green area produced to eliminate "luck of the bounce" from the game (Bale, 1994). Golf developers, not surprisingly, tend to seek out scenic areas for course location, choosing to place courses near beaches and rivers, on mountains and hills, and near other naturally outstanding features. The production of a new golf course can require recontouring of terrain; modern technology has made it possible for golf courses to be situated in previously inaccessible areas of the world. As a result, deserts have been "greened," marshes drained, artificial lakes dug, trees removed, and mountains dynamited to produce ideal golfing conditions. These conditions are sustained through the importation of new topsoils to ensure golf-friendly surfaces, the application of chemicals to maintain the natural green course appearance, and sophisticated machinery to create suitable uniformity of surface and grass length (Adams, 1987). The result can be spectacular, as the extensive debate in the golf media surrounding the 100 most beautiful courses in the world illustrates. Environmentalists, however, have been quick to criticize.

The "scorched earth" practice of new course design—in which the old topology is replaced by a completely new one—can involve the importation of foreign soils, sand, grass types, and vegetation. Much research has shown that fairways, greens, and bunkers support a limited number of species compared to natural environments. In addition, fairways, often up to 90 meters wide for beginner-friendly courses, create barriers between populations of indigenous species of flora and fauna, preventing long-term sustainability of these communities.

Water consumption is an often-cited problem (Plumarom, 1992; Markwick, 2000). Golf courses need substantial amounts of water for irrigation purposes. Once the needs of clubhouses, hotels, and swimming pools at larger golf resorts have been added, the result can be a major strain on an already-scarce resource. This is especially applicable in areas of low rainfall, although the application of modern technology has helped in some areas. For instance, the Emirates Golf Club (Dubai) is irrigated with water from a specially constructed desalination plant. Elsewhere, in areas such as California, Arizona (United States), Greece, the interior of Spain, or parts of the Far East, water shortages caused by golf development are a problem.

Another complaint against golf is chemical usage. In some areas, especially in extreme climates or where foreign grasses and vegetation have been imported, the production of a green surface suitable for golf has required the application of large amounts of chemicals which include herbicides, pesticides, coloring agents, and fertilizers (McCormack, 1991, cited in Bale, 1994). Some of these chemicals can be carcinogenic and harmful to greenkeepers due to repeated contact (Tsutomu, 1991). Alternatively, water runoff from courses can contaminate neighboring water supplies, kill wildlife, and affect local agriculture or residential areas. Plumarom (1992) illustrated this problem with reference to cases in Japan, Thailand, and South Korea.

## Golf's Response

Supporters of golf have been swift to come to its defense, pointing out that its development diversifies economies and provides valuable greenbelt spaces and wildlife refuge areas in regions that are already developed (Terman, 1997). It is pointed out that golf turfgrass can act as an effective biological filter, helping to maintain air and water quality and to aid in the reduction of erosion. It is also felt that the game has been unfairly victimized, with golf course development being singled out for criticism when in reality it is mainly the modern industrialization of regions that has led to the destruction of valuable wetlands and habitats. Instead, it is asserted that golf development is a method of recapturing lost industrial land, such as landfills and quarries, recycling these areas for recreational benefit.

Despite these and other defenses the golf industry is slowly beginning to acknowledge—persuaded by the dearth of scientific evidence linking the game to environmental problems—that it has to adopt a much more environmentally friendly attitude. In 1990, the United States Golf Association (USGA) teamed up with Audubon International to form the Audubon Cooperative Sanctuary Program (ACSP) for golf courses. Its aim was to provide an educational and awareness program for designers, managers, and golfers to help them understand environmental issues and to manage golf in a better way for wildlife and the environment. The ACSP also runs a certification system for golf courses conforming to a set of prescribed environmental guidelines. These guidelines include:

1. Water quality management—constant monitoring of chemical levels in ponds and lakes to make sure they are free of contaminants
2. Wildlife conservation—creation of habitats where native animals can thrive
3. Integrative pest management—keeping pest management usage to a minimum
4. Use of different forms of wildlife to help combat pest problems
5. Waste reduction—recycling of waste wherever possible

6. Energy conservation—reduction of energy usage throughout the golf complex
7. Water conservation—minimization of water usage both on and off the golf course (Audubon International, 2000)

To date, over 2,400 golf courses have become members of ACSP (about 16 percent of the golf courses in the United States) and over 100 of them are now fully certified. In addition, the USGA has spent over $18 million on environmental research since 1991, and the ACSP has received endorsements from, among others, the Golf Course Superintendents Association of America (GCSAA), the Professional Golfers' Association (PGA), the American Society of Golf Course Architects (ASGCA), and the Royal Canadian Golf Association (RCGA) (Dodson, 1997).

In Europe, a joint initiative among the European Golf Association (EGA), the Royal and Ancient Golf Club of St. Andrews, and the PGA European Tour led to the establishment of the European Golf Association Ecology Unit in 1994. The unit's goals included:

1. Establishing a solid, factual understanding of the environmental attributes of golf courses;
2. Developing awareness of the environmental aspects of golf courses through a program of positive ecological initiatives;
3. Encouraging a higher standard of environmental performance throughout the golfing community; and
4. Providing a serious contribution to the European environmental debate. (EGA Ecology Unit, 1998)

This unit has since been superseded by an independent body, the Committed to Green Foundation, which was launched on September 28, 1997, by European Commissioner Jacques Santer during the Ryder cup held at Valderrama, southern Spain. Committed to Green aims to show how well-managed golf courses can benefit the environment and the community through the conservation of nature, landscape, cultural heritage, water resource management, pollution control, energy efficiency, waste management, education, and public awareness.

The three targets for the Committed to Green campaign are:

1. Existing facilities: to encourage improvement of environmental performance and demonstrate good practice via the Committed to Green recognition program
2. New projects: to ensure they are developed in accordance with appropriate environmental guidelines
3. Major events: to use the strong media interest to promote environmental awareness to support Committed to Green in the wider sporting community (Stubbs, 1995)

The golf industry conveys a greater corporate sensibility toward environmentalism than it did twenty years ago, particularly in the United States and Europe. However, the effectiveness of this campaign is a matter of great debate. The mere fact that the game's administrators and leading proponents are working so hard on the issue suggests that golf does have a problem to solve. This is particularly true in developing golf destinations where, up to now, golf development has gone largely unchecked by social, legal, and environmental constraints.

## CASE STUDIES

Two case studies are presented in this section, Pinehurst Resort, North Carolina, and Tobs Kenya Golf Safaris. They are presented in order to illustrate the contrasts between a large, world-renowned, well-established golf resort at one end of the golf tourism spectrum, and a small, developing golf tourism operation on the other.

### Pinehurst Resort, North Carolina

With eight golf courses Pinehurst Resort is the largest golf resort in the world and the only single resort with that many courses (see Figure 6.2). Not content with this, the resort is planning additional courses, with the ninth Pinehurst scheduled to open in late 2003. Golf at Pinehurst dates back to 1897 when the first course, a nine-hole links course, was laid out on land owned by the Tufts family. Donald Ross built the now famous No. 2 course in 1907 and added No. 3 in

FIGURE 6.2. Pinehurst Resort, North Carolina. (Photo used with permission of Pinehurst Resort.)

1910. The remaining courses were built throughout the past century. Pinehurst No. 8 was completed in 1996. Pinehurst has hosted many national and international tournaments, notably the PGA Championships, U.S. Opens, and a Ryder Cup in 1951. After a significant gap the U.S. Open returned to Pinehurst in 1999 and based on the success of that tournament, Pinehurst was awarded the 2005 U.S. Open.

The entire Pinehurst Resort, owned by ClubCorp, is a magnificent development spread over 5,500 acres of undulating sand hills and pine forest areas. Pinehurst No. 2 is currently voted third-best golf course in the world and the resort as a whole attracts golfers from all directions. Pinehurst consists of three hotels, eight eighteen-hole championship golf courses, twenty-four tennis courts, three croquet courts, a 200-acre lake suitable for sailing, canoeing, kayaking, and fishing, two outdoor swimming pools, and a fitness center. The resort sits within Moore County which contains another forty golf courses. As it has few other amenities, this area is a true golf tourism destination.

## Value of Golf Tourism to Moore County

Average Daily Expenditure in 1999

$ 111,953 hotels, motels, resorts for lodging

160,537 food and beverage purchases

230,244 recreation at golf courses and tennis facilities

127,444 other retail purchases at a variety of shops and antique stores

46,471 transportation

27, 460 miscellaneous

$ 704,110 Total daily spend by visitors to Moore County*

(*It is not known what percentage of this average was foreign visitors.)

- This spend supports over 5,700 jobs in the local economy with a daily payroll of $197,780.
- State and local taxes generate $62,740 daily.
- Golf tourism in Moore County is worth $257 million annually. (U.S. Travel Data Center North Carolina State University Visitor Study, 1999)

The projected visitation for 2003 is 1,508,780 guests staying in a combination of hotels, condominiums, and private housing. Pinehurst Resort recognizes that to continue to attract visitors it must maintain its unique character. To ensure this, a program of sustainable tourism with the following aims is being implemented:

- *Environmental protection.* Environmentally friendly greenkeeping practices have been instituted, including certification as an Audubon Cooperative Sanctuary and the distinction of being the first resort to enroll in the Safe Harbor Program for endangered species.
- *Focus on authenticity.* Efforts to preserve the authentic aspects of local heritage and culture are being made, including handicrafts, art, music, language, architectural landscape traditions, and history.
- *Recognize that tourism has limits.* Knowing the carrying capacity of the resort aids in decisions regarding protection of scenic views and vistas, planting trees, landscaping of parking lots, and controlling signage.
- *Enhance the journey as well as the destination.* Development of historic heritage corridors, biking paths, hiking trails, and other forms of alternative transportation helps shape the overall experience. (Moore County Convention and Visitors Bureau, 2000)

## The Development of a New Golf Tourism Destination— Tobs Kenya Golf Safaris

Tobs Kenya Golf Safaris is the first and only tour operator in Kenya that specializes in golf (see Figure 6.3). Kenya has thirty-eight golf courses of which twelve have eighteen holes, ten are used for championship events, and six are within twenty miles of Nairobi— Kenya's capital. Established in 1991 the company has added Kenya's well-kept golf secret to its already well-established attributes of wildlife, beaches, climate, good hotels, and friendly people.

After registration of the company in September 1991 its founder, Tob Cohen, set about advertising the product through the manufacture and distribution of an expensive glossy brochure to 500 golf clubs. In addition, an advertisement was placed in *Golf World* magazine. This marketing campaign was an unmitigated failure, resulting in just one booking. Later, Kenya Golf Safaris switched its marketing focus to Swiss, German, and Dutch golf markets, as these groups were known to be already interested in Kenya for tourism purposes and represented the longer staying, higher spending section of the visiting population. In 1996 Tobs Kenya Golf Safaris opened new of-

FIGURE 6.3. Mount Kenya Golf Club. (Photo used with permission of Tobs Kenya Golf Safaris.)

fices in Nairobi and developed a Web site, the first tourism Web site in East Africa, <www.kenya-golf-safaris.com>. These new tactics, along with joining IAGTO in 1998 and attendance of the second World Golf tourism Convention in Athens, led to a tripling of the company's golf turnover and the opportunity to organize the prestigious United Nations conference appointments in Africa.

Tobs Kenya Golf Safaris aims to attract 5,000 visitors per year to Kenya. These visitors are golf tourists first and safari and beach tourists second. The major supplier countries, in descending order of size, are Holland, Switzerland, France, United States, and Canada. To date no golf tourists have traveled from the United Kingdom, which is a surprise since there are thirty-five golf tour operators there. Kenya is also an ex-colony, and the United Kingdom is the biggest supplier of general tourists to Kenya.

The average stay for a golf tourist to Kenya is nine days (with seventeen days being the longest and four-day incentive trips the shortest). These tourists spend between $150 and $250 (U.S.) per day depending on whether safaris are included in their golf program (this is the case in 80 percent of cases).

The Kenya Tourist Board (KTB) has been unable to aid the development of golf tourism due to the fact that it has been an effective organization only for the past three years, and only recently has the KTB been interested in marketing Kenya as a golf destination. Before this time only safaris and beach holidays were promoted. In 1998 the Kenya Golf Marketing Alliance was formed with the mission statement of "putting Kenya on the map as a quality Golf Destination," (Kenya Golf Marketing Alliance, 2000, p. 2). To this end, the resources of golf and related tourism inputs such as the KTB, reputable golf tour operators, airlines, hotels, and golf clubs are being harnessed. It is expected that in the near future Kenya will be recognized throughout the world not just for safaris but as a golf destination as well.

## CONCLUSION

Golf is clearly in its ascendancy; the numbers of players and courses worldwide is on the increase. Subsequently, as this market has grown the number of golf tourism destinations has increased sharply. These destinations have the backing of investors, developers, and tour operators ready to build and market these new infrastructures to a hungry golf population. In the foreseeable future it can be expected that the golf tourism market will continue to expand and diversify with golf tourists traveling to different destinations to explore new golf experiences. It cannot be long before relatively untapped destinations such as China and South America, with their huge resources and expanding golf populations, enter the fray.

As long as golf continues to be the preserve of the higher-spending and longer-staying tourist, it can be predicted that tourism destinations will continue to develop golf facilities to achieve their economic aims of growth, program diversity, and increased profitability. However, caution is in order: in recent years golf developers worldwide have found it relatively easy to obtain land to build golf courses—in some cases with complete disregard for local environments and cultures. If escalation of opposition to golf development is to be avoided then developers, managers, golf associations, and governments will need to continue to their trend toward lower-impact golf courses and demonstrate to a much greater extent the benefits for all people affected by golf tourism.

## RELEVANT WEB SITES

Amateur Golf Information: http://www.amateur-golf.com
Audubon International's Cooperative Sanctuary Program for Golf
    Courses: http://www.audubonintl.org/programs/acss/ golf.htm
Committed to Green Foundation: http://www.committedtogreen.org
European Golf Association Ecology Unit: www.golfecology.co.uk
International Association of Golf Tour Operators: www.iagto.com
National Golf Foundation: www.ngf.org
Royal and Ancient Golf Club: www.randa.org
United States Golf Association: www.usga.org

## REFERENCES

Adams, R. (1987). Same name, different game, *Sport Place*, 1 (2): 29-35.

Association Argentina De Golf (2000). <http://www.argengolf.org>. Accessed online December 4.

Audubon International (2000). <http://www.audubonintl.org>. Accessed online December 12.

Australian Golf Union (2000). About the AGU. <http://www.agu.org.au/about/theagu/default.sps>. Accessed online December 4.

Bale, J. (1994). *Landscapes of Modern Sport*. London: Leicester University Press.

Barrett, T. (1994). *The Daily Telegraph Golf Chronicle*. London: Hodder and Stoughton.

Beditz, J.F. (1994). The development and growth of the U.S. golf market. *Science and Golf II: Proceedings of the World Scientific Congress of Golf*. In Cochran, A.J. and Farally, (Eds.). London: M.R.E. and F.N. Spon.

Blais, P. (1997). Destination Morocco? It's not far off. *Golf Course News: Newspaper for the Golf Course Industry*, February, p. 59.

Brasch, R. (1972). *How did Sports Begin* London: Longman.

Campbell, M. (1994). *The Encyclopaedia of Golf*. London: Dorling Kindersley.

Cartier, C. (1998). Megadevelopment in Malaysia: From heritage landscapes to "leisurescapes" in Melaka's tourism sector. *Singapore Journal of Tropical Geography*, 1 (19): 151-176, Part 2.

Connell, J. (1999). Beyond Manila: Walls, malls and private spaces. *Environment and Planning*, 31: 417-439.

Davies, D. and Davies, P. (1999). *Beyond the fairways: The past, present and future of world golf*. CollinsWillow.

Dodson R. (1997). *Perception, reality and the future*. Golf Course Management, Publication of Golf Course Superintendents Association of America, February: 192.

European Golf Association (EGA) (2000). List of member federations, unions and associations.

European Golf Association Ecology Unit (1998). The ecology unit. <http://www. golfecology.com>. Accessed online December 11, 2000.

Gluckman, R. (1997). No slowdown seen in Asia's hottest market. *Golf Course News: Newspaper for the Golf Industry,* June: 35.

Gold Developments (1997). Alliance to Bring Golf to Urban Areas. November 10, p. 1.

Green, R. (1993). *The Illustrated Encyclopaedia of Golf.* London: CollinsWillow.

Haywood, L.J., Kew, F.C., Bramham, J., Spink, J., and Henry H. (1993). *Understanding Leisure.* Cheltenham, UK: Thornes Publishers

International Association of Golf Tour Operators (IAGTO) (2002). Fact Sheet. <http://www.iagto.com>. Accessed online May 2.

Kenya Golf Marketing Alliance (2000). Membership Package Handbook.

Klein, B S. (1996). The responsibility challenge. *Golfweek: America's Golf Newspaper* November 23: 3.

Llewelyn-Davies in association with Water Management Consultants (1997). *Golf course development subject study: Final Report.* London: Llewelyn-Davies.

Maguire, T. (1999). Insights and intelligence on consumer markets: Getting in the swing of things. *American Demographics,* January: 16-19.

Markwick, M.C. (2000). Golf tourism development, stakeholders differing discourses and alternative agendas: The case of Malta. *Tourism Management,* 21: 515-524.

Mintel (1996). General Household Survey.

Mintel (Aug. 1999). Mintel Participation in Golf. <http://sinatra2.mintel.com>. Accessed Dec. 4, 2000.

Moore County Convention and Visitors Bureau (2000).

National Golf Foundation (NGF) (1998). The U.S. Golf Travel Market. Florida: NGF.

National Golf Foundation (NGF) (2000). *Golf Facilities in the US,* 2000 Edition. Florida: NGF.

National Golf Foundation (NGF) (2002). *Golf Participation in the US,* Accessed online <http://www.ngfior/faq/#/>, July 5.

New Zealand Golf Association (NZGA) (2000). <http://nzga.co.nz/facts/index> Accessed online December 4.

Olmstead, L. (1997). African golfari: ultimate getaways. *The Washington Golf Monthly.* April: 132-133.

Pleumarom, A. (1992). Course and effect: golf tourism in Thailand. *Ecologist,* 22 (3): 104-110.

Priestley, G.K. and Ashworth, G.J. (1995). *Sports Tourism: the Case of Golf. Tourism and Spatial Transformations.* Wallingford: CAB Publishing.

Royal and Ancient Golf Club of St. Andrews Development Panel (1990). *The Demand for Golf.* St. Andrews: RAGC.

Sports Marketing Surveys (2000).

Storey, K.R. (1994). Targeting for success—the European golf market. *Science and golf II: Proceedings of the World Scientific Congress of Golf.* In Cochran, A.J. and Farally, London: M.R.E. and F.N. Spon.

Strickland, V. (1997). If you build it they will come: Puerto Rico's determination to become a world class destination. *Golf Course Management,* Golf Course Superintendents Association of America, January: 196.

Stubbs, D. (1995). Environmental guidelines for new golf course development in Europe. <http://www.golfecology.com/publics/development/develop.htm>. Accessed online January 26.

Sulaiman, M.S. (1996). Islands within islands: Exclusive tourism and sustainable utilization of coastal resources in Zanzibar. In Bruguglio, L., Butler, R., Harrison, D., and Filho, W.L. (Eds.). *Sustainable Tourism in Islands and Small States Case Studies* (pp. 32-49). London: Cassell.

Sullivan, M. (1996). Market segments: The Japanese golf holiday market. *Travel and Tourism Analyst,* 2: 58-71.

Takeda, A. (1996). Japan's Golf Courses and the Environment. <http://www. amrican.edu/ projects/mandala/TED/JPGOLF>. Accessed online May 8, 2000.

Terman, M. R. (1997). Natural links: Naturalistic golf courses as wildlife habitat. *Landscape and Urban Planning,* 38: 183-197.

Tsutomu, K. (1991). The political economy of golf. *AMPO Japan-Asia Quarterly Review,* 22(4), pp. 47-54.

Turespaña (2000). Golf Tourism Survey.

US Travel Data Center (1999). North Carolina State University Visitor Study.

Van Hengel, S.J.H. (1985). *Early Golf.* Vanduz: Frank P. Van Eck.

Zaitsu, H., Takeshita, S., Meshizuka, T., and Kawashima, K. (1994). Golf course development in Japan: Its abnormal supply and demand. *Science and Golf II: Proceedings of the World Scientific Congress of Golf* (pp. 562-568). In Cochran, A.J. and Farally, M.R.E. (Eds.). London: F.N. Spon.

Chapter 7

# Adventure Tourism

## Paul Beedie

### INTRODUCTION

Most of us in the developed world live in urban areas. Mountains, lakes, oceans, jungles, desert islands, and other wild places represent escape locations that offer excitement, stimulation, and potential adventure. This dislocation of self from the ordinary to the extraordinary appears to provide a pleasurable experience that is central to tourism (Rojek and Urry, 1997). Adventure tourism offers adventure holidays. Clients are tourists in so much as they buy an experience that is usually packaged for maximum efficiency. Existing tourist theory purports to explain tourist behavior in relation to mass tourism (MacCannell, 1976; Urry 1990; Rojek and Urry, 1997), leaving the contemporary adventure tourist scene underresearched and therefore underrepresented in academic terms.

Adventure tourism brings together travel, sport, and outdoor recreation. It might be considered a growing subset of tourism (Christiansen, 1990; Trauer, 1999), but an experiential engagement makes adventure tourism distinctive. This chapter will discuss adventure tourism, a huge and diverse topic (see Figure 7.1), by focusing on adventure tourism in mountains. Mountain-based adventure tourism has extended the breadth of traditional mountaineering (climbing and walking) so that, today, in mountains throughout the world, mountaineering has been fragmented, reinvented, and redefined. Climbing is now adventure climbing or sports climbing; abseiling has become an end in itself; hill walking has been redefined as trekking; scrambling has emerged as a hybrid activity with its own definitive guidebooks; cycling has moved off-road as mountain biking; canyoning has emerged as an adventure activity as has bungee jumping. Hudson

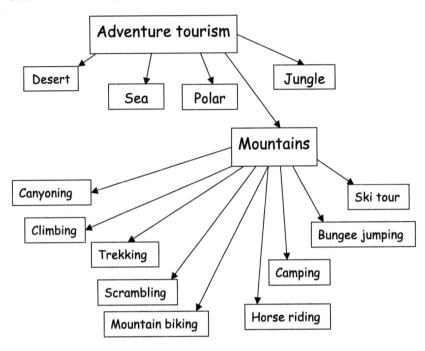

FIGURE 7.1. Diversity in Adventure Tourism.

(2000) has provided a study of the skiing industry, a sport that has undergone similar fragmentation and diversification. For example, it is now possible to go snow rafting at Seefeld in Austria <www.orange. net>. In addition, mountains are common as spectacular backdrops for activities such as white-water rafting and hang gliding (see Figure 7.2).

All of these activities to a greater or lesser extent have been packaged for adventure tourism. Mountains are particularly attractive destinations as they offer a range of activity options in a setting steeped in actual and symbolic representations of adventure: an opportunity to experience what Hamilton-Smith (1993, p. 10) would call "serious leisure." Mountains are wild, rugged places that attract bad weather and contain objective dangers, such as exposure to extreme elemental conditions and loose rock, which make mountain recreation activities inherently risky and hazardous. However, it is such uncertainty and

FIGURE 7.2. Hang gliding in the Himalayas. (Photo by P. Beedie.)

potential for personal harm that generates excitement by setting such undertakings in a context of challenge and adventure. There are, therefore, issues about marketing and management emerging from the commodification of mountains in the name of adventure tourism. This chapter, in particular, examines three central ideas to illuminate how mountain-based adventure tourism has evolved. These are:

- The management role of guides and mountaineering experts
- Brochures, guidebooks, Web sites, and other marketing materials
- The influence of technological innovation, particularly in relation to access and the ongoing redefinition of risk in the mountains

The following analysis of mountain adventure tourism will also draw on two specific examples: trekking in Nepal, and the Foundry Climbing Centre in the United Kingdom. This chapter offers an overview of adventure tourism and begins a process of theorizing this fast-growing phenomenon.

## THE COMMODIFICATION OF ADVENTURE

Perhaps the most significant factor in the development of adventure tourism is the extent to which we really engage in adventure. Price (1978) suggests we cannot have "adventure by numbers," as adventure is more about uncertainty of outcome (Miles and Priest, 2000). Price (1978) argues that any planned outdoor recreation cannot be called an adventure. Yet this is precisely how adventure tourism is marketed. There exists, therefore, something of a paradox whereby the more detailed, planned, and logistically smooth an adventure tourist itinerary becomes, the more removed the experience is from the notion of adventure. The three factors outlined previously—experts, brochures, and technology—combine to create a cushioning zone between the normal, home, and urban location of everyday life and the extraordinary experience of the adventure holiday. This idea is illuminated by the concept of frames (see Figure 7.3). Most of us in the developed world live our lives in an urban frame, insulated from less desirable elements of the real world by warm houses, hot water, electricity, beds, hygienic food, and other comforts. A part of our expressive selves reacts against this through an attraction to the perceived adventure of activities in wild places. However, our "habitus" (Bourdieu, 1984) travels with us, and it has been suggested that we rarely, if ever, actually leave the urban frame behind when we travel through the wilderness (Greenway, 1995). It is not surprising, therefore, to find clients on safaris in Tanzania expecting "fluffy white towels and snake-proof tents" (Beedie, 2002: 15). Mountaineering offers a frame of reference, but numerous frames overlap simultaneously: this is expressed diagrammatically in Figure 7.3.

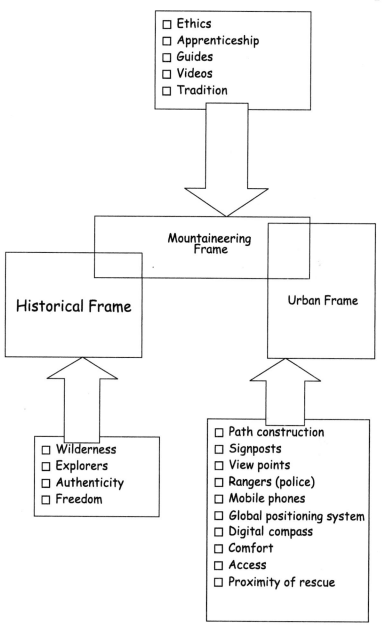

FIGURE 7.3. Frames: Influences on the Boundaries of Mountaineering.

Overlapping frames lead to ambivalent boundaries. As adventure moves closer to tourism, boundaries become hazy. The situation is exacerbated by the fact that many adventure tourists are GRAMPIES, that is, people who are "growing, retired, and moneyed, in good physical and emotional health" (Christiansen, 1990: 440). The average age of explorer clients is now forty-one years, and 77 percent are over thirty years. In his survey of the socioeconomic characteristics of North American wilderness users, Hendon suggests that such people are predominantly "white, educated, and middle-class" (Hendon, 1991: 111). The capital transfer equation, money for experience, is positively correlated so that the more exotic and adventurous the holiday purchased, the greater the cost. WorldWide Journeys has five-day safaris on the Skeleton Coast of Namibia from £1820 per person (WorldWide Journeys, 2000: 30); Naturetrek offer fourteen days in Canada with an itinerary called "The Great Whales and Fall Migration" for £2795 per person (*Birds* magazine of the RSPB, winter 2000: 25) and a journalistic estimate of the cost of climbing Mount Everest is £110,600 (*Observer Magazine,* 2000: 7), although this cost is for a group, not an individual. Of this last total, £46,700 is the cost of the permit required just to set foot on Everest, a clear example of the commodification of mountains. When clients are paying thousands of pounds for an adventure holiday, their standard of living, and by implication their expectations of comfort, will be high. Adventure tourism companies tread a careful line between selling adventure as an idea and delivering adventure as an experience. Figure 7.4 demonstrates the stages a client may move through in the journey from ordinary to extraordinary and back again.

## WHAT IS ADVENTURE TOURISM?

There is a great deal of discussion about definitions of tourism (Sharpley, 1994: 29-32), but few attempts to define adventure tourism. For purposes of discussion, adventure tourism encompasses several major ideas. First, adventure tourism involves practical engagement for the tourist. There is a physical effort involved, to a greater or lesser extent, which from some perspectives is closer to work than vacation. This embodied experience is an important point of discussion. Outdoor physical challenge, which may have positive side effects such as

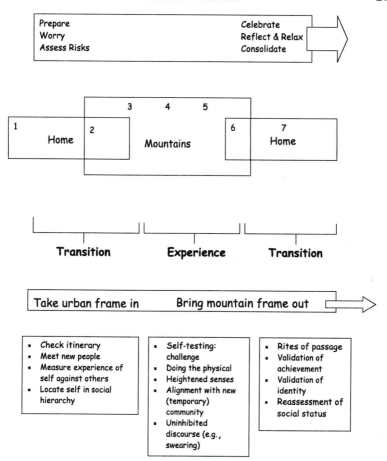

FIGURE 7.4. Leaving and Coming Back: The Extraordinary Experience.

weight loss, physique development, suntan, and related stress reduction, may be influenced by cultural forces in developed countries. Visser (1994: 16), for example, discusses the way cultural perspectives of tanned skin changed throughout the twentieth century.

Second, adventure tourism is a business enterprise. As with other industries competition characterizes the market and big companies have a tendency to dominate. Small independent companies offering specific personalized itineraries, such as White Peak Mountaineering, find it difficult to compete with large international companies, such as Explore,

Himalayan Kingdoms, and Exodus. The range and diversity of the holidays offered by the bigger companies is enormous. Explore WorldWide, for example, includes wildlife safaris in Tanzania, cultural touring in Vietnam, ethnic or tribal encounters in Borneo, sail touring such as the Philippines Island Adventure, hikes up Kilimanjaro, rafting down the Zambezi, the Kimberley wilderness experience in Australia, and Central Asia overland. Some companies—Jagged Globe and Foundry Mountain Activities are two British-based examples—specialize in mountaineering within adventure tourism.

Rubens (1999: 26) describes adventurous activities as either broad or narrow. The broad view of mountain-based adventure tourism encompasses activities such as multi-day trekking journeys which make sustained physical demands on the participant and in which the adventure element is sustained at a relatively low level. The narrow view is exemplified by activities such as abseiling, which offer an intense, highly charged, but short-lived experience. In Hamilton-Smith's (1993) terminology the former might be considered the more serious form of leisure. Adventure tourism embraces both broad and narrow activities and thereby maximizes its appeal to a full range of paying clientele. Adventure tourists in general have in common the financial capacity to pay for their expensive holidays. Beyond this similarity the range of clients is as great as the nature of the activities offered. Working and retired people are represented. The extent to which retired clients take longer trips is unknown. Existing research (Beedie, 2002) finds no obvious correlation between working commitments and length of holidays taken.

## MOUNTAINS AND COMMODIFICATION

The suggestion that those of us in developed countries have more leisure time resulting from a more efficient approach to work, advanced technology, and a better standard of living, is generally challenged by the whole notion of packaged holidays. Packages for mountain-based adventure tourism have been created by companies that bring together people in two areas of expertise. First, a company needs mountaineers, preferably Union Internationale Association Guides de Mantagne (UIAGM) qualified mountain guides (although local knowledge appears to be more important than qualifications to some companies, which may be irrelevant in some underdeveloped countries keen on exploiting the economic potential of their mountains by attracting tourists). Second, a company needs marketing expertise that can develop culturally embedded notions of a romantic "gaze" (Urry, 1990, 1995; Short, 1991). Adventure tourist companies are, therefore, run by experts with specialized knowledge (Giddens, 1990).

Evidence suggests that, professionals at least, are working longer hours and have more fragmented and complex social lives today than at any other time in history. It is the relative effortlessness of booking a vacation in the form of a package that appeals to adventure tourists because many, by their own admission, do not have the time to make the arrangements for themselves. It appears that the phenomenon Godbey (cited in Christiansen, 1990) has called "time-deepening" is operating: we use technology to save time, enabling us to work longer but to maximize leisure activities. Adventure tourists are typically rich monetarily but poor in time. They want to squeeze as much experience into as short a time as possible. Lifestyles of clients therefore reinforce the commodification of mountains by encouraging the package format.

At the same time mountain mythology is embedded with romantic notions of exploration, journey, and searching. Such ideas become attractive in our modern social world where fragmentation and complexity are the norm. This is because exploration implies finding, thereby suggesting potential stability in a world that is increasingly destabilized. Brochures and, increasingly, electronic media are important reference points for adventure tourists. When we buy a holiday we are paying for the expectation that we will gain something: a suntan, greater knowledge, new experiences, and new (perhaps temporary) social identities for example. This process of commodification has always included distinctive places such as cultural foci and beaches, but mountains too are increasingly viewed from this mechanistic and economic perspective (Johnson and Edwards, 1994).

Technology is having a profound influence on adventure tourism. For example, we may buy the latest ice axes, trekking poles, or climbing boots with the expectation that these will make us more accomplished climbers or trekkers. Our investment is seen as a way of making progress within these activities. Furthermore, commodification is creating an opportunity to both enter and make progress within the social world of the mountaineer. Access routes are changing. It is no longer necessary to serve an apprenticeship of walking and climbing in lower hills under the tutelage of experienced peers before being allowed to move into more challenging environments and engage with the more demanding aspects of mountaineering. Experienced mountaineers who have served their apprenticeships commonly voice their disapproval at such fast-tracking (Collister, 1984; Scott, 1994). Adventure companies and the packages they offer create the possibility of bypassing this traditional social requirement and moving directly to the more exotic challenges of the highest mountains. Adventure tourism is thus superimposing itself on existing social structures in mountaineering. A recent documentary suggested that paying to be guided to the summit of Everest was now the accepted mode of ascent, an illustration of the social impact of adventure tourism (BBC, 2001). The commodification of mountains has, therefore, had at least two consequences. First, mountains, which formerly held few positive attractions because they were considered the home of trolls and dragons (Bernbaum, 1997), have been reinvented as locations in which it is possible to accumulate symbolic capital. Second, this capital potential is being packaged and sold by adventure tourist companies. The following section expands the discussion by making connections to existing theory.

## THEORETICAL CONNECTIONS

What we choose to do in our leisure time has much to do with how we see ourselves as individuals and as members of groups (Goffman, 1959; Kelly, 1983; Jenkins, 1996). Bauman (1996) encapsulates the relationship between what we do and who we are. He draws analogies between such terms as "pilgrim" and "tourist" to theorize the cultural changes concerning the central issue of identity. He argues that the pilgrim, a conceptualization predating the tourist, had a clear sense of place. When we were pilgrims, he argues, we had a sense of direction but we were always striving for the future, never living in the present. By contrast, our contemporary social world is characterized by a complexity, fragmentation, and ambivalence that makes it impossible to conceive a future with any sense of certainty and conviction. As tourists we therefore live for the present, a conceptualization that explains our desire(s) for instant gratification, thrill, and the "buzz" of the moment. Mountain activities, particularly those involving ropes and/or positions of exposure, clearly offer such potential (see Figure 7.5).

Bauman's (1996) work helps to explain the ongoing dynamic between mountaineering and adventure tourism. Mountaineers who have served an apprenticeship are closer to pilgrims because they possess a clear sense of protocol and direction. Adventure tourists are closer to Bauman's postmodern conceptualizations, or the posttourist (Feifer, 1985). Their experience appears to be different from that of true mountaineers. The true mountaineer is something of a free-roving spirit, sometimes flaunting rules and management strategies and remaining closer to the ideals of historical explorers. These people reject the notion of hiring a guide and instead rely upon their own carefully constructed accumulation of skill and experience to explore the mountain while simultaneously avoiding the objective dangers inherent in such activity. Adventure tourists, by contrast, have their experiences defined for them through a combination of several outside influences including a dependence on guides, existing sources of information about mountains, and the protection afforded by con-

FIGURE 7.5. Crevasse jumping on the Bosson glacier at Chamonix in France. (Photo by P. Beedie.)

stantly improving equipment and other resources such as mountain rescue possibilities. One of the problems, however, is that it is increasingly difficult to operate independently. If we do plan our own expeditions we must still turn to guidebooks, chartered flights, and liaison officers to facilitate our arrangements and are, to no small degree, guided by such systems.

Such dependence becomes acceptable because of the capital potential of participation. It is the mountaineering objective that matters so it becomes less logical to engage with difficulties that can be eliminated by utilizing the systems that already exist. Moreover, this makes more sense because achieving an adventurous objective requires some kind of social validation to be meaningful. Through experiential engagement, adventure tourists accumulate physical capital. According to Bourdieu (1986), physical capital translates to cultural capital which determines "distinction" and thereby social identity. Bourdieu's work asserts that "the appeal of sport and leisure practices to social groups lies in distinctive uses of the body. These practices act as taste signifiers in a constant struggle to gain or maintain distinction" (Jarvie and Maguire, 1994: 184). According to Bourdieu, we gravitate toward those social fields that offer us the greatest potential capital. Such appears to be the case in mountaineering where the highest, longest, and hardest routes require a greater investment, which translates into greater benefits in the form of physical capital (Bourdieu, 1986). With mountaineering, this capital has become more easily accessible to a greater number of people. However, this is occurring in a context of control within which adventure tourism can be located. Guides are part of the structure of this control, and paying clientele help to sustain it. Thus, despite ongoing changes to the social scene, the distinctive position of guides is maintained.

One of the changes that has facilitated this development is the commodification of mountain spaces. Edensor (1998) is concerned with tourist spaces. Heterogeneous space, he explains, is about freedom to move and self-expression. Enclavic space is about constraint and convention. Mountains are symbolic of freedom and adventure and therefore seem more closely aligned to the conceptualization of heterogeneous space. However, today we can see a shift to the enclavic: many mountains have urbanized by providing footpaths and signposts, access agreements, bylaws, car parks, rest areas with refreshments, and rangers (see Figure 7.3). Such developments are in many instances management responses to increasing demands upon a fragile mountain environment; however, adventure tourism has made a significant contribution to that demand.

New social forms are superseding mountaineering club structures, that is, the way mountaineers have traditionally organized themselves. Johnson and Edwards (1994) acknowledge a significant increase in the number of those enjoying mountain recreation, many of whom who will not belong to a mountaineering club. Increasingly, they argue, this increase is closely aligned with changes in the relationship between people and mountains as the latter become increasingly commodified. Clearly such an influx of participants has not been the sole responsibility of mountaineering clubs. Indeed, the enduring tradition surrounding the notion of apprenticeship appears outdated in the postmodern conditions in which Bauman (1991; 1996) suggests we currently live. It is therefore more likely that any new social configurations that are recognizable under present social circumstances are closer to Hetherington's (1996) conceptualization of "sociations." The characteristics of sociations are dominated by temporariness and transition. Perhaps the enduring message is to live for the moment.

Paying clientele feed the commercial interests of companies that can control the process of capital acquisition from the "dream stage" (brochures and slide shows) right through the mountain experience itself (choreography of the trek, expedition, or climb) through reinforcement of achievements (post trip reunions), which in turn circles forward to the next "dream phase." By paying for mountain-based adventure holidays, clients are contributing to changes in the social world of mountaineering. The remaining sections present data to support such theoretical ideas. Two contrasting case studies explore degrees of the exotic in adventure tourism. Research findings from company managers, guides, client brochures, and magazines are utilized to explore salient issues in the contemporary mountain adventure tourism scene.

## *CASE STUDY 1: TREKKING IN NEPAL*

*High Mountain Sports* magazine sums up why a particular client chose to vacation in the biggest mountains in the world:

The prospect of a trek in the Himalayas stimulates the taste for adventure, the imagination can run wild before you go. Whatever the circumstances you are resolved to have a good time. Trips to the mountains are as much for talking about once they are completed as they are for the actual participation. (Greaves, 1990: 38)

Trekking in Nepal was founded by Jimmy Roberts. He was responsible for setting up the first trekking agency in Kathmandu. As a Western trekker/entrepreneur he settled in Nepal and, together with other prominent Westerners such as Mike Cheyney, provided the impetus for rapid expansion of this form of tourism in the country. Barely thirty years later there are over 200 trekking agencies in Kathmandu alone (Scott, 1994). In the period between 1950 and 1965 most unclimbed mountains in the Himalayas were conquered. This became the golden age of Himalayan mountaineering (Frison-Roche and Jouty, 1996). The Chinese invasion of Tibet effectively closed access to the Himalayas from the north in 1950, but Nepal simultaneously opened its borders to adventure tourists and travelers. In 1958 Colonel J. Roberts was appointed to the newly created post of military attaché at the British Embassy in Kathmandu. He retired from the army shortly thereafter but continued living in Kathmandu.

From his adopted home in Kathmandu, Roberts set about applying the wealth of experience he gained from his own exploratory journeys and expeditions throughout the greater Himalayas over a period of many years to the pragmatic considerations of how to earn a living now that he had retired from the military. Trek, originally a Boer word referring to a pioneering exodus, in the context of the Himalayas came to mean travel through the mountains using predominantly lightweight camping equipment (see Figure 7.6).

The concept Roberts introduced in Nepal brought together the traditional perspectives of the Victorian-Edwardian gentleman traveler (heavy duty tent, bath, crockery, and camp furniture) which he had observed in Kashmir and his own experiences of Himalayan expeditions. This latter perspective was certainly more austere, pragmatic, and lightweight. For example, in planning for his early treks for eight people Roberts initially wrote eight tents down in his notes but subsequently changed this to four when his lightweight rationale led him to exclaim, "let 'em share!" (Roberts, 1994: 53).

FIGURE 7.6. Rudimentary accommodation at Hoper in the Karakoram Himalayas. (Photo by P. Beedie.)

So the principle of paying clients needing a degree of comfort, but not to the detriment of progress through the mountains, was established as early as 1964 when Roberts officially retired from the army. In that same year his trekking agency, Mountain Travel, was registered with the Nepalese government and he put out advertisements in *Holiday* magazine. When requests for further information arrived, he had to send out handwritten replies as Kathmandu did not possess a typewriter. This is a far cry from the instantaneous electronic communication we enjoy today via fax machines and e-mail.

As a result of his early advertising efforts Roberts ran his first trek in 1965. He guided three women into the Khumbu area below Everest. It was his first trek and it set a precedent that threw an economic lifeline to the poverty-stricken Khumbu, which was suffering through declining trade with Tibet, itself a manifestation of the Chinese occupation of that country. The Khumbu embraced trekking tourism and now, predominantly through its geographical proximity to Everest, it has become one of the most popular trekking areas in the Himalayas. In 1976 both India and Pakistan, recognizing the tourist potential of their own sections of the Greater Himalayas, opened their borders. In the 1980s China followed the trend and allowed tourists into its Tibetan enclave. But it is Nepal that has led the way and set the precedents for trekking developments. In the words of Roberts, "Nepal did not invent hotels or aeroplanes but it did invent trekking tourism as we know it today" (Roberts, 1994: 55).

In 1987, 40,000 trekking permits were issued by the Nepalese authorities. By 1992 this figure had risen to 72,000. Trekking is making a major contribution to the Nepalese economy (Roberts, 1994). In 1994, 300,000 tourists visited Nepal, the majority of them arriving at Kathmandu. The government projection was 1 million tourists by the year 2000 (Scott, 1994). Roberts would argue that the average trekker stays in the country longer than more conventional tourists and therefore contributes more to the economy than tourists who do little more than visit the sights in Kathmandu or Pokara. Roberts, although a trekker/entrepreneur himself, sees the benefits of his and others' initiatives for the Sherpas, particularly in poor areas such as the Khumbu (Cleare, 1998).

Others such as Doug Scott comment on the less welcome (to a Westerner) aspects of the development of a trekking infrastructure in Nepal. Scott is an internationally respected mountaineer with first ascents to his credit all over the world. He has organized and/or taken part in mountaineering and trekking expeditions in Nepal for many years. He was a successful summiteer on Bonington's 1975 Everest southwest face expedition, for example. He has also been able to earn a living from his climbs and expeditions for the majority of his working life. Scott's lavishly illustrated book *Himalayan Climber* (1992) contains many spectacular photographs of climbs and treks in Nepal as well as other parts of the Himalayas. Scott condemns the "high mountain tourist" (Scott, 1994: 57) and calls for severe constraints on trekking in Nepal. He argues that the commodification of Nepal's mountains is causing harm to both the land and the culture (see Figure 7.7). In addition, he argues that the right to explore the Himalayan mountains should be accessible only to those who have served a long mountaineering apprenticeship. Scott is a cofounder of the Specialist Trekking Cooperative which is a body run by Sherpas with a view to protecting them from the excesses of a free market economy. The embryonic monetary Nepalese economy does not have the controls common to a more sophisticated Western country. In this respect the

FIGURE 7.7. Trekking in the Himalayas: Scott (1994) argues that the commodification of Nepal's mountains is causing harm to both the land and the culture. (Photo by P. Beedie.)

cooperative serves a similar role to trade unions in the United Kingdom. In common with independent trekker/entrepreneurs Scott has concerns about the well-being of the indigenous people of Nepal when faced with the cultural and economic upheaval of the past thirty years. Yet he has also contributed to the commercialization of trekking himself as the mountains have afforded him a living.

Most trekking itineraries will be tight because the organizers want to be seen as providing value for money. The route, the spectacular views, and the ensuing photo opportunities will have been determined for the trekker. The views may indeed correspond to what the guidebooks, coffee table books, and brochures identify as spectacular, such as the sight of K2 from Concordia, for example (O'Connor, 1990; Renouf, 1990; Evans, 1986), but equally they may not. Therefore an element of social control is linked to what is politically and economically expedient. The highlights of a trek are signaled and signposted by brochures, posters, and ultimately by personal photographs and informal exchanges between trekkers. These are mechanisms through which the need for a mountain wilderness experience is generated. The tension evident between the old and traditional and the new structures and systems of adventure tourism is not unique to exotic mountain settings such as the Himalayas. Indeed, the holiday impetus is present in developed countries. The following section expands on the British adventure tourism base and its relationship to mountaineering.

## INFLUENCES UPON BRITISH ADVENTURE TOURISM

Three phases have occurred in the history of British mountaineering. Adventure tourism is a part of the latest phase from about the 1970s to the present day. Before this, in the first phase from the mid-nineteenth century to about 1930, was the era of the middle- and upper-class mountaineer. In this phase a leisured and wealthy elite were responsible for developing mountain-based sport and recreations. In the middle phase, between about 1930 and 1970, there were a number of important developments—notably, a significant increase in people walking and climbing from the working classes and the consolidation of an ethos that connected individual ambition to ability via a "mountain activity apprenticeship" (Scott, 1994; Connor, 1999). Connor, for example, discusses the position of the "blackboy," a title given to new members who were inexperienced as mountaineers, in the Creagh Dhu climbing club (Connor, 1999: 47-49). Mountain and moorland walking became a mass participation recreation in the same middle period (see Wallace, 1993: 1-17, for a discussion concerning the emergence of walking as a "respectable" recreation). Today, adventure tourists can bypass this apprenticeship and move quickly toward an accumulation of substantial mountaineering capital.

Paying to be guided in wild mountain country is not new. It has existed for as long as people have climbed, walked, and skied for sport. However, the social context of the mountain activity has changed. First came the Victorian amateur mountaineers who employed guides for their local knowledge (Frison-Roche and Jouty, 1996; Bernstein, 1989; Stephen, 1936). Then came the fiercely independent working-class mountaineers who challenged the land-owning hegemony (Donnelly, 1986). An alternative somewhat anarchic tradition emerged, typified by the Rock and Ice Club in Manchester, England (Whillans and Omerod, 1971; Gray, 1979;

Birkett, 1983; Peascod, 1985). Poor in leisure time and money, these climbers and walkers established a self-taught tradition that reflected the apprenticeships of the shipyards and factories from which they emerged. More recently this mode of engagement has been bypassed by aspirant climbers and walkers who are also poor in terms of leisure time but, significantly wealthy in a material sense. These people are adventure tourists. They rely on the expertise of others to provide the wherewithal to complete their adventure.

## THE ROLE OF THE GUIDE

Experts choreograph the formative experiences of their clients in mountains and offer suggestions as to future excursions. The mountain instructor who leads the treks, scrambles, and climbs that are the practical engagement in mountain adventure tourism is a professional who has gained his or her status through the accumulation of experience and technical expertise, which is usually represented by relevant qualifications. Qualifications convey status so that instructors, in turn, can convey authority. In the mountains, the guide is the expert. Guides can shape the mountaineering experience for paying clients in a number of ways. These methods operate to enhance the economic interests of the guide or company, and reinforce and ultimately define what is acceptable mountaineering practice. First, there are contributions to articles in magazines, video representations, and brochure designs. Second, a form of control over clientele is exerted through the establishment of grading criteria for walks, treks, climbs, and expeditions. Third, in the mountains, the guide choreographs the detail of the experience by selecting where to walk, when to stop to admire the view, how the group is positioned on and off the rope, and so forth. The following data illustrate these points.

Many mountain days are wet and windy with clouds and poor visibility. Such a situation is common in British mountains but may appear threatening to those who lack experience, particularly when images of blue skies and dry rocks, which are commonly found in outdoor magazines, are mismatched with reality. Such a situation does, however, have a positive side for one guide: "I like getting up there and showing them how its done by sorting it out. It might be claggy, but we'll still find our way around. It establishes our credentials" (Beedie, 2002: 256). When asked whether clients were directed in their choices by his recommendations, one director replied:

> I think it's largely our recommendation, I don't think the brochure yet adequately reflects what we can do. We are learning as we go along, but I think it's fair to say that most people have come because I've suggested the idea to them. . . . The first contact is with me, the Web site, or the brochure. Second is gathering information by measuring themselves against the things we are describing. (Beedie, 2002: 263)

The guide's greater experience is further demonstrated by discussing details of the mountains to be attempted. In a very direct way this can occur at the start of the actual route. For example, below the impressive east face of Naranjo de Bulnes in northern Spain, a guide described the route to his clients:

> . . . it starts up these grooves, climbs out onto a big stance below a short unprotected wall, up this and trending left to that huge red corner which can be an epic struggle . . . up the wall above and onto the crest behind that pinnacle . . . emerging onto the summit ridge beyond where we can see from here. (Beedie, 2002: 118)

In a less obvious way, general discussion, whether out in the hills or at the pub or hostel, gives the guide an opportunity to describe details of routes that are of concern to the client. For example, on the isle of Skye, the Inaccessible Pinnacle is considered to be the hardest of all Munros (a Munro is a distinctive Scottish mountain over 3,000 feet) to ascend because it requires hands-on rock climbing whichever route is chosen. Climbing the "In Pinn" is a key objective for many clients. One client said, "I'm going to climb this today because although I might be back at this spot by myself at some time in the future I'm never going to be here with guides and all these ropes" (Beedie, 2002: 240). On the summit of the Inaccessible Pinnacle, where he had been organizing the lowering off of each summiting client, the guide asked if anyone else wanted to come up while he was there. No one else did, and, having completed the main task of the day, he promptly did a handstand on the summit (see Figure 7.8).

FIGURE 7.8. Climbing the Inaccessible Pinnacle on the Cuillin Ridge, Isle of Skye, Scotland. (Photo by P. Beedie.)

Having briefed the clients about what to wear, what to carry, and about the objectives for the day and how the logistics might unfold given the prevalent weather conditions, guide and clients emerge from the bothy, hostel, or car to begin the day in the mountains. Here, the role that the guide performs transforms from words to action. The guide becomes the director of operations, an actor (Goffman, 1959), or a choreographer (Edensor, 1998). Behavior on the hills becomes a performance. The guide does what his title suggests and the clients follow or are guided. Defending an accusation that he might have to haul a client up a route, one guide's response was:

> ... the whole skill of guiding clients in the mountains is to use route choice and rope work in ways that hopefully eliminate the need to haul anyone up anything. Skill and experience are always more important than strength. (Beedie, 2002: 279)

The guide therefore appears to exude confidence based on good route choice and sensible use of tools such as rope, slings, and carabiners. The performance is consistent and professional; if it were otherwise the guide would get no business.

The lack of experience that some clients have in British mountains can put pressure on the guide to achieve, particularly when the client expects to see a return on their financial investment in the trip. This was succinctly expressed by one guide:

> When a client is paying to achieve a specific aim in the mountains, and the weather is good, they never experience the down side of the mountains—like bad weather—that prevents you getting up. So they don't appreciate it in the same way we do. They have no real experience as a yardstick. They don't understand why you can't just go and do anything in the mountains. (Beedie, 2002: 259)

The gulf between a client's grasp of a situation and the guide's may be considerable, as the following extract from a guide illustrates:

> I think that the reason they [the clients] are buying in to the experience is that they want to be organized by someone. If they researched the trip, trained, planned it, made the contacts, and sorted out travel for themselves then they wouldn't come to FMA [Foundry Mountain Activities]; they'd go by themselves. What they need is some indication of when they should be getting up, what they should pack, and what they should do in order to get to the top. I had to take a pair of leather casual shoes out of Hugh's rucksack, for example. It's our job to get that balance right, so that it is happening in the background without being too up front. Because if you are going to take a military approach to it then it wouldn't be a holiday. But it needs to be sufficiently thought through and controlled that the background activity is maximising [sic] a client's chances of achieving the objective.

And having a good time along the way . . . A lot of people today are working very hard and putting in long hours. Living in London, say, people don't have time to join a mountaineering club or to go out and gain mountain skills. So they short-circuit it and go straight in with people who have been around the mountains a bit and know what's out there to be done. (Beedie, 2002: 281)

## THE CONTROL OF INFORMATION

Extensive literature, many videos, and numerous magazines covering mountain recreation. Guides take photographs, for example, and many of these appear in brochures and at company slide-show presentations. These direct us toward objectives. One guide, who is also a director of an adventure tourism company, had this view on the brochures:

> The manufacturers are very keen to be associated with us and our guides, who get their badges and logos seen around. So that when the clients are going away on trips, connections are being made, as in, "I do like that jacket that he's got on, it looks comfortable and stylish and it's quick-drying and warm." At the moment we've got Wild Country, Lowe, and others all thinking that way. We have the latest gear and technology for our kit as well, so the clients feel cutting edge. We've got "offset friends" now with odd-shaped cams; we've got the newest harnesses and the sexiest chalk-bags. The clients see all this gear in operation and can see what they do or don't like. They go away from us right up to date on everything. We can show our commercial connections on our Web site, including Petzl, Wild Country, and so on. We are offering a good product here, but any good product has to continue to hit the spot in terms of what people are looking for. Image is about imagination. Them projecting themselves into what they want to do and what they want to be wearing when they do it. That's why the equipment shops take great care in their presentation by having lots of action poses and spectacular pictures on the walls. We can learn from that. (Beedie, 2002: 281-282)

Part of the control that experts place on mountain adventure tourism relates to measurement. If our mountaineering experiences equate to the accumulation of capital, then it seems logical that we will be interested in certain criteria such as how far, how high, and how difficult a walking route or a climb may be. To make such an assessment there is a need for objective criteria that categorize our activities. Rock climbs have always been graded using, in the traditional British context, a combination of overall seriousness (moderate, difficult, severe, very severe, extremely severe) with a numerical representation of the hardest moves on any one pitch (for example, the range 4a, 4b, and 4c generally covers the severe to very severe categories). It is therefore possible for a climber to know the grade of climb being undertaken. The grade of a new climb is established by the team completing the first ascent and then moderated by subsequent climbers. Over time the route is written up in a guidebook and revisited; the grade is adjusted as necessary every time the guidebook is updated. Guides and other experienced or expert climbers control this process, implicit in which is a hierarchy of achievement. Climbing guidebooks, which may have additional features such as a star system to distinguish the best climbs, therefore direct us toward certain crags and mountains at the expense of ignoring others. For any climber, including the paying client, the outlined system simultaneously creates feedback about the level of any specific achievement and a ladder of possibilities for the future.

Since the emergence of adventure tourism in the last third of the twentieth century, such measuring criteria have been applied to both walking and, more recently, scrambling routes. Grading criteria, which were much cruder and more embryonic in brochures as recently as six to eight years ago, now dominate certain pages as marketing expediency recognizes the implicit attractions of capital accumulation alongside the more immediate considerations of demonstrating a duty of care to clients by matching their experience to specific itineraries. This process of grading and rationalization is not exclusive to paying clientele in adventure tourism but is part of broader processes of cultural change. The case of scrambling is a particularly interesting example. A spate of scrambling guidebooks has been published over the past ten years focusing on popular mountain regions such as Snowdonia and the Lake District. Most British mountains can be ascended by simply walking a route. Some have climbing routes on their steeper faces. Scrambling offers a hybrid activity between these two extremes. Scrambling routes offer interesting ways up mountains that are off the beaten path but not as serious as climbs. Nevertheless, sound judgment concerning route selection and movement over potentially loose rock is paramount, and it is no coincidence that adventure tourism companies are among the experts competing for clients interested in this activity. Foundry Mountain Activities (FMA) offers a "Scrambles in Snowdonia" course (FMA Brochure, 2000). It follows that, once such an activity becomes established as part of the British mountain scene, a grading system will emerge whereby levels can be quantified of achievement. *The Black Cuillin Ridge Scrambler's Guide* provides an example:

> In the descriptions each scramble has been graded . . . many of the routes are not literally easy, sometimes even by climbing standards, and drawing distinctions within the very wide "easy" classification should assist those in need of guidance in this matter. (Bull, 1980: 10-11)

The criteria for grading, and to some extent the geographical context, are established by experts.

## THE IMPORTANCE OF
## TECHNOLOGICAL DEVELOPMENTS

Technology has had a general impact on mountain sport in that it is easier to get to the mountains by roads and air travel, for example. More specifically, technological developments impact practical matters such as how comfortable we are able to feel in adverse weather. Comfort is about clothing and equipment (physical), and also about connections to the outside world (psychological). A guide commented:

> I think we have to be careful about pushing too far. It is interesting how many clients take mobile phones. Nowhere on our kit lists does it say "take a mobile phone," yet most clients have them. So it is no longer about leaving everything behind. (Beedie, 2002: 282)

Clothing makes us feel more comfortable but equipment is more than this. It is a facilitator. For example, trekking poles aid balance and movement in rough terrain and climbing shoes with sticky soles aid movement on rock. Using such technology, ordinary people can now attempt walks and climbs that were once preserved for an elite group of dedicated mountaineers (see Figure 7.9).

Figure 7.3 illustrated how frames can merge, and here is another example. The boundaries between tourist and climber become blurred, as the mountain is engineered for safety. For the clients undertaking more demanding mountaineering holidays, as in offered by Jagged Globe and FMA, there is resentment at being viewed as tourists when they clearly identify more strongly with climbers. Indeed, their accumulated experience may be considerable.

A glance through any of the mountain activity magazines will consolidate for the reader an image of the contemporary mountain scene. This literature is full of spectacular images of mountains and those who use them for sport and recreation. The pictures and text are amply complemented by advertisements from retailers and manufacturers and almost every one of these magazines has a gear assessment section. It could be argued that these magazines influence behavior in their readers in two ways. The first is through the concept of the role model. Climbers and walkers at the cutting edge of mountaineering developments offer us a level of performance to which we can aspire.

FIGURE 7.9. Guiding made safe: A climber clipped to a metal wire in the Austrian Tyrol. (Photo by P. Beedie.)

These significant individuals, whether consciously, unconsciously, or by more subtle means such as editorial expediency, set the trends. Recent front-cover photographs from magazines show British climbers in exciting positions wearing shorts and singlets (*High Mountain Sports,* 1999b; *Summit,* 1999) climbing in sticky rubber rock boots but without helmets. This has become popular attire for many climbers. Another example is the spectacular cover shot of a climber involved in deepwater soloing (*High Mountain Sports,* 1999a). This variety of rock climbing, in which the climber wears nothing but swimming gear and rock boots (although the photograph discussed clearly shows two armbands clipped to the climber's waist) and climbs unroped up and around cliffs that drop directly into the sea, is becoming very popular. Published next to articles in the press (*High Mountain Sports,* 1999a: 14-17) are advertisements depicting a new video of this activity (*High Mountain Sports,* 2000: 89; *Summit,* 1999: 33). Deepwater soloing is not just for pioneering experts as dialogue with one client suggests: "More and more climbers, particularly like me from London, are heading for the south coast. It's cool, and there are some wicked routes!" (Beedie, 2002: 210).

Another example of the power these magazines have with regard to influencing behavior among climbers in general is that few climbers wear helmets. The magazines show that aspirant "hard" climbers rarely wear helmets (*High Mountain Sports,* 1999a: 26-29; 1999b: 12-15; *Summit,* 1999: 9). In contrast, off-road cycling images clearly connect helmet and rider (*Trail,* 1998a: 112-113, 116-117; 1999: 136-137, for example). A similar analysis from walking magazines demonstrates how trekking poles, a walking accessory integrated from skiing, have become an important part of a hill walker's presentation (see Figure 7.7) (*Trail,* 1998b: 7, 12, 15, 83, 108; 1998a: 19, 62-65, 87, 109; *The Great Outdoors,* 1995: cover).

A second way that magazines might influence presentation and behavior is through the ubiquitous gear section. Here, experienced outdoor practitioners wear specific garments or use certain pieces of equipment for a period of time and then report on them. These reports are organized thematically, edited, and presented via the magazines. In the final assessment certain criteria are established, commonly objectively definable ones such as cost, size, weight, capacity, waterproofing, and some more subjective criteria such as feel and comfort, and direct comparisons made usually with a star system. It is clear from discussions with clients that the gear section is popular with readers. For example, one client bought his waterproof jacket and trousers on the recommendation of the gear reviewer in *Trail* magazine. Indeed, he has a subscription to *Trail* magazine:

> . . . not just because it is packed full of useful information but also because their introductory offer included a free K.I.S.U. [a lightweight emergency shelter] which has got to be worth sixty quid by itself! (Beedie, 2002: 211)

The presence of experts (Bauman, 1991:200; Giddens, 1990) supersedes the need for the individual to make choices for himself or herself. Sometimes, however, when those choices have already been made, it is merely an endorsement of choice that an individual seeks. One male client, with an impressive list of guided mountain ascents from around the world, has accumulated mountaineering experiences that might be the envy of many experts in this field. He had, however, brought four pairs of boots to a pretrip gathering because "I still need to sort out my crampon situation" (Beedie, 2002: 277). His decision still needed to be deferred to the expert even though technology and fashion have now merged.

We are safer and more comfortable in mountains today than at any time in the past. However, when people accept a certain insulation from the elements, and this is combined with a deferment of decision making to experts who guide the mountain experience in every sense of the word, the nature of the experience is changed. The idea of adventure, crucial to the sport of mountaineering, is diminished in relation to an increase in the business of tourism. The following case study demonstrates the extent to which adventure tourism has absorbed characteristics of business.

## *CASE STUDY 2: THE FOUNDRY CLIMBING CENTRE*

The opening paragraph from the Foundry Mountain Activities Web site encapsulates the notion of mountain-based adventure tourism:

> Great Adventure holidays encompass many superb mountain challenges. They offer something for everyone with a taste for mountains and adventure. With the focus on a specific achievement or ascent, each trip is selected for its unique qualities; they

aim to sample the best that an area has to offer and range from a weekend in Britain to several weeks in the Himalayas. Many of our Great Adventures are suitable for the novice and require nothing more than good health. Others are physically testing and require hill fitness and some technical ability. We will guide, teach skills and can even hire you the right gear. Many of our clients choose to tick off several over the years as their ability improves. There will be many more to choose from in the future as we search for outstanding things to do around the world. Order an itinerary or call the office to choose the right trip and join us for a satisfactory combination of stunning scenery, new skills and a real personal achievement. (<www.greatadventures. co.uk/great.html>)

Foundry Mountain Activities (FMA) began in 1991 as a service to groups of novices who wanted to use the new Foundry indoor climbing wall to learn how to climb (Figure 7.10). To more fully understand how FMA has expanded to include adventure tourism within its present activities it is instructive to examine the history of the Foundry Climbing Centre.

Sheffield has always been a geographical focus for the British climbing and mountaineering scene. It is a substantial urban area close to the Peak District, which contains a multitude of gritstone and limestone climbing venues amid its sweeping moorlands (the Dark Peak) and deeply incised valleys (the White Peak). Sheffield has an active mountaineering history emphasized by the close juxtaposition of city and what has been, since 1951, a national park (Milburn, 1997). Political activity to generate access to climbing and walking possibilities in the Peak District can be traced back at least as far as the formation of the Commons and Open Spaces Preservation Society in 1865, which had an influential group in Sheffield. Climbers and walkers were united in their desire to practice their respective activities in the Peak District, however climbing has an integral hierarchy of achievement built into the activity through the grading system and is more overtly competitive than walking. The result is that climbers performing at the cutting edge of the activity are concerned with an exploration of technical difficulty. Standards in climbing, aided by guidebooks and technical innovation, have evolved with each generation of climbers. The 1970s saw the beginnings of scientifically based training regimes in the climbing scene and Sheffield became famous for its "climbing cellars." In these esoteric attics, garages, and other improvized indoor spaces, cutting-edge climbers trained on homemade plywood and wooden holds, through the winter months in particular, and emerged each time the sun came out long enough to allow rock climbing in the Peak District to be a pleasurable experience. The Foundry indoor climbing wall opened in 1991 and, without any advertising other than word of mouth, immediately catered to 500 climbers a day throughout the winter of 1991-1992. The market for this dedicated climbing facility was already in place.

FIGURE 7.10. The Foundry Climbing Centre, Sheffield, United Kingdom. (Photo by P. Beedie.)

The site on Mowbray Street was identified in 1990. Three climbing businessmen, Paul Reeve (working in telecommunications), Jerry Moffat (a professional climber of international renown), and Mark Valence (the founder of outdoor retail manufacturers Wild Country), entered into partnership to develop the site as an indoor climbing complex. Indoor climbing walls for training and introducing novices to the activity had existed for many years in Britain, but many were designed by architects, not climbers, and most were part of a bigger sport-and-leisure complex that compromised the wall's potential for use by serious climbing clientele. The Foundry, in contrast, claimed to be the first dedicated indoor climbing wall in Britain. Mile End in London opened in 1988 and has been constantly developed ever since, but the Foundry was of a different scale with more potential to expand both upward and sideways.

The early success of the Foundry occurred for a number of reasons, including a ready-made market, the dedicated nature of the facility, and Sheffield's proximity to the M1 motorway, which facilitated a national attraction of users from as far away as London, Bristol, Manchester, and Newcastle. Other factors accounting for its early success included opportunities to climb day or night, training facilities, social factors such as meeting points for climbers, opportunities for display and identity formation, and opportunities for formal and informal competition. The Foundry clearly fulfilled a niche market through the provision of an indoor, minimum-risk environment. Perhaps the most important point to consider, however, is the way in which the climbing experience was beginning to change. The Foundry offered an indoor adventure; it was varied and offered attractive and spectacular climbing that was exciting, even thrilling, but the risks were probably more closely aligned to potential social gaffs, such as wearing the wrong clothes, than they were to objective dangers (there is certainly no danger of rock falls and it is rare to see climbers wearing helmets when climbing at the Foundry). The experience is managed and facilitated by experts, and the parameters are closely defined and controlled. This is part of the attraction.

Such was the initial success of the Foundry wall, where climbers were prepared to pay £3.50 to £4.50 for a climbing session. Dedicated climbing centers mushroomed in other British cities: Mile End (London), Rock Face (Birmingham), Werbergh's Church (Bristol), Berghaus Wall (Newcastle), Rope Race (Stockport), and The Edge (Sheffield). Attendance at the Foundry began to fall in the 1990s, which was exacerbated by the seasonal variations that had always existed. Peaks of attendance usually occur from late autumn through spring, and weekly peaks on Wednesdays and weekends. The Foundry responded to this competition by diversifying its offerings, and it is this process that has created the critical mass that sustains the Foundry Climbing Centre today. Over a period of several years the following facilities and services were added to the Centre: Foundry Mountain Activities; travel and insurance packages aligned to membership initiatives; a sports injuries facility; training room, bouldering wall (low-level unroped climbing), and a second leading wall called The Furnace; a climbing shop (part of the Outside chain); changing rooms, showers; a warm-up traversing wall in a corridor; a café and viewing gallery; the Spider Club (for children aged six to eleven), and the Junior Club (for children aged eleven to sixteen); and a climbing holds factory (S7, owned by climber Ben Moon). Moreover, in 1997, a branch of the adventure tourist company Himalayan Kingdoms, which specializes in expeditions to mountain summits, located itself at the Foundry Climbing Centre and has since consolidated its position in the world market and renamed itself Jagged Globe. A similar but smaller-scale metamorphosis was undertaken by Tim Gould, director of Foundry Mountain Activities. Recognizing the potential of the adventure tourist market, and taking advantage of the critical mass generated by the center's diversification and the arrival of Jagged Globe in particular, FMA expanded its activities from basic climbing courses, outdoor education, and management training to include adventure tourism in the form of its program of Great Adventures. The most popular courses in the FMA brochure for adventure tourists are the itineraries based around the Cuillin Ridge on Skye Island, Scotland, and Naranjo de Bulnes, a spectacular mountain in the Picos de Europa in Northern Spain. FMA and Jagged Globe operate symbiotically to support each other's adventure tourist itineraries because they are not direct rivals in the marketplace. Rather, they both benefit from their location at the Foundry Climbing Centre in Sheffield.

## CONCLUSION: THE FUTURE

We are living longer and many of us are retiring sooner. It is estimated that by 2040 over half the population in the developed world will be over fifty. This means more people in good health with a more informed global perspective—more GRAMPIES—thus more adventure tourists. The lines between adventure and mainstream tourism will become less clearly defined. Adventure will become more accessible and achievable for more people. Moreover, adventure holidays will become more attractive as the collection of experiences begins to undermine the more materialistic elements of consumer society. This is consistent with Bourdieu's (1986) notion of symbolic capital.

The world is becoming increasingly familiar through media-generated symbols and images. Enclavic space that was once predominant in urban areas and tourist honeypots is invading the wilderness. In addition, in a social sense the "old school," for example, of mountaineers and mountaineering traditions, will continue to be eroded and soon will exist only in museums and heritage centers— although these too will become tourists attractions. New social configurations, such as associations, will emerge as we become more playful in our sense of identity and more confident in enjoying the adventure tourist vacation in whichever way we like.

Adventure tourism will become more akin to business enterprise, or will even become an industry comparable to skiing as the market becomes dominated by a relatively small number of international companies. Each company will retain a substantial nucleus of clientele that might be described as "serial adventure tourists." Currently, 60 percent of all Himalayan Kingdom clients have already completed at least one holiday with the company. The big companies will survive because of the breadth of itineraries they can offer, thus retaining the attractiveness of the novel and new. Mountains will move away from notions of heterogeneous space as enclavic controls gain ground. Our curiosity about adventure and the need to be challenged will not diminish, but the tension that currently exists between old and new traditions of mountaineering will become irrelevant as the mechanisms controlling how adventure is packaged and sold become more sophisticated. An example is the way that itineraries are currently packaged as environmentally sensitive, an idea that empathizes with our existing knowledgeable and educated perspective on environmental impact.

Adventure tourism will continue to grow, and the risks inherent in the activities will appear to diminish as our knowledge, experience and technical capacity increases. However, the risks can never be eliminated; there will continue to be disasters such as the one on Everest in 1996 and the rafting tragedy in Austria in 1999. The higher the profile of such mishaps in the media, paradoxically, the more attractive adventure tourism becomes—not least because there is almost certainly an immediate response from management and other authorities, which reaffirms our perceived control over nature. The physical component of adventure tourism is a crucial part of the attraction: it is seductive and alluring because it makes us feel alive. Adventure tourism allows the expressive and the irrational in us all out to play, and the more people that realize the exhilaration is possible, the more they will want to participate in it.

### *RELEVANT WEB SITES*

www.bugbog.com: Diverse range of cultural adventures, well-organized example of an electronic brochure.

www.greatadventures.co.uk: Foundry Mountain Activities Web site.

www.rockandice.co.uk: Small company offering specialized courses including training.

www.jagged-globe.co.uk: International market leader for ascents of world's most famous mountains. Note the grading system.

www.lonelyplanet.com: *The* guidebooks for international travel.

www.tangentexp.demon.co.uk: Small but highly specialized adventure holidays in Greenland.

www.fieldandtrek.com: British company selling equipment and clothing for outdoor recreation, specializing in mail order. Free brochure on request.

www.9feet.com: Cutting edge Web presentations appealing predominantly to "latest generation" of adventurers.

www.snozonemk.co.uk: Skiing on real snow indoors—part of a huge outdoor recreation shopping mall at Milton Keynes. This is where dreams are nurtured!

### REFERENCES

Bauman, Z. (1991). *Modernity and Ambivalence.* Cambridge: Polity Press.

Bauman, Z. (1996). From pilgrim to tourist—or a short history of identity. In Hall, S. and Du Gay, P. (Eds.) *Questions of Cultural Identity,* (pp. 15-35). London: Sage.

Beedie, P. (2002). *Mountain-Based Adventure Tourism*. Doctoral thesis. Unpublished.

Bernbaum, E. (1997). *Sacred Mountains of the World*. London: University of California Press.

Bernstein, J. [1965] (1989). *Ascent: The Invention of Mountain Climbing and Its Practice*. New York: Simon and Schuster.

*Birds* Magazine (2000). Winter: Royal Society for the Protection of Birds.

Birkett, B. (1983). *Lakeland's Greatest Pioneers*. London: Robert Hale.

Bourdieu, P. (1986). *Distinction*. London: Routledge.

British Broadcasting Corporation (BBC) (2001). Death on Everest: An exploration of adventure tourism, broadcast: August 10.

Bull, S. (1980). *Black Cuillin Ridge Scrambler's Guide*. Edinburgh: Scottish Mountaineering Trust.

Christiansen, D. (1990). Adventure tourism. In Miles, J. and Priest, S. (1990) *Adventure Education*, (pp. 432-441). State College, PA: Venture Publishing.

Cleare, J. (1998). Obituary for Jimmy Roberts. *High Mountain Sports*, 183:66-67.

Collister, R. (1984). Adventure versus the mountain. *The Alpine Journal*, 89:123-125.

Connor, J. (1999). *Creagh Dhu Climber: The Life and Times of John Cunningham*. Hong Kong: Ernest Press.

Donnelly, P. (1986). The paradox of parks: Politics of recreational landuse before and after the mass trespass. *Leisure Studies*, 5(2):187-200.

Edensor, T. (1998). *Tourists at the Taj*. London: Routledge.

Evans, I. (1986). Karakoram trek. *High Mountain Sports*, 42:31-33.

Feifer, M. (1985). *Going Places*. London: Macmillan.

Foundry Mountain Activities (2000). Brochure. Sheffield.

Frison-Roche, R. and Jouty, S. (1996). *A History of Mountain Climbing*. New York: Flammarion.

Giddens, A. (1990). *The Consequences of Modernity*. Cambridge: Polity Press.

Goffman, E. (1959). *The Presentation of Self in Everyday Life*. Harmondsworth: Penguin.

Gray, D. (1979). *Rope Boy*. London: Gollancz.

*The Great Outdoors* (1995). April.

Greaves, V. (1990). A Himalayan Trek. *High Mountain Sports*, 97:38-39.

Greenway, R. (1995). Healing by the wilderness experience. In Rothenberg, D. (Ed.), *Wild Ideas* (pp. 182-193). Minnesota: University of Minnesota Press.

Hamilton-Smith, E. (1993). In the Austalian bush: Some reflections on serious leisure. *World Recreation and Leisure*, 35(1):10-13.

Hendon, W. (1991). The wilderness as a source of recreation and renewal. *American Journal of Economics and Sociology*, 50(1):106-112.

Hetherington, K. (1996). Identity Formation, Space and Social Centrality. *Theory, Culture and Society*, 13(4):33-52.

*High Mountain Sports* (1999a). October, 203.

*High Mountain Sports* (1999b). September, 202.

*High Mountain Sports* (2000). January, 206.

Hudson, S. (2000). *Snow Business: A Study of the International Ski Industry*. London: Cassell.

Jarvie, G. and Maguire, J. (1994). *Sport and Leisure in Social Thought*. London: Routledge.

Jenkins, R. (1996). *Social Identity*. London: Routledge.

Johnson, B. and Edwards, T. (1994). The commodification of mountaineering. *Annals of Tourism Research*, 21(3):459-478.

Kelly, J. (1983). *Leisure Identities and Interactions*. London: George Allen and Unwin.

MacCannell, D. (1976). *The Tourist: A New Theory of The Leisure Class*. London: Macmillan.

Milburn, G. (1997). *The First Fifty Years of The British Mountaineering Council*. Manchester:BMC.

Miles, J. and Priest, S. (2000). *Adventure Programming*. State College, PA:Venture Publishing Inc.

*Observer Magazine* (2000). The cost of climbing Everest. September 10:7.

O'Connor, B. (1990). *Adventure Treks: Nepal*. Marlborough: Crowood Press.

Peascod, B. (1985). *Journey After Dawn*. Milnthorpe: Cicerone Press.

Price, T. [1974] (1978). Adventure by numbers. In Wilson, K. (1978) *The Games Climbers Play* (pp. 646-651). London: Diadem.

Renouf, L. (1990). Trek to K2. *High Mountain Sports*, 92:24-25.

Roberts, J. (1994). Trek: The Himalayan odyssey. *High Mountain Sports*, 140:50-55.

Rojek, C. and Urry, J. (1997). *Touring Cultures*. London: Routledge.

Rubens, D. (1999). Effort or performance: Keys to motivated learners in the outdoors. *Horizons*, 4:26-28.

Scott, D. (1992). *Himalayan Climber*. London: Diadem.

Scott, D. (1994). Trekking commentary. *High Mountain Sports*, 134:56-59.

Sharpley, R. (1994). *Tourism, Tourists and Society*. Huntingdon: Elm Publications.

Short, J. (1991). *Imagined Country: Environment, Culture and Society*. London: Routledge.

Stephen, L. [1894] (1936). *The Playground of Europe*. Oxford: Blackwell.

*Summit* (1999). Autumn, 15.

*Trail* (1998a). December.

*Trail* (1998b). May.

*Trail* (1999). February.

Trauer, B. (1999). Conceptualising adventure tourism and travel placed in the Australian context. Unpublished paper, University of Lancaster.

Urry, J. (1990). *The Tourist Gaze*. London: Sage.

Urry, J. (1995). *Consuming Places*. London: Routledge.

Visser, M. (1994). *The Way We Are*. Harmondsworth: Penguin.

Wallace, A. (1993). *Walking, Literature and English Culture*. Oxford: Clarendon Press.

Whillans, D. and Omerod, A. (1971). *Don Whillans: Portrait of A Mountaineer*. London: Heinemann.
Worldwide Journeys and Expeditions. (2000). Brochure. London.

## *Additional Sources of Information*

Bartlett, P. (1993). *The Undiscovered Country: The Reason We Climb*. Hong Kong: The Ernest Press.
Bezruchka, S. (1997). *Trekking in Nepal: A Travellers Guide*. Leicester: Cordee.
Cloke, P. and Perkins, H. (1998a). Cracking the canyon with the awesome foursome: Representations of adventure tourism in New Zealand. *Environment and Planning D: Society and Space,* 16:185-218.
Cloke, P. and Perkins, H. (1998b). Pushing the limits: Place, promotion and adventure tourism in the South Island of New Zealand. In Perkins, H. and Cushman, G. (1998). *Time Out: Leisure, Recreation and Tourism in New Zealand and Australia* (pp. 127-141). Auckland: Longman.
Lorimer, H. (2000). *De-Bagging The Munros: The Promotion and Commodification of Scotland's Mountains*. Glasgow: LSA Conference Paper.
Melucci, A. (1996). *The Playing Self: Person and Meaning in the Planetary Society*. Cambridge: Cambridge University Press.
Reed, D. (1997). *Nepal: The Rough Guide*. Reading: Penguin Books Ltd.
Weiler, B. and Hall, C. (1992). *Special Interest Tourism*. London: Belhaven Press.

# Chapter 8

# The Business of Adventure Tourism

Ross Cloutier

## INTRODUCTION

As the demand for adventure activities has increased, so has the interest of providers of commercial adventure in activities becoming profitable. The effort expended by a whole generation of outdoor recreationists to have their high-risk endeavors become widely recognized, economically viable, and socially acceptable activities has resulted in a completely new service industry of adventure tourism. As adventure sports have evolved from what has historically been seen by much of society as antiestablishment behavior to a more mainstream, significant economic generator, increasing emphasis has been placed upon their business operations and profit potential. This chapter considers a number of selected topics that pertain to the operation of an adventure tourism business.

## THE EVOLUTION FROM LIFESTYLE TO BUSINESS

Adventure tourism has developed partially because of the benefits that the lifestyle brings to those who work in it. International travel and extensive time outdoors in risk-supporting environments are activities that many adventurers seek out and thrive in. The ability to paddle, climb, or ski the majority of the year, explore new and exotic lands, and be responsible for much of the excitement and enthusiasm guests experience in the wilderness all affirm the desirability of the adventure tourism lifestyle.

Just as adventure tourism has its roots in its desirable lifestyle, its future lies in the application of business techniques. There has been tremendous recognition within the adventure guiding and tourism industries over the past decade of the potential profit in adventure sport activities. The application of good business management principles is no longer thought of as unnecessary; it is now a crucial element to ensure a financially rewarding living from the lifestyle of adventure.

Many longtime guides and adventurers have sacrificed large portions of their skiing or paddling time to take on the challenge of company start-ups and the pursuit of financial controls, marketing knowledge, personnel management, or Internet expertise as ways to improve their potential to make a living in the adventure industry. Their personal contacts from many years of working in the field form the basis for business start-ups, marketing contacts, training programs, and contract or consulting work. Entrepreneurial initiative and business skills have become important components to blend with outdoor-related skills in order for an adventure business to succeed and for the adventurer to make a living in their field of expertise.

Although development of commercial adventure activities is rooted in small, home-based businesses, the trend today is toward larger and more sophisticated operations. Economies of scale and scope have become desirable in order to compete for clients. This trend will continue, along with the accompanying demand for the necessary business skills to operate such firms.

## THE BUSINESS MOSAIC

For the guide in transition to becoming a business owner or new entrant to the industry, it is sometimes difficult to identify the necessary business skill sets required to be successful in business. Figure 8.1 illustrates the major knowledge areas that business owners need to acquire to operate a business effectively. In business activities, as in sport activities, individuals may have more aptitude or interest in certain areas over others such as marketing, over accounting, or administration over staff management. However, a healthy business needs these skills, and they must be either developed or hired within the staff group.

*Administration skills* refer to the logistical, planning, and administrative actions necessary for the business to operate. This may include business structure, permits, insurance, correspondence, filing, scheduling, and other administrative functions.

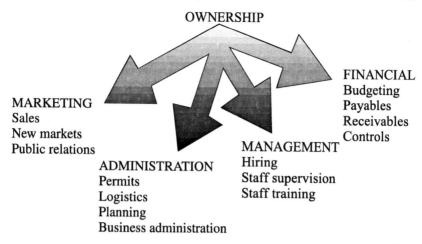

OWNERSHIP

MARKETING
Sales
New markets
Public relations

FINANCIAL
Budgeting
Payables
Receivables
Controls

ADMINISTRATION
Permits
Logistics
Planning
Business administration

MANAGEMENT
Hiring
Staff supervision
Staff training

PROFIT and VIABILITY

FIGURE 8.1. The business mosaic.

*Source:* Cloutier, K.R. (1998). *The Business of Adventure: Developing an Adventure Tourism Business.* Kamloops, BC: Bhudak Consultants, Ltd., p. 27. (Reprinted by permission.)

*Management skills* refer to the management of an office and guiding staff, in-house training requirements, risk management and safety controls, and other management functions that will make the business function effectively.

*Financial skills* refer to the planning and management of budgets, the management of money coming in and going out of the business, the allocation of financial resources to other elements, such as marketing, finding sources of investment funds, and the application of suitable financial controls to meet financial projections.

*Marketing skills* refer to the ability to identify new clientele, to clearly communicate the products offered to the customers, to price and sell the product, and to maintain a positive product and company image in the public eye.

## ADVENTURE BUSINESS ADMINISTRATION

### Business Structure

One of the decisions that must be made when starting a business concerns the legal form that the organization of the business will take. In many countries, this decision may include deciding whether the business should operate under a proprietorship in which the owner remains personally responsible for all business liabilities. Any income is claimed as personal income for tax purposes. Alternatively, the business could attempt to limit the liability of its owners and operate as a corporation. Aside from liability advantages a corporation may be sold more easily if it is a separate legal entity and the incorporated firm's structure is more receptive to investors through the sale of stock.

### Business Development Stages

Small businesses pass through identifiable life cycle or development stages as they grow and develop. Different businesses do not develop at the same speed, and many may stay in one stage for considerable periods of time. The transition from one stage to another often brings new and unique issues to deal with, and crises may develop as the business requires new levels of expertise or investment to thrive. Business owners need to be able to identify where their business is on its development curve and what additional management skills and financial resources are required to assist in the transition from one stage to another. Figure 8.2 shows the typical stages of business development that an adventure business goes through.

#### Inception and Incubation

The inception and incubation stages include the development of an idea and vision. The main priorities are those of its originator. Primary efforts revolve around creating a commercially viable product and testing it the marketplace. Emphasis is on creating a positive cash flow and developing sellable products. Products will evolve from either a market- or product-driven perspective. Market-driven products are developed when client demands dictate the types of adventure activities the business offers. Product-driven products are those not

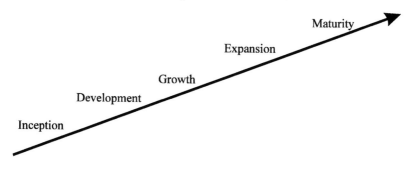

FIGURE 8.2. Business development stages.

driven by client demand but more upon the skills or interests of the operator.

## Development and Survival

Development and survival stages revolve around the development of both the business organization and its products. Many small adventure businesses remain in this stage for long periods of time. To develop the business there is a need to access financing to finance its operations and to finance the purchase of fixed assets. As the need for sales growth increases, so does the necessity to expand the customer base. This means diversifying, offering new products, increasing marketing channels, and possibly operating in new geographic locations. Such expansion affects the amount of control owners can have over operational matters and, as a result, many owners resist doing this.

## Growth

The growth stage typifies much of the adventure industry at the end of the twentieth century. Through the 1980s many adventure products were both developed and proven viable; the 1990s provided significant growth for the industry as a whole and for businesses that held a market position. By the time a business reaches this stage, it is likely to be profitable but may not be generating much equity for the owners since earnings may need to be retained and invested back into the business to finance further growth.

In most cases owners are able to sell a business at this point for substantial gains.

Businesses at this stage still require hands-on involvement of the owners in operational matters, however there are a limited number of individuals who possess this type of experience and who also have access to the funds necessary to purchase a business at this stage. Those who do have access to this level of financing may not feel comfortable with the financial risk associated with such a purchase. These factors create exit barriers to owners who want out of their businesses but find them too large to sell to another person with similar skills and interests. As a result, the adventure industry sees investors who are not necessarily adventurers entering the industry by buying businesses.

When owners of adventure businesses find they are unable to sell their business, it often has the result of making the business worth more "alive" than "dead." That is, the owner ends up operating the business to be able to take out money on an annual basis from operations rather than from the sale of the business.

Amalgamations, consolidations, and joint ventures are beginning to characterize the growth development stage within the adventure industry as ways for companies to become more cost-effective and to enable them to access new, further-afield trip offerings. In some cases, cost savings of up to 30 percent in overhead and administration are found as a result of amalgamating; in most cases this is as much or more than the business's profit percentage.

*Expansion and Maturity*

The expansion stage of a business is its period of maturation and includes activities such as acquisitions, franchising, and large market-growth drives for reasons of market power or defensive posturing. This is the most profitable stage for a business. In reality, relatively few adventure businesses have achieved this level. Most adventure operations are too new in their life cycle to have gone through the growth stage. However, successful examples include Mountain Travel Sobek, Canadian Mountain Holidays, and World Expeditions.

Cost controls, professional management, formal accounting systems, worldwide staff management, and markets characterize firms of this stage. Professionals needed for their business expertise, rather than their interest in adventure sports, will have been incorporated into the company's personnel by this stage.

## Business Start-Up versus Purchase

To date the majority of adventure businesses have been built from the ground up as a way of entering the marketplace. Entry barriers have been so few and surmountable that almost anyone with a desire to enter could do so. This has resulted in a plethora of new companies, most of which do not generate adequate revenue to survive more than a few years, while a smaller number have become successful and have established a market niche and long-term position in the marketplace.

Becoming more common as a way of entering the adventure industry is the practice of purchasing an existing business that has been developed from inception to the point where there is something tangible to sell, either in the way of facilities and equipment, or in terms of a customer base. A problem inherent in purchasing an existing business is how to value the business. There is obvious worth in a business's sweat equity, assets, permits, goodwill, and mailing lists—less clear is how to assign a monetary value to each of these items.

Each method of entry has obvious benefits. Starting a business from nothing enables a start-up group to enter the industry slowly, feeling its way along and thus determining both its own interest and that of its projected market. Purchasing a business has the effect of shorting the cycle of business development for the purchasing group since the business is acquired at a more advanced stage; much of the early uncertainty has been resolved and the sweat equity required in the early stages has already been contributed. Acquiring an existing business involves higher initial costs because the assets, goodwill, and sweat equity is being purchased all at once. However, the result may be a higher chance that the business will be successful.

Purchasing a business will undoubtedly become an increasingly important method of entering the adventure industry as influences such as lack of land use permits and saturation of market segments become more common in a mature industry.

## ADVENTURE BUSINESS MANAGEMENT

### Guides

Adventure tourism is a customer service industry which means that the focus of product development and how this product is presented is driven largely by customer needs and desires. This also means that members of the staff who come in direct contact with guests must focus on the guest and provide excellent service.

Individuals have historically been drawn to work within the various adventure activities because of a primary interest in an outdoor, travel-oriented lifestyle. These lifestyle operators have started most past and present adventure businesses. However, aside from their lifestyle interests, it often takes people some time to develop a client-centered approach and the necessary personal characteristics that make them successful in the industry.

Leading groups into a wilderness environment requires a broad range of skills and expertise on the part of guides. Figure 8.3 shows the types of skills that guides need to acquire to competently lead commercial groups. The diagram clearly shows the integrated nature of the knowledge, skills, and abilities of five primary task areas: interpersonal, safety, technique, environment, and culture.

The possession of an engaging personality and good *interpersonal skills* is paramount for leaders who are involved in working with both individuals and groups in instructional situations that can sometimes be long and stressful. A self-inventory might include an assessment of personal character, values, communication skills, leadership modeling, teaching ability, attitude, and judgment.

*Safety* refers to the all-encompassing nature of the guide's role in keeping guests healthy and safe with respect to hazards in the wilderness. This includes aspects of hygiene, diet, medical treatment and care, search and rescue, and the management of emergencies.

*Technique* refers to the requirement for a guide to be a highly skilled expert in the primary activity undertaken and with secondary and tertiary activities such as equipment use, equipment care, and food preparation. There is an expectation that the guide will have skills and background knowledge that far surpass the functioning levels of trip participants.

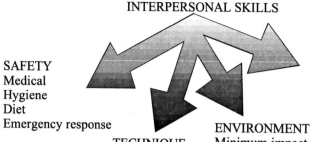

INTERPERSONAL SKILLS

SAFETY
Medical
Hygiene
Diet
Emergency response

TECHNIQUE
Skill performance
Food service
Equipment use
Qualifications

ENVIRONMENT
Minimum impact
Pollution
Education
Sustainable use

CULTURE
Languages
Art
Archaeology
Natural history
Anthropology

**EXPERIENCE and JUDGMENT**

FIGURE 8.3. The guiding mosaic.

*Environmental knowledge* refers to the guide's ability to impart to guests a respect for and an understanding of the natural resources upon which the adventure industry depends. This may include techniques of minimum-impact camping, educating guests as to pollution and litter control, or educating local residents in a third-world culture with respect to environmental stewardship or pollution issues. The larger picture may include teaching guests about land-use preservation or zoning issues to protect the natural resource base for future generations to use.

*Culture* refers to aspects of both foreign culture and local heritage. Guides who are leading groups in foreign countries are obliged to have a good understanding of the local language, art, archaeology, natural history, and anthropology. Part of the ability to add value to a guest's trip is to assist with the interpretation of the local culture and its people. Guides who are leading foreign clientele on local trips also have an obligation to interpret the heritage, history, and natural history. In most cases, people travel to other cultures, and others travel to ours, to explore and understand the diversity and differences between the two.

The underlying principle of the development of good guides is the necessity for broad experience levels and good judgment. It has been said that good judgment is the result of bad experience, and it is exactly this principle that is shown as the underlying aspect of guiding. It is imperative—regardless of a guide's academic background or industry qualification—that the experience level is broad, and judgment in both relaxed and stressful times is accurate.

## ADVENTURE BUSINESS FINANCE

The management of finances within a business is critical to the success of any firm. Within the adventure industry, financial management is playing a larger role in the viability of companies. As the adventure industry raises expectations and becomes more professional, and as companies become larger and more global, the financial officer of the company must manage the finances of both local and international operations. An understanding of finance is also critical to business owners who must determine how to finance the start-up or expansion of their dreams. Decision making concerning corporate strategies, investment decisions, cash flow difficulties, dividend payments, international politics, and currency exchanges is becoming more and more important for adventure companies.

### Current Asset Management

The financial manager must carefully allocate the resources of the company: cash, marketable securities, accounts receivable, and inventory.

Cash balances are largely determined by cash flowing through the company on a daily, weekly, monthly, or seasonal basis as determined by the type of business. Cash flow relies on the timeliness of customer payments and the speed at which suppliers and creditors request payments. The primary consideration in managing the cash flow is to ensure that the stream of revenue and expenses within a business is properly synchronized.

The sale of an adventure service to a guest produces either a cash sale or an account receivable (on credit), which will be collected some time in the future. When the account receivable is collected it becomes cash. By providing customers with credit (accounts receivable) one is making it easier for them to purchase services (which is positive), while at the same time reducing the amount of cash on hand (which is negative). For example, this credit may be provided offering thirty, sixty, or ninety days for customers to pay, requiring only a deposit at the point of sale and allowing the remainder of the fee to be paid later, or by allowing customers to purchase with short-term financing techniques such as credit cards. Decisions must be made thoughtfully regarding an accounts receivable policy, recognizing that it is a double-edged sword. On one hand it facilitates the sale, while on the other there is an opportunity cost to the business in not immediately having the cash on hand to invest or to pay for operating costs.

## Financing

Business managers access sources of funds that are external to the company when cash flows are inadequate for certain needs. Short-term funds are generally used to finance current operating expenses and temporary current assets while long-term funds are generally used to finance more permanent fixed assets. A business requires access to capital for start-up costs, the purchase of fixed assets, operating costs, and ultimately for expansion purposes. The business manager's choice of financing sources is one of the most important business decisions that will be made. Appropriate financing requires the forecasting and planning of future capital needs to have suitable access to funds for the business. It must also minimize the cost of these funds as much as possible. The issues become those of appropriate timing as well as affordability.

### Short-Term Financing

Short-term funds are those that generally need to be repaid in less than one year and might include credit cards, bank credit, and credit from suppliers.

The seasonal operating cycles that force adventure companies to incur highly fluctuating operating costs often make the need for various forms of short-term credit a necessity. Many small businesses do not have access to long-term capital and are forced to rely heavily on short-term bank and trade credit. This is risky for the company because if sales lag and cash flows are not as projected, the business may not be able to meet its short-term credit obligations.

*Savings, Friends, and Start-Ups.* The major sources of capital for adventure businesses during their start-up are often the personal savings, equipment, and credit of the business owners and a small circle of family and friends. This is generally a combination of personal cash savings that provide the initial start-up funds, the transfer of personal equipment to the business for operating use, and any short-term personal credit sources such as credit cards or lines of bank credit. This personal commitment by the owner is often combined with loans, or cosigners on loans, such as friends or relatives in order to expand the capital base available.

*Trade Credit.* Trade credit is provided when the manufacturer or seller of goods or services extends payment credit for a determined period of time (e.g., thirty days) and allows the purchaser to pay at a later date. For example, a rafting business is taking advantage of trade credit when it purchases its daily food at the local grocery store on account and receives an invoice at the end of every month. Over 40 percent of short-term financing is in the form of accounts payable (trade credit) (Block, Hirt, and Short, 1994, p. 282).

*Bank Credit.* Banks may provide short-term loans or lines of credit to businesses for the financing of operational or seasonal cash flow needs. In this case, the bank will primarily be concerned with the business's ability to generate adequate cash flow to meet payment demands.

## Long-Term Financing

Long-term funds generally consist of debt or equity financing terms of two years or more. They include stock, bank loans, the issuance of bonds, and mortgages. To protect against not being able to carry short-term financing during low cash flow periods, companies may rely on long-term financing to purchase fixed assets as well as to finance a portion of current asset (cash) needs. Established companies or companies with collateral tend to have better access to long-term funds than newer companies or those without a significant asset base. This is an issue for many adventure businesses today, and one which restricts the growth of many viable operations (and in fact the entire adventure industry) since they may not have the stability or the appropriate assets that banks or investors require to lend or invest long-term capital. As a result, many businesses operate using more expensive short-term credit.

*Common Stock.* Common stock (share) represents the ownership interest of the firm. Normally, each share represents one vote in electing the company's board of directors. The board members are responsible to the stockholders, and the stockholders have the authority to elect a new board if desired. As a form of financing, common stock provides the corporation's equity. Corporations sometimes create two classes of common stock, one of which does not have voting rights.

*Preferred Stock.* Preferred stock is a form of stock that has a fixed dividend (interest similar to a bond) which must be paid before common stock dividends can be paid. It has two important preferences over common stock: preference as to payment of dividends and preference as to stockholders' claims on the assets of the business in the event of bankruptcy. It is an equity security and represents an ownership interest in the company.

*Corporate Bond.* Bonds are long-term debt agreements issued by corporations (or governments) generally in units of $1,000 principal value per bond. Each bond represents two promises by the issuing organization: the promise to repay the $1,000 principal value at maturity and the promise to pay the stated interest rate (coupon rate) when due. Bonds are seeing increasing use by larger adventure companies as a way to raise capital.

*Lease Financing.* A long-term lease is an alternative to the purchase of an asset with borrowed funds. Such lease obligations are a form of long-term financing that must be shown on the balance sheet as debt. Leases are typically used as a form of financing when: (a) the business lacks the credit to purchase the asset but has the cash flow to pay the lease; (b) no down payment is required, which may assist the business's cash flow; (c) there may be tax benefits to leasing; and/or (d) risk-management considerations determine that it is better not to own the asset (i.e., vehicles).

*Mortgages.* Mortgages are loan agreements between a business and an investor or bank that require equipment or real estate as collateral for the loan. The issuance of the loan is tied directly to the value of the asset.

### Fixed and Variable Costs

The term *cost* can have different meanings depending on the context in which it is used. Costs are classified as either *fixed* or *variable*. Fixed costs are those expenses that do not vary with sales—expenses incurred whether or not any sales are made. Fixed costs may include such things as: marketing, insurance, depreciation, and administration costs.

Variable costs are expenses that vary directly with sales—those incurred only if sales are made and trips operate—and are often called operating expenses. Variable costs may include such things as: guest food, program expenses, wages for contracted guides, and transportation expenses.

Any revenue which remains after the business covers all variable and fixed costs is excess and becomes profit (net income) which the owners may spend as they see fit. If revenues do not cover both variable and fixed costs, the business loses money in that time period. When revenue covers both variable and fixed costs exactly the business breaks even.

### Bottom-Up Budgeting

One of the first financial tools that both guides and adventure operators develop is the bottom-up budgeting of a proposed trip. Bottom-up budgeting entails the construction of a trip budget that calculates and balances the trip revenue from participant registration numbers as well as the total costs of operating the trip.[1]

Total revenue is easily calculated by multiplying the number of expected trip participants by the amount charged for the trip. Total costs of the trip include the per-participant costs incurred by running the trip (variable costs), as well as a contribution to the firm's annual fixed costs and profit. The break-even point for the trip is calculated as the point at which the sales revenue covers:

1. The trip's per-participant operating expenses
2. A suitable portion of the firm's annual fixed expenses
3. A suitable portion of the firm's annual profit expectations

In order to construct bottom-up income statements for a business (or an individual trip budget) one must be able to accurately calculate both revenue and expense for the period.

## RISK MANAGEMENT

### What Risk Management Is

Risk management is a rational approach to the problem of dealing with the risks faced by a business. It is about managing or optimizing risks; it is not necessarily about eliminating them, because risk is inherent in adventure activities—and should remain so. Risk management is concerned with all types of risk, regardless of whether they are insurable or not, and it deals with choosing appropriate techniques for dealing with the hazards that the business could face.

Risk management should be viewed as a process, not as an individual technique or item. The risk-management process consists of:

- Determining exposure levels acceptable to the planning organization and its guests
- Identifying hazards to the business
- Evaluating those hazards
- Selecting finance and control alternatives
- Implementing mitigation strategies
- Planning appropriate responses to emergency incidents

Ultimately, the long list of things to be considered when developing a risk management strategy will be determined by the first bullet point—determining exposure levels that are acceptable to the organization and its guests.

The level of risk management applied is relative to business and guest tolerances. This is an important concept to grasp. Different businesses and their guests will have different tolerances to risk. Mitigating risk to a point below this will begin to impact guest experiences. There is no expectation by the court that all risk shall be eliminated from adventure activities because there is recognition that risk is inherent in adventure.

### Perspectives on Risk Management

Risk management is practiced for a variety of reasons and it is easy for a business operator to fall into the trap of adopting a narrow view of why it is carried out. Carrying out risk management to protect a business from litigation is often the first question to be answered: Did the business conform to statute and common law, and if it is sued, will it win? In addition, this question is easily expanded to include financial considerations: Will the business survive the incident and how can it reduce the financial consequences?

A higher-level consideration is the public relations impact: How will the business look in the public eye, and will the incident affect its image? A discerning operator will recognize that accidents result in increased publicity and media coverage, and very often, an incident will increase call volume for a business. How the incident is handled, however, becomes important to how the public perceives the business. Good accident management often results in increased business and public attention. Accidents tend to result in widespread media attention and publicity that most businesses could not afford to buy. Adventure consumers have short memories and a strong affinity for self-denial, thinking, "An accident will not happen to me."

The highest level of scrutiny for evaluating a risk-management program is likely the ethical and moral one. In other words, did the business display morally excellent behavior acceptable to the profession? Judgment by peers is made according to such criteria as justice, virtue, integrity, honesty, and fairness. The industry as a whole will judge whether the risk management practices carried out by the business met these criteria. For example, in waivers, the inclusion of negligence in assumption of risk statements is allowed by some legal jurisdictions, but is it really ethical or moral, and is it a principle on which the adventure industry should be able to rely? One perspective held by an increasing number of legal jurisdictions and operators is that requiring clients to sign away their rights to sue, even where the business is negligent, is unethical, if not immoral. Risk management at this level considers whether the business conforms to the expanded, ideal code of moral principles associated with a profession and whether the techniques applied conform with generally accepted societal standards of goodness or rightness.

Ultimately, risk management should create a balance between legal strategies intended to protect the worth and life of the business and the underlying professional and ethical values of its personnel. Whether the marketplace and insurance industry will accept the increased cost and higher risk of such an ethical approach remains to be seen.

## *Risk Management Techniques*

Risk management is acted out in a combination of risk-control and risk-financing techniques (see Figure 8.4). Risk-control techniques are intended to reduce or eliminate incidents; they include exposure avoidance, loss prevention, loss reduction, and loss sharing. Risk-financing techniques deal with financial considerations and include risk transfer through insurance, risk transfer through contract, risk transfer through participant assumption, and risk retention on the part of the organization. These risk-control and risk-financing techniques are carried out both before and after an incident through preventive and response strategies. In addition, guides and business operators both participate in pre- and postincident activities throughout the entire risk management process.

## *Risk Management Planning*

Risk management planning is carried out by developing a series of planning and policy documents for a business (see Figure 8.5). These documents might include any combination of materials developed under four primary categories: general business concerns, trip planning, staff training, and client materials.

### Risk Management Is:

**■ Risk Control**

- Exposure avoidance
  - (not engaging)
- Loss prevention
  - (frequency)
- Loss reduction
  - (severity)
- Loss sharing

**■ Risk Financing**

- Risk transfer
  - (insurance)
- Risk transfer
  - (employee contract)
  - (volenti)
- Risk retention
  - (absorb)

FIGURE 8.4. Risk control and risk finance.

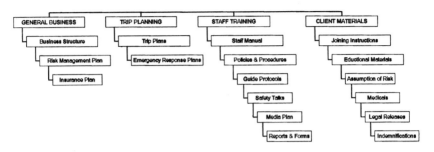

FIGURE 8.5. Risk management documentation.

## Business Documentation

General business documentation that can also serve as risk management documentation includes incorporation documents, risk management plans, and insurance plans. Incorporation documents play a role because they deal with such relevant topics as legal status, asset holdings, shareholder agreements, buyout clauses, and ownership structures—all topics that provide risk exposure to the ongoing business operations of the firm.

The risk management plan outlines policies and procedures that a business will use to mitigate or respond to crisis and emergency situations affecting the business. It is a basic document that explains corporate philosophy and standard operating procedures. It identifies hazards to the business and develops policies and strategies to deal with them. These hazards may include such problems as loss of permits, loss of insurance, vehicle accidents, and undertrained staff.

An insurance plan determines what assets and hazards to the business will be insured and what level of risk will be retained through insurance deductibles. Insurance is one of the most important and most common risk management tools available, and a well-thought-out plan of what needs to be insured, how the wording in a policy should read, and how much insurance to buy must be carefully considered.

## Trip Planning Documentation

Trip planning documentation includes pretrip plans and emergency-response plans. The purpose of these documents is to demonstrate that adequate planning has been carried out prior to a trip's operation, to determine the logistics required to support a trip, and to outline how the business will respond to emergencies caused by hazards on the trip. Many legal jurisdictions now expect trips to be planned in writing, that educational objectives will match the client's exposure to risk, and that trip itineraries will be progressive in the nature of their delivery. In addition, many jurisdictions require written emergency response plans.

## Staff-Training Documentation

The intent of developing staff-training materials such as staff manuals, policies and procedures, guide emergency protocols, safety talk outlines, media plans, and report formats is to provide adequate training and resources to frontline staff who are responsible for both preventing and responding to potential incidents. Staff must be trained in company emergency response policies. Guides must present safety talks to clients, and proactive strategy must be developed for how to deal with the media.

## Client Documentation

Materials that are developed for clients also act as risk management documents because their intent is to prepare and educate the participant about what is involved in the trip. In addition, the effectiveness of any defense will rest largely on the preparedness of the guest, how well he or she understood the risks involved, and how clearly these risks were accepted. Client documentation includes marketing materials, joining instructions, information packages, and release contracts. These materials must be written with care—giving thought to their marketing value as well as their risk management implications.

A well-organized and well-run business will develop and implement the complete spectrum of these planning processes, in all four areas.

## SUMMARY

Operating an adventure business has changed significantly in the past few years. The adventure industry is characterized by a move toward bigger business and more professional management. The lifestyle-oriented business manager is under continual pressure to approach the business more professionally, particularly in terms of administration, finance, marketing, operations, and risk management. The industry trend is toward increasing involvement of government regulatory bodies and industry governing bodies with regard to operating standards, legal liability, and risk management. The bar will continue to rise. The successful adventure business will be the one that responds to these trends and professionalizes both its operations and its management.

## CASE STUDY:
## CANADIAN MOUNTAIN HOLIDAYS (CMH)

### By Simon Hudson

One of the fastest growing sectors of the adventure tourism industry is helitourism. Under this catchy compound name several subcategories have evolved which offer the public a diverse range of activities encompassing everything from helifly-fishing to helipicnicking. Although winter heliskiing has been around for decades, summer heli-tourism is relatively new. Canadian Mountain Holidays (CMH), a helicopter pioneer, was founded in 1965 and operates in eleven mountain areas of southeastern British Columbia (see Figure 8.6).

The Banff-based company has annual revenue of $44 million (Canadian), and claims a 70 percent repeat-booking figure. CMH holds leasehold rights in British Columbia to more than 20,000 square kilometers of remote territory in the Purcell, Cariboo, Selkirk, and Monashee mountain ranges. At several times the size of its next competitor in heliski visits, its operations include thirty helicopters, and seven remote lodges—many accessible in winter only by helicopter (see Figure 8.7). Lodges have been designed specifically to meet the needs of helitourists. Each has a dining room for serving food and a fully stocked lounge, and each is equipped with a sauna and jacuzzi. There is even a resident qualified massage practitioner to help renew tired muscles.

Austrian mountain guide Hans Gmoser started the company in Canada over thirty-five years ago. In 1965 he hit upon the idea of ferrying hard-core, thrill-seeking skiers to virgin powder by helicopter.

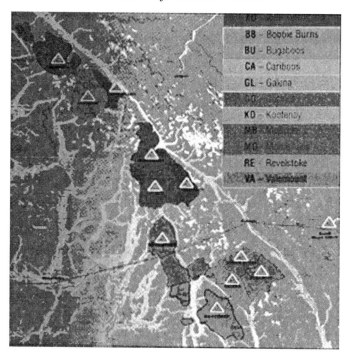

Key:
- BB – Bobbie Burns
- BU – Bugaboos
- CA – Cariboos
- GL – Galena
- GO –
- KO – Kootenay
- MB –
- MG –
- RE – Revelstoke
- VA – Valemount

FIGURE 8.6. The eleven mountain areas in which CMH operates. (Photo courtesy of CMH; used with permission.)

Initially, accommodation was very basic and elite skiers were willing to endure certain deprivations. That first year, eighteen skiers came for one week, equipped with their own sleeping gear. Despite the outdoor plumbing and being towed behind a snowmobile for twenty-eight miles from the nearest highway to reach the camp, the skiers were so enthusiastic about the experience that they decided to tell all their friends. The next year, seventy guests arrived over a six-week period, and the following year 150 came over a ten-week period. Gmoser decided it was time to expand, so with $115,000 borrowed from friends and skiing clientele, the Bugaboo Lodge was built in 1967-1968. By 1969, attendance had grown to 440 and the lodge was expanded. Demand kept increasing so Gmoser just kept building lodges.

In 1978 Gmoser expanded his helicopter service to hikers and began to improve the facilities at the lodges to attract customers in the summer as well as winter. Growth of CMH continued until 1982 when the

FIGURE 8.7. Many of the CMH lodges are accessible in winter only by helicopter. (Photo courtesy of CMH; used with permission.)

recession, along with a series of accidents, contributed to a decline in demand. Operating procedures were tightened until 1986 when demand began to increase dramatically. Once again, new ski areas were opened, lodges were built or expanded, and helihiking grew to include most lodges during the summer. In 1996, Alpine Helicopters, a British Columbia firm that had been CMH's helicopter supplier since 1981, acquired the company. Two years later, Intrawest Corp. of Vancouver purchased a 45 percent stake in the parent company of CMH. Intrawest may decide to buy the remaining 55 percent after five years.

There are three main strands to its business: heliskiing, helihiking, and mountaineering.

## Heliskiing

Although heliskiing has spread to the United States, Europe, South America, New Zealand, and even to Russia's Kamchatka peninsula, Canadian operators are the industry's unquestioned leaders. Heliskiing is an activity favored by well-heeled adventure travelers and has markedly increased in the past few decades. In 1999, 92,000 heliskier days were recorded in Canada—8,000 more than the year before and a sizeable 28,000 more than in 1994-1995. According to the B.C. Helicopter and Snowcat Ski Operators Association, gross revenues from high mountain skiing now generates between $80 and $100 million (Canadian) annually. This growth made CMH an attractive purchase prospect for industry giant Intrawest. In justifying Intrawest's investment in CMH, Daniel Jarvis, chief financial officer, said that helicopter skiing was the one element of the sport missing from its ski network, noting that it offers a predictable stream of revenue and demand exceeds supply. Also, because the skiing takes place at high altitudes, there is less concern that warm winters will melt snow and ruin conditions (see Figure 8.8).

Since its inception over thirty-five years ago, CMH has hosted over 106,000 skier weeks. These skiers have logged approximately 5.9 million runs for a combined total of over 12.4 billion vertical feet. Each winter, CMH sells some 7,000 holidays and actually has a waiting list of around 3,000. About 50 percent of customers are from the United States, and 40 percent are from Europe. A seven-day package costs about $6,000 (Canadian) which includes 100,000 vertical feet of skiing; accommodation for seven nights; all meals, snacks, and soft drinks; return transport from Calgary by bus; and all taxes.

Most clients are white-collar professionals, and physicians are a large market segment. Special interest weeks have been created to cater to groups that perhaps feature an evening lecture series on selected topics. CMH does not advertise its heliskiing holidays, relying more on encouraged word of mouth. This strategy has been successful for them largely because the product appeals to a certain type of person. These skiers are likely to socialize with people of similar means and interests, and often return the following year with a friend. Most of the guests are male, the average age is forty-five, and the majority earn over $200,000 (Canadian) per annum.

Eight lodges host forty-four guests, one holds thirty-three, and two are for private groups of ten skiers. Although there are no telephones or television antennas, the lodges are fully equipped and self-contained. On arrival each skier is outfitted with an avalanche transceiver (a beacon that sends out a signal to rescuers in case of an avalanche) and each group carries a radio and rescue pack with a shovel and a probe. On the first day, all guests are trained to search with the de-

FIGURE 8.8. Heliskiing offers a predictable stream of revenue as it takes place at such high altitude. (Photo courtesy of CMH; used with permission.)

vices. Vertical feet is a badge of honor. An 8,000-meter day is good, but 10,000 meters is better. By the end of the week, most people meet and exceed their 30,500-meter guarantee (see Figure 8.9). Prior to or after a guest's heliskiing week, CMH will prepare a customized itinerary that could include ski touring, ice climbing, sleigh rides, or a bobsled run.

In terms of competition, Canada's second largest heliskiing company is Mike Wiegele Helicopter Skiing. Wiegele operates a 7,800-square-kilometer area using up to six helicopters based in tiny Blue River, British Columbia. There are also operators that offer heliskiing by the day working out of Whistler Resort, Golden, or Panorama. Custom-designed packages are also becoming more common. For example, Canadian adventure specialists High Sky have put together

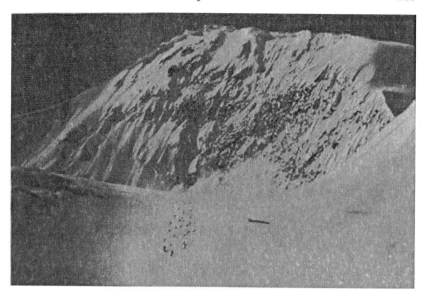

FIGURE 8.9. By the end of the week most skiers meet and exceed their 30,500-meter guarantee at CMH. (Photo courtesy of CMH; used with permission.)

a special women-only heliskiing package to compete with CMH who have been offering women's weeks since 1989. Competition to CMH has also increased due to the popularity of snowcat skiing. Snowcats are large, truck-like vehicles that run on tracks instead of wheels. Like helicopters, they carry powder enthusiasts to high mountain areas that do not have lifts or groomed trails. New snowcat skiing operations have sprung up all over, from southwestern Colorado to British Columbia, and existing companies are expanding and upgrading in response to the growing demand.

*Helihiking*

CMH invented helihiking (an abbreviation for helicopter-assisted hiking) in 1978. They run excursions, June to September, from five mountain lodges used by heliskiers in the winter. Each CMH lodge has about 386 square miles of wilderness all to itself. Participants, who range in age from eight to eighty, can cover as little as 20 meters or as much as 16 kilometers in a day. CMH provides a variety of helihiking vacations ranging from one to eight days. Packages include meals, insulated hooded jackets, top-quality hiking boots, wind pants, rain ponchos, daypacks, water bottles, snacks, and even sunscreen. All-inclusive packages range from family adventures and photography workshops to alpine ecology. Prices depend on the lodge and dates. Stays can be at one or a combination of five lodges, and three-night helihiking packages cost approximately $1,500 (Canadian). Helicopters transport guests to remote wilderness areas around British Columbia where they can decide from day to day whether they want to make like mountaineers scaling steep ridges, or leisurely stroll along the glaciers and flowered meadows (see Figure 8.10).

In twenty-two years of operation, CMH has served over 40,000 visitors. The company says that guests are of all ages and from all over the world. The common desire is to see beautiful, remote mountains in comfort and safety. They are seeing a tremendous increase in parents traveling with children and in response they have created a specific family adventure package with a multitude of activities and events with children in mind. They have also noticed that people are

FIGURE 8.10. Helicopters transport guests to remote wilderness areas around British Columbia for helihiking excursions. (Photo courtesy of CMH; used with permission.)

looking for a variety of activities, and they now offer white-water rafting, horseback riding, and fly-fishing in addition to hiking. Other specialty programs that have proved to be popular are the *National Geographic* programs and affinity groups, such as Stanford University Alumni.

## Mountaineering

The mountaineering program was created to satisfy the needs of helihiking guests who wanted more skills, more challenge, and more accomplishments. With a helicopter, guests can access four different peaks in four days, whereas normally it would take four weeks. On mountaineering holidays, guides create groups of eleven guests with similar abilities. The guide then chooses the route for the day ranging from beginner to advanced. There is a small guest-to-guide ratio, ranging from two to one to six to one, depending on the adventure.

To take one of these holidays, guests do not have to be experienced climbers but are expected to be in good physical condition. A three-night mountaineering package costs about $2,000 (Canadian), and includes accommodation, food, equipment, guides, helicopter flights, and transportation to and from Banff or Calgary. CMH also offers personalized mountain guides at a cost of $650 (Canadian) per day.

## Management and Marketing at CMH

According to Chief Marketing Officer Marty von Neudegg, CMH is just a bunch of mountain guides taking people into the mountains to have fun, and the company philosophy reflects this attitude. The company's greatest marketing vehicle is encouraged word of mouth and the company does very little advertising. Von Neudegg says there are three marketing areas for the company: sales, advertising, and service. Ninety percent of the marketing budget is spent on the latter to encourage customer loyalty. CMH produces colorful brochures for each of its three brands (with winter brochures produced in six languages); expensive videos are made for all three activities in up to six languages, and a Web site exists for each. CMH also hosts "An Evening with CMH" throughout North America, Europe, Japan, and Australia. These are invitation-only evenings where past guests are invited to bring their friends to an evening with CMH staff and guides. These events are very successful; 75 percent of all attendees book a holiday with CMH.

When CMH began marketing in Europe during the late 1960s and early 1970s, there was no knowledge of heliskiing in Canada. Rather than follow the normal route of mass media advertising, CMH chose to place no advertising at all. Instead, they employ one agent in each country, and this person must know the products and their market intimately. Initially, they sold heliskiing one person at a time. This was many years before the term "one-to-one" marketing had been used. Although the distribution system has become more sophisticated over the years, these ten agents in Europe still exist and bring in 40 percent of the total winter business. For the U.S. and Canadian markets, CMH employs its own travel agency based in Banff.

CMH is also part of the Adventure Collection, a group of six adventure companies that have joined together to form an alliance based on the principle that each company is deeply committed to the environment in which they travel. This is not a marketing alliance but rather a group formed to demonstrate that tourism can be a positive force rather than a negative one. The group's primary focus is to communicate environmental and cultural messages. They print a collective brochure which is sent to guests of all six companies, and they jointly promote each other's trips. They also combine itineraries to create new trips to give travelers more choices.

Operations behind the scenes include the planning and training of staff and guides, computer support, updating reservations systems, maintaining the buildings, dealing with government and land issues, and environmental and wildlife research. Environmental sensitivity has always been a priority at CMH, but in the past decade growing environmental awareness and opposition to tourist activities by environmentalists has forced the company to communicate its environmental initiatives. In its brochures, CMH describes its wildlife programs, in which all wildlife sightings are reported; its garbage, waste management, and recycling programs; its fuel management initiatives; and its ongoing research activities.

### Human Resource Management

To run their operation CMH employs over 500 people, and training is not taken lightly. Successful mountain guides have to be part diplomat, mountaineer, entertainer, weather expert, teacher, and paramedic. All CMH guides have to be certified members of internationally recognized guide associations before they join the company. They also attend annual training sessions and, on an ongoing basis, take refresher courses in avalanche hazard evaluation and stabilization, weather analysis, and emergency medical techniques. They bring a wide background of experience and come from Canada, the United States, Switzerland, Germany, Great Britain, France, Austria, Italy, Australia, and New Zealand. All mountaineering guides are either International Federation of Mountain Guides Association (IFMGA) mountain guides or Association of Canadian Mountain Guides (ACMG) alpine and assistant alpine guides.

### Risk Management

Risks inherent in heliskiing cannot be completely eliminated. Some elements of risk are more manageable, but others are not. Guests in the winter are asked to accept this fact by signing a CMH heliski waiver. A safety briefing and training on arrival ensures each guest understands these risks. CMH is a member of the British Columbia Helicopter and Snowcat Skiing Operators Association. This association sets strict safety standards for operating a helicopter skiing area. CMH is proud of its flying safety record. The company has transported thousands of helihikers and heliskiers without injury in its twin-engine helicopters, which seats up to fourteen passengers each (see Figure 8.11). Each chopper is inspected daily by a certified engineer, and every CMH pilot has logged a minimum of 2,500 hours in helicopters. A safety lecture is also mandatory for guests.

CMH has developed a comprehensive snow and avalanche management system. This includes procedures for collecting weather and snow information, evaluating snowpack stability, assessing hazards in the terrain, and determining a skiing program. In each area, a snow safety guide, separate from the skiing program, makes additional observations to facilitate more informed decisions by the guiding team. Observations are shared between all CMH areas on a daily radio exchange and relayed to the Canadian Avalanche Center. In spite of all these efforts there have been thirty-two fatalities since 1965, twenty-three of them in eight avalanche accidents. CMH does not try to hide

FIGURE 8.11. Each CMH helicopter seats up to fourteen passengers. (Photo courtesy of CMH; used with permission.)

the fact that heliskiing is inherently risky, as all this information is found on their Web site.

### Future Challenges

Although the company is optimistic about its future, certain industry constraints may limit growth. The size of a heliskiing area is an obstacle in terms of the Canadian government granting tenure, and the government is concerned that no monopoly or oligopoly situations should result from the granting of tenure. There is also the problem of safety and public image. Over the past few decades there have been several major avalanche accidents that have received a great deal of media coverage (the response to the death of a British CMH client in February 2001, for example). As a result, the public image of heliskiing is that of a high risk, dangerous sport. Therefore it is essential therefore that CMH assure the public that they use only the highest guiding standards possible and that all guides have taken avalanche and first aid courses in addition to heliskiing guide certification. As mentioned previously, growing environmental awareness and opposition to tourist activities by environmentalists have forced the company to communicate its environmental initiatives. These environmental constraints could have a serious impact on the future of CMH. In addition, a potential conflict exists in terms of alternate resource uses. For example, there are problems of conflict with other wilderness users. Finally, although CMH does not seem to be significantly affected by recession, a major worldwide depression or a serious fuel shortage would certainly present a challenge to the company.

## *RELEVANT WEB SITES*

Above the Clouds: www.aboveclouds.com
Adventure Centre: www.adventurecentre.com
Adventure Planet: www.adventureplanet.com
Adventureseek: www.adventureseek.com
Destination Wilderness: www.wildernesstrips.com
Gorp: www.gorp.com
Canadian Mountain Holidays Heliskiing: cmhski.com
CMH Helihiking: cmhhike.com
CMH Mountaineering: cmhmountaineering.com
The Adventure Collection: adventurecollection.com

## NOTE

1. Top-down budgeting (applicable to a wide variety of applications such as trip budgets, marketing budgets, insurance budgets, etc.) occurs when a business determines it has a certain amount of money for the specific function, and the task must then be carried out for this amount of money. For example, insurance coverage bought with x amount of money "because it is what we think we can afford" is a top-down insurance budget. A bottom-up budget would ask: What are our risks? Which risks do we need to insure (and which do we transfer or retain)? Based on this decision what will it cost us to buy adequate insurance for our needs?

# BIBLIOGRAPHY

Block, S., Hirt, G., and Short, D. (1994). *Foundations of Financial Management.* Burr Ridge, IL: Irwin, Inc.

Cloutier, K.R. (2000). *Legal Liability and Risk Management for Adventure Businesses.* Kamloops, BC: Bhudak Consultants Ltd.

Cloutier, K.R. (1998). *The Business of Adventure: Developing an Adventure Tourism Business.* Kamloops, BC: Bhudak Consultants Ltd.

Daft, R. and Fitzgerald, P. (1992). *Management,* First Canadian Edition. Toronto: Holt, Rindhart and Winston of Canada Ltd.

DuBrin, A. and Ireland, D. (1993). *Management and Organization,* Second Edition. Cincinnati, OH: South-Western Publishing Co.

Garrison, R., Chesley, G., and Carroll, R. (1996). *Managerial Accounting,* Third Canadian Edition. Burr Ridge, IL: Irwin, Inc.

Lustig, P. and Schwab, B. (1991). *Managerial Finance in a Canadian Setting,* Fourth Edition. Toronto: Butterworths Ltd.

Siegel, J., Shim, J., and Dauber, N. (1994). *Corporate Controller's Handbook of Financial Management,* Englewood Cliffs, NJ: Prentice Hall.

# Chapter 9

# Spa and Health Tourism

## Michael Hall

### INTRODUCTION

The popular media image of health or spa tourism—that of over-weight or unhealthy people being pampered at some sort of "health farm" or "fat farm"—may appear to bear little relation to the popular image of sports tourism. Such popular images can be deceiving. For many involved with sport as a recreational and tourism pursuit, the improvement or maintenance of one's heath is a major motivation for participation and travel. Indeed, as Hall (1992) noted in an earlier review of health, adventure, and sports tourism, all three types of tourism are functionally related in terms of travel motivations and social values, which emphasize improving an individual's quality of life and which all involve relatively active participation, often in outdoor settings.

Since the 1980s, Western society has witnessed a marked trend among sections of the population toward more active, experientially oriented outdoor leisure activities in response to increasingly sedentary work patterns, which may also be regarded as a response to problems of urbanism and contemporary lifestyles (Mitchell, 1983). Indeed, the present resurgence of public interest in adventure, health, and sport parallels the attention given to the physical, moral, and spiritual "damage" of urban living at the turn of the twenty-first century in North America, Europe, and Australia, and the resultant growth in national parks, sport, and physical education as formal recreational activities and spaces (Altmeyer, 1976; Nash, 1982; Hall, 1985). In the contemporary travel setting, escape from a mundane, alienating urban environment has been long recognized as a major motivating force in tourism, while the physical activity possible through health or sport tourism provides the outlet for potential personal rewards (e.g., Crompton, 1979; Iso-Ahola, 1980, 1982). In addition, the desire for a healthy lifestyle, which is a significant intrinsic reward of travel, is a component of tourism behavior and products that has become increasingly important in recent years. Finally, one can note the role of fashion and the significance of body image as an influence on individual motivations to attend beauty clinics and spas. Indeed, Tarlow and Muehsam (1992) argue that cities with large medical facilities, such as Houston's Texas Medical Center, will use these structures as a springboard for new economic vitality through "sanitourism." These hospital centers will cater to the ill and offer programs such as stress reduction to patients' loved ones, while health-conscious individuals seeking to maintain their personal well-being will turn to hospitals for fully monitored, individually tailored health programs. Whatever the reason, the tourism industry undoubtedly recognizes spa and health tourism as one of the fastest-growing areas of contemporary tourism ("Spa Popularity," 1998).

This chapter provides a review of health and spa tourism, its growing significance for the tourism industry, and its use as a component of economic development strategies. First, the issue of defining health and spa tourism is discussed. This is followed by a brief historical overview of the development of health and spa tourism. Then aspects of the supply side of health and spa tourism are reviewed before issues of demand are examined. This chapter also notes the importance of an aging society as an influential factor in current and future demand, which suggests that health tourism will become an even larger component of tourism development and flow in the twenty-first century.

## DEFINING HEALTH AND SPA TOURISM

Health tourism was defined by the International Union of Tourist Organizations (IUTO), the forerunner to the World Tourism Organization, as "the provision of health facilities utilizing the natural resources of the country, in particular mineral water and climate" (IUTO, 1973: 7). Goeldner (1989: 7), in a review of the health tourism literature, defined health tourism as "(1) staying away from home, (2) health [as the] most important motive, and (3) done in a leisure setting." Goodrich and Goodrich (1987: 217) and Goodrich (1994) define health tourism in terms of the narrower concept of health care tourism as "the attempt on the part of a tourist facility (e.g. hotel) or destination (e.g., Baden, Switzerland) to attract tourists by deliberately promoting its health care services and facilities, in addition to its regular tourist amenities." Goeldner (1989) recognized five components of the health tourism market, each identifying a specific market segment:

1. Sun and fun activities
2. Engaging in healthy activities, but health is not the central motive (adventure and sports tourism activities such as hiking, cycling, or golf)
3. Principle motive for travel is health (e.g., a sea cruise or travel to a different climate)
4. Travel for sauna, massage, and other health activities (spa resort)
5. Medical treatment

As Figure 9.1 illustrates, segments three to five comprise the subjects usually recognized as constituting the health and spa travel market, as it is in these categories that health is the primary motive for travel. However, although this classification is useful for identifying elements of the demand for health and spa tourism, it fails to acknowledge the importance that health products and spas play in destination or attraction marketing and promotion or as a component of tourism development strategies. Therefore, for the purpose of this chapter, health tourism is defined as

> a commercial phenomena of industrial society which involves a person traveling overnight away from the normal home environment for the express benefit of maintaining or improving health, and the supply and promotion of facilities and destinations which seek to provide such benefits.

Spa tourism is a component of health tourism that relates to the provision of specific health facilities and destinations which traditionally include the provision of mineral waters but which may also be used to refer to tourist resorts that integrate health facilities with accommodation. Nevertheless, it should be noted that use of the term *health tourism* is not widespread in the Anglo-American tourism lit-

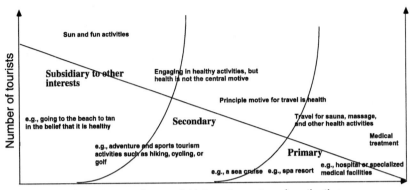

FIGURE 9.1. Characteristics of health and spa tourism segments in relation to motivation and size of market.

erature, nor is it widely recognized in the tourism industry. For example, in an exploratory study of health tourism in the Caribbean, in which interviews were conducted with twenty-eight tourist officials at twenty-eight Caribbean tourist offices in Miami and New York, only seven Caribbean resorts were found to specifically advertise their health facilities to tourists. The Caribbean tourist offices had never before heard of the term health care tourism and did not try to promote their respective islands along that dimension; neither had the Miami travel agents ever heard of the term (Goodrich, 1994).

The idea of health tourism is much more widespread in Europe which has a long tradition of using spas for health tourism purposes of the middle classes as well as the elite or aristocracy. Indeed, the democratic nature of the use of spas is such that in a number of European countries such visits may be covered under health insurance schemes. As the following discussion illustrates, in an increasingly health-, fitness-, and body image-conscious world, health tourism has developed as a small yet extremely significant market segment that includes developed countries such as Austria (Ender, 1989), France (Guignand, 1989; Mesplier-Pinet, 1990), Germany (Carone, 1989; Godau, 1989), Hungary (Goodrich and Goodrich, 1987), Iceland (Millward, 2000), Israel (Bar-On, 1989; Niv, 1989), Italy (Becheri, 1989), New Zealand (Hall and Kearsley, 2001), and Switzerland

(Lanquar, 1989), and is growing in the developing world including China (Wu, 1994), Cuba (Wolff, 1992; Goodrich, 1993), the Caribbean (Goodrich, 1994), India, and Malaysia ("Malaysia," 1998).

## HISTORICAL DIMENSIONS OF HEALTH AND SPA TOURISM

The relationship between the generation of positive health and travel has a long history and shares a number of relationships. The use of waters at mineral spas and hot springs has been popular since Roman times, and the "taking to the waters" of the elites of seventeenth-century Europe provided one of the foundations for the modern pleasure resort concept (Lowenthal, 1962; Hembry 1990; Mackaman, 1993; Towner, 1996; Chambers, 1999). In the United Kingdom, the development of seaside resorts, such as Margate or Southend, had its genesis in the British aristocracy's belief in the curative powers of sea air (the "ozone," as it was described) and bathing in sea waters, though not initially in the sea itself. In the mid-nineteenth century the combination of improved transport accessibility to leisure because of the growth of the railways and economic accessibility because of rapidly increasing per capita incomes for the new middle classes led to the popularization among middle classes of what was previously available only to the rich. However, middle-class and, later, working-class access to seaside resorts was built upon not only the desire for the health benefits of recreation away from the industrial centers but also the continued belief in the curative value of the seaside (Pimlott, 1947; Walvin, 1978; Walton, 1983; Towner, 1996).

In mainland Europe, many cities have grown up around mineral springs and health spas. Examples of such cities include Baden, Lausanne, St. Moritz, and Interlaken in Switzerland; Baden-Baden and Wiesbaden in Germany; Vienna, Austria; and Budapest, Hungary (Goodrich and Goodrich, 1987; Towner, 1996). People have used mineral water since ancient times to cure such ailments as rheumatism, skin infections, and poor digestion. The waters from some foreign springs are imported to the United States, including Apolinaris from Germany, Hunyadi-Janos from Hungary, and Vichy from France. Indeed, the sale of bottled water, including the export of brands such as Perrier from France, is perhaps testimony to the continued belief in the healthy characteristics of mineral water. In Europe, mineral springs have long been the focus of health tourism, although in recent times seaside and mountain resorts have also developed with the intention of appealing to the health tourism market, particularly to corporate businesspersons and their partners. In the United States and Canada, mineral springs also provided opportunities for the development of spa tourism around which national parks were created (e.g., Runte, 1972, 1973, 1974a,b, 1977, 1979, 1990; Buchholtz, 1983; Mark, 1991). However, the spa tourism concept has considerably broadened to include resorts that are not based on hot springs but instead focus on other natural resource attributes such as climate. Similarly, in New Zealand, mineral springs were originally set aside as health resorts by the government to promote international tourism and domestic health improvements. More recently the major spa resorts at destinations such as Rotorua and Hanmer Springs have become geared toward the Asian market and the wealthier domestic tourist (Hall and Kearsley, 2001). Two examples are the Radium and Priest Hot Springs at the Polynesian Spa, Rotorua (see Figure 9.2) and the Rotorua Museum of Art and History—Te Whare Taonga O Te Arawa (see Figure 9.3). The latter is housed in the magnificent bathhouse building situated in beautiful Government Gardens. The bathhouse, constructed as a therapeutic spa in 1908, is listed as a category one historic building and is believed to be the most photographed building in New Zealand.

In addition, the use of travel to improve an individual's health, for instance through sea cruising or a change in climate, has long been a motive for travel (Mathieson and Wall, 1982; Wright, 1988; Hall and Rudkin, 1996). In the nineteenth century, wealthy tuberculosis sufferers in Northern Europe, including authors such as D. H. Lawrence and Robert Louis Stevenson, traveled to and lived in the Mediterranean, southwest United States, or even in the South Pacific to improve their health. Arguably, such movements predate some of the second home retirement migration to these same areas from colder northern climates for similar health-related motivations today.

## SUPPLY OF HEALTH AND SPA TOURISM

The provision of health and spa resorts is in part related to the availability of suitable natural resources including mineral springs or attractive amenity landscapes or climates. However, the resource also

FIGURE 9.2. The Radium and Priest Hot Springs at the Polynesian Spa, Rotorua, New Zealand. (Photo by C. M. Hall.)

has to be developed and promoted before it becomes available to the tourism market. Historically, government has had a major role to play in development, along with private-sector players such as railway companies and, more recently, travel companies (Ward, 1998). Nevertheless, there is significant variation in the role of government. Although governments play a gradually less important ownership role in spa and health resorts in Western countries, the importance that governments attach to tourism as a mechanism for economic development has grown in significance.

One of the most active governments with respect to health tourism is that of Israel. The Israeli government has established health resorts in the Dead Sea, Tiberius, and Kinneret regions. The Tiberius hot springs have been used as a spa area since Roman times. Israel, in recognizing the "promotion of health tourism as an issue of national importance," passed a special law regulating health tourism and established a Health Spa Authority (Niv, 1989: 32). The Health Spa Authority has a variety of tasks including health spa development, classification of land and services, research, encouragement of visita-

FIGURE 9.3. Rotorua Museum of Art and History—Te Whare Taonga O Te Arawa, New Zealand. (Photo by C. M. Hall.)

tion, publicity, "to initiate and encourage the search for therapeutic springs," and "to encourage, plan and promote the production and sale of mineral water and similar products" (Niv, 1989: 32). "The law regulates all aspects of developing and promoting health tourism, and guarantees priority for the advancement and marketing of sites endowed with the necessary features. The law emphasizes that in regions clearly suited to health tourism, only projects directly or indirectly related to this sphere will be approved for development" (Niv, 1989: 32). Israel has developed a network of vacation balneological centers for the treatment of noncontagious diseases that do not impose limitations on daily living such as dermatological ailments, particularly psoriasis, and rheumatic conditions. The spas along Israel's Dead Sea coast attract thousands of psoriasis sufferers from Scandinavia, with much of the vacation's costs covered by national health plans (Tarlow and Muehsam, 1992).

The traditional notion of spa tourism in Italy changed substantially in the 1980s with the rapid expansion of what Becheri (1989: 17) described as "thermal spring tourism of well being," which includes massage centers, health clubs and centers, fitness, marine therapies, diet therapies and physiotherapies, beauty treatments, detoxify treatments, sports and exercise, steam bath, hydrotherapies, health education, and relaxation techniques. Health tourists may also combine health motivations with other interests. For instance, at the Hamat Gader site in northern Israel, "vacationers combine a visit to this ancient archeological site with independent bathing in the thermal pool" (Niv, 1989: 31).

In the United States, the traditional spa concept has been modified to account for the broader interest in health and fitness. America's fitness spas constitute a service industry that is presently riding the crest of recent strong interest in physical conditioning (Robey, 1985; Rea, 1987). Spa participants are typically younger persons who are concerned about their appearance, confident in their own state of conditioning, and interested in a number of both active and passive pursuits (Olsen and Granzin, 1989). Similarly, Becheri (1989) has argued that the broader concept of health tourism, including the pursuit of a healthy lifestyle in the general population, provides a basis for the relaunch of traditional thermal spring tourism in Italy.

In Northern Europe, Iceland's mineral rich geothermal waters are also being exploited for the health tourism industry. The Blue Lagoon health resort in the southwest region of the country is a prime example. The high silica content of the hot waters is said to have properties that can alleviate skin disorders. A major expansion was completed there in July 1999 with further development planned through 2002. From the government of Iceland's perspective, the development of spa tourism is complementary to the wilderness and outdoor recreation opportunities that the country already offers international tourists—tourism that also provides a mechanism of expanding the regional economic base ("Investors Invited," 2000; Millward, 2000).

In the United States, health-related pursuits have become a significant component of tourism in the southwest, and in Florida and Hawaii. This is true in part because of the role retirement migration to those regions has played. The active involvement of government has also had an impact. For example, the state of Hawaii has focused on health tourism, along with ecotourism and meetings, incentive travel, conventions, and exhibitions industry (MICE) tourism, as a means of diversifying the state's tourism industry and economic development strategy. Indeed, as part of Hawaii's health tourism initiative, Governor Ben Cayetano met with Mayo Clinic officials in an attempt to get

Mayo to establish a presence in the state (Kertesz, 1995). A more amusing and probably unintentional dimension of Hawaii's promotion of health tourism is the development of Viagra-related tourism. Because of the relative ease in access to Viagra in Hawaii compared to Japan, it has been reported that Japanese men have traveled to Hawaii as part of organized tours to try the drug and utilize its effects (Memminger, 1998). Although the accuracy of such news reports is debatable, they do indicate the value of available medical services to those who can afford them as a factor in influencing travel patterns.

Cuba earns some US$25 million a year from international health tourists (Robinson, 1997). According to the Cuban agency Servimed, which handles 70 percent of the foreign patients, 5,365 overseas health tourists came in 1996, mainly from Latin America, along with 1,218 Europeans and 92 Americans. Cuban hospitals and clinics offer a wide range of procedures for foreigners, including low-cost face-lifts and liposuction, and innovative treatments for night blindness, vitiligo, and neurological disorders. The newest attractions are drug and alcohol addiction centers and refurbished medical spas, including mineral springs used by Americans prior to the revolution. There are several reasons for the attractiveness of Cuba as a health tourism destination, including the relatively low cost of Cuban medical services for foreign visitors (they are free for Cubans), the high quality of its medical services, and its Spanish language (Wolff, 1992).

The attractiveness of Cuba as a health tourist destination has undoubtedly been enhanced by high-profile users of its health services, such as the Argentinian soccer star Diego Maradona who visited the island for treatment of his drug addiction. Given the continuation of the American trade embargo on Cuba, health tourism is an important means of attracting foreign exchange to pay for drugs and medications normally unavailable to the Cuban population (Calzon, 2000). However, it is likely that health tourism will continue to grow once normal diplomatic and trade relations between the United States and Cuba are established as its relatively cheap medical services will become available to the American market in general, and the retirement market in Florida in particular.

Another region not normally associated with health tourism that is increasingly focusing on product development is south India, particularly the states of Tamil Nadu, Karnataka, and Kerala, which are jointly promoting themselves as health tourism destinations with Sri Lanka and the Maldives ("Destination: India," 1998). Joint packages are being marketed to Germans, French, Taiwanese, and Singaporeans. The packages incorporate the beach destinations of the Maldives, Buddhist sites of Sri Lanka, and culture and cruises from the three southern Indian states. A ten-day extension to south India after traveling to the Maldives includes wildlife, temples, fairs, and festivals of Tamil Nadu and Karnataka, and also includes Ayurvedic health spas and cruises of Kerala's rivers. Southern India is a big draw for tourists, as rates are 40 percent lower than the Maldives. Awareness of Ayurvedic medicine is increasing in Western Europe and Southeast Asia, particularly in Malaysia and Singapore. Ayurvedic medicine is thus a significant factor in attracting foreign visitors to the region. Indeed, visitors from Singapore to Chennai increased from 23,379 in 1996 to 79,480 in 1997 ("Destination: India," 1998).

## DEMAND FOR HEALTH AND SPA TOURISM

According to Goodrich (1993), the health tourism concept suggests at least two possible approaches to segmentation of the consumer market: health and income. On the basis of health, appeals could be directed at people with various afflictions and illnesses, such as high cholesterol levels and obesity, who would form the core health segment. Within this segment, certain groups are more akin to the spa and beauty break market ("Destination: India," 1998). This appeals to people who wish to maintain a healthy appearance. The second possible approach is for destinations or hotels and resorts to cater to the high-income travelers who can afford high prices for health services.

For example, in the case of Malaysia, the target group for health tourism is the middle-income earner in neighboring ASEAN (Association of South East Asian) countries. In many of these countries, medical bills for the middle and upper classes are paid either by health management organizations or employer-sponsored medical insurance. These payers are the target group. For most payers from developed countries, Malaysia can now offer services of the same quality at cheaper prices. According to the Malaysian government, the standard of medical treatment and care found locally is on par or even better than what is found in other countries, and is at least 2.5

times cheaper than in Singapore. Potential consumers in developing countries such as Myanmar, Vietnam, Laos, Iraq, and other Middle Eastern countries that lack quality medical facilities have also been targeted, particularly in relation to cultural and religious factors in health care, which Malaysia can cater to. Significantly, the values of health tourism in Malaysia are recognized in terms of the person seeking treatment as well as their accompanying family.

For example, the health ministry reached an agreement with the immigration department to allow medical visitors to Malaysia to receive visa approvals in one week. "Fast track" visa clearance has also been introduced through which the visiting patient can seek the assistance of an immigration department official at the point of entry for quick clearance. In late August 1998, Health Minister Datuk Chua Jui Ming said patients and relatives or friends accompanying them were to be given priority in the renewal of visas or social visit passes if their stay extended beyond three months ("Malaysia," 1998).

Balneotherapy and spa tourism have long been important components of European travel motivations (Witt and Witt, 1989). Mesplier-Pinet (1990) reported that 1 percent of the population of France, 2 percent of the population of Italy, 2.5 percent of the population of West Germany, and 3 percent of the population of Poland engaged regularly in visits to traditional thermal resorts. The costs of many domestic visitors to European spas is borne by the state as a component of national health care delivery (Bar-On, 1989; Mesplier-Pinet, 1990). For example, in Italy, approximately 85 percent of domestic thermal spring tourists are government financed. However, in 1987, so many employees were exploiting their ability to take time off work to have thermal spring treatment that the Italian high court acted to contain health service expenditures and labor costs, and to reduce the abuse of government sponsorship of thermalists (Becheri, 1989). In Eastern Europe, governments were also the main sponsors of domestic health tourism at spa centers prior to the collapse of communism (Mesplier-Pinet, 1990; Hall, 1991). Since the early 1990s, many state spas have been taken over by the private sector though the state continues to use spas as a component of health services.

According to Niv (1989: 30), Israel is endowed with four basic characteristics that can transform it into a leading international center for health tourism:

1. Good natural resources
2. Year-round stable, comfortable climate
3. One of the world's most progressive medical systems
4. Attractive scenic locations that have a calming effect on patients

Nevertheless, he also noted that the health tourism market is made up of different groups:

The average customer of health clinics could be thought of as an independent, self-employed professional or a high-level manager, thirty-five, forty or, fifty years of age, who has achieved economic success in life and who, now, turns his or her thoughts to the restoration of the body.

The thermal spring patient is on average older, with very little or no motivation and with a considerably lower income. On the plus side, he or she shows a certain habit toward the treatments which he or she repeats every year (Becheri, 1989: 17).

In contrast, Goodrich (1994) observed that the primary tourist users of health-oriented resorts in the Caribbean tended to be younger adults between the ages of twenty-five and forty-five, white, and predominantly from the United States. Goodrich's research is most likely oriented toward the more active form of spa resort. However, although recreational activity is undoubtedly encouraged at the majority of spa and health resorts, it is readily apparent that the most dominant factor shaping demand for spa and health tourism is the rapidly aging population that seeks to retain good health and fitness in retirement.

Currently, 11 percent of the world's population is age sixty and above. By 2050, 20 percent will be sixty years or older; and by 2150, over 30 percent will be sixty years or older. In addition, the older population itself is still aging (United Nations, 1998). The health revolution, which has given millions of elderly persons relatively good health well into their eighties, has also helped to drive tourism's growth in general, and health-related travel in particular. The population of forty-five to sixty-four-year-olds will grow nearly five times faster than the total population between 2000 and 2010; between 2010 and 2030, the population over sixty-five will grow eight times faster than the total population (Tarlow and Muehsam, 1992). The increase in the number of very old people (aged eighty-plus years) between 1950 and 2050 is projected to grow by a factor of eight to ten times on the global scale. On current trends, by 2150, about one-third of the older population will be eighty years or older. As well as a general aging of the world's population there are also substantial regional differences in the aged population. For example, currently one out of five Europeans is sixty years or older, but one out of twenty Africans is sixty years or older. In some developed countries today, the proportion of older persons is close to one in five. According to the United Nations, during the first half of the twenty-first century that proportion will reach one in four and, in some countries, one in two (United Nations, Division for Social Policy and Development, 1998). Given that the vast majority of the world's tourists come from developed countries, such a demographic shift will clearly have substantial implications for the international health tourism industry. Not only may particular types of tourism continue to grow in popularity, such as cruising, but second homes, retirement homes, and the provision of health facilities for retirees may become increasingly important in destination development strategies. For example, areas of the European Mediterranean, the Iberian Peninsula, and the southwestern United States and Florida are already subject to substantial seasonal and permanent retirement migration (e.g., Williams, King, and Warnes, 1997) that is designed to further healthy retirement lifestyles.

In the United States the number of persons age sixty-five and older has grown faster than the general population. The Travel Industry Association of America estimated that by the year 2000 the elderly would comprise approximately one-fourth of the nation's population (Tarlow and Muehsam, 1992). With people living longer following retirement, the lifestyles of the mature traveler will have a substantial influence on the development and supply of tourism infrastructure. For example, *Modern Maturity,* a North American lifestyles magazine for the over-fifty market surveyed its subscribers about their travel habits and preferences. Over 37 percent traveled three to five times a year; 46 percent preferred car travel over any other type of transportation; 42 percent indicated that the purpose of their trip was to relax; 39 percent preferred just their partner as a traveling companion; 46 percent preferred to go to museums over any other tourist attraction; and 67 percent stayed in hotels ("Results," 1999: 12). This group will have the most available free time of any segment of the population, and it will also have the greatest amount of disposable income. Already, travelers over age sixty make up well over 30 percent of all room nights sold within the American lodging industry. Elder travelers spend more nights away from home (8.2) than do travelers under age fifty (4.8), according to the American Association of Retired Persons ("Results," 1999). Financially and physically able elderly will significantly increase the demand for leisure travel with health-related tourism being a significant component of growth in the retirement travel market (Tarlow and Muehsam, 1992).

One dimension that has not been adequately examined in the research on the demand for health tourism is its possibly highly gendered nature. Arguably, in contemporary industrial society, women's bodily experience appears to be largely structured through their sexual attractiveness, and men's bodily experiences are primarily structured through the category of health and the functionality of their bodies (i.e., men recognize the need to stay slim to avoid ill health and therefore utilize sport and exercise as leisure time activities) (Valentine, 1999). One possible interpretation of this situation is that if men think of their bodies in "active" terms, they may be more inclined to pursue the sports dimension of health tourism while women, who are more concerned with their appearance and therefore perceive their bodies as "passive" objects (Wolf, 1990; Saltonstall, 1993), are more concerned with the spa aspects of health tourism. Such an observation clearly has implications in the relationship of leisure and tourism practices and in the nature of demands for health tourism product.

## CONCLUSION

Health tourism and spa tourism have had a long and significant history. In recent years health tourism has undergone significant renewal and expansion. Evidence in this review suggests that the health tourism market is developing into two distinct yet related resort segments: resorts in which the emphasis is on improving overall health and fitness and promoting well-being, and resorts specifically geared toward providing medical services to clients suffering from disease. It should be noted that these segments will have considerable overlap and their respective popularity will depend as much on medical and social trends as it will on successful advertising and promotion. Most significant of these trends are the aging of society in the developed world and the growth of retirement migration in pursuit of healthier lifestyles. Health tourism also appears to be significant for those groups in society that seek physical conditioning programs, places to relieve stress, and centers for spiritual renewal. In the case of the latter, the successful promotion of Javanese Lulur massage, Russian Platza massage, Ayurvedic health spas, or traditional Chinese medicine in the West (Wu, 1994; Urquhart, 2000), may well signal the possible integration of various aspects of health tourism with spirituality and alternative medicine. For the more active tourist it is possible, as Tarlow and Muehsam (1992) have argued, that these centers will become sports fantasy programs where individuals will test their physical condition and act out their athletic dreams. Regardless of these possibilities, it is apparent that the mainstream hospitality providers such as hotels and restaurants adjust their facilities to accommodate health demands. For example, standard fare at most five-star resorts includes all-purpose weight and aerobic facilities, and fat-free/low-calorie and cholesterol-conscious eating plans.

The continued growth of health awareness in industrial society, the significance of image to identity, and the continued aging of society all point to the expansion of health-oriented tourism well into the twenty-first century. The traditional spa resort areas of Europe, North America, and Australia will likely maintain their appeal, often with augmented product offerings, some of which may be more closely related to traditional forms of sports tourism such as skiing. Spa tourism lies at the core of the foundation of modern mass tourism. Relatively dormant for much of the past century, spa and health tourism is now poised to reclaim its position at the core of the tourist experience and as one of the most important drivers in determining travel patterns.

## REFERENCES

Altmeyer, G. (1976). Three Ideas of Nature in Canada, 1893-1914. *Journal of Canadian Studies,*11(3), 21-36.
Bar-On, R. (1989). Cost-Benefit Considerations for Spa Treatments, Illustrated by the Dead Sea and Arad, Israel. *Revue de Tourisme,* 44(4), 12-15.
Becheri, E. (1989). From Thermalism to Health Tourism. *Revue de Tourisme,* 44(4), 15-19.

Buchholtz, C.W. (1983). *Rocky Mountain National Park: A History*. Boulder: Colorado Associated University Press.

Calzon, F. (2000). The Americas: Want a Radical Face Lift? Try Revolutionary Cuba. *The Wall Street Journal* (Eastern Edition), January 21, A19.

Carone, G. (1989). Pour un Thermalisme Différent—Considérations sur le Cas de l'Italie. Revue de Tourisme, 44(3), 23-26.

Chambers, T.A. (1999). *Fashionable Disease: Promoting Health and Leisure at Saratoga Springs, New York and the Virginia Springs, 1790-1860*. Unpublished doctoral dissertation. Williamsburg: Department of History, College of William and Mary.

Crompton, J.L. (1979). Motivations for Pleasure Vacation. *Annals of Tourism Research*, 6, 408-424.

"Destination: India: Kerala: Offering Tourists Health Spas and Exotic Cruises", (1998). *Travel Trade Gazette Asia*, October 30.

Ender, W. (1989). Diversifikation des Kurörtlichen Angebots, Möglichkeiten und Grenzen. *Revue de Tourisme*, 44(3), 16-22.

Godau, A. (1989). Das kur- und Bäderwesen der DDR—Bestandteil des Tourismus und des Sozialistischen Gesundheitsschutzes. *Revue de Tourisme*, 44(4), 20-22.

Goeldner, C. (1989). 39th Congress AIEST: English Workshop Summary. *Revue de Tourisme*, 44(4), 6-7.

Goodrich, J.N. (1993). Socialist Cuba: A Study of Health Tourism. *Journal of Travel Research*, 32(1), 36-42.

Goodrich, J.N. (1994). Health tourism: A New Positioning Strategy for Tourist Destinations. *Journal of International Consumer Marketing* 6(3/4), 227-237.

Goodrich, J.N. and Goodrich, G.E. (1987). Health-care Tourism—An Exploratory Study. *Tourism Management*, 8, 217-222.

Guignand, A. (1989). Thermalisme et Remise en Forme dans les Villages de Vacances Familiaux. *Revue de Tourisme*, 44(4), 23-25.

Hall, C.M. (1985). Outdoor Recreation and National Identity: A Comparative Analysis of Australia and Canada. *Journal of Canadian Culture*, 2(2), 25-39.

Hall, C.M. (1992). Review. Adventure, Health and Sports Tourism. In Weiler, B. and Hall, C.M. (Eds.), *Special Interest Tourism* (pp.141-158). London: Belhaven Press.

Hall, C.M. and Kearsley, G.W. (2001). *Tourism in New Zealand: An Introduction*. Melbourne: Oxford University Press.

Hall, C.M. and Rudkin, B. (1996). Health and Tourism in the Pacific. In Hall, C.M. and Page, S. (Eds.), *Tourism in the Pacific: Issues and Cases* (pp.130-145). London: Routledge.

Hall, D.R. (1991). *Tourism and Economic Development in Eastern Europe and the Soviet Union*. London: Belhaven Press.

Hembry, P.M. (1990). *The English Spa, 1560-1815: a Social History*. London: Athlone Press.

International Union of Tourism Organisations (IUTO) (1973). *Health Tourism*. Geneva: United Nations.

"Investors Invited to Pick Icelanders' Brains" (2000). *Corporate Location,* 1st Quarter: 48, 53-55.

Iso-Ahola, S.E. (1980). *The Social Psychology of Leisure and Recreation.* Dubuque: William C. Brown.

Iso-Ahola, S.E. (1982). Toward a Social Psychology Theory of Tourism Motivation: A Rejoinder. *Annals of Tourism Research,* 9, 256-261.

Kertesz, L. (1995). Hawaii Governor Woos Mayo Clinic. *Modern Healthcare.* 25(36), 54.

Lanquar, R. (1989). La Filière du Tourisme de Santé. *Revue de Tourisme,* 44(4), 25-30.

Lowenthal, D. (1962). Tourists and Thermalists. *Geographical Review,* 52(1), 124-127.

Mackaman, D.P. (1993). *Doctoring on Vacation: Medicine and Culture at the Spas of Nineteenth-Century France.* Unpublished doctoral dissertation. Berkeley: University of California.

"Malaysia: Government to Promote Health and Medical Tourism Industry," (1998). *International Market Insight Trade Inquiries,* October 21: 1.

Mark, S. (1991). Planning and Development at Rim Village. In *Administrative History, Crater Lake National Park, Oregon.* Seattle: U.S. Department of the Interior, National Park Service.

Mathieson, A. and Wall, G. (1982). *Tourism Economic, Physical and Social Impacts,* Harlow: Longman Scientific and Technical.

Memminger, C. (1998). Japanese Men Are Pioneers in Viagra Tour. *Boston Globe* (City Edition). June 15, A5.

Mesplier-Pinet, J. (1990). Thermalisme et Curistes: Les Contraintes. *Revue de Tourisme,* 45(2), 10-17.

Millward, T. (2000). The Hottest Economy in Scandinavia. *Corporate Location,* 1st Quarter 2000, pp. 38-47.

Mitchell, R.G. (1983). *Mountain Experience: The Psychology and Sociology of Adventure.* Chicago: The University of Chicago Press.

Nash, R. (1982). *Wilderness and the American Mind,* Second Edition. New Haven: Yale University Press.

Niv, A. (1989). Health Tourism in Israel: A Developing Industry. *Revue de Tourisme,* 44(4), 30-32.

Olsen, J.A. and Granzin, K.L. (1989). Life Style Segmentation in a Service Industry: The Case of Fitness Spas. *Visions in Leisure and Business: An International Journal of Personal Services, Programming and Administration,* 8(3), 4-20.

Pimlott, J.A.R. (1947). *The Englishman's Holiday: A Social History.* London: Faber.

Rea, P.S. (1987). Using Recreation to Promote Fitness. *Parks and Recreation,* 22(July), 32-36.

Results of Travel Survey (1999). *Modern Maturity,* January 12.

Robey, B. (1985). Life on a Treadmill. *American Demographics,* 7, 4-5.

Robinson, L. (1997). A Vacation in Havana: Sun, Fun, and Surgery. *U.S. News and World Report* 122(17), 42-43.

Runte, A. (1972). Yellowstone: It's Useless, So Why Not a Park. *National Parks and Conservation Magazine: The Environment Journal*, 46(March), 4-7.

Runte, A. (1973). "Worthless" Lands—Our National Parks: The Enigmatic Past and Uncertain Future of America's Scenic Wonderlands, *American West*, 10(May), 4-11.

Runte, A. (1974a). Pragmatic Alliance: Western Railroads and the National Parks. *National Parks and Conservation Magazine: The Environmental Journal*, 48(April), 14-21.

Runte, A. (1974b). Yosemite Valley Railroad Highway of History. *National Parks and Conservation Magazine: The Environmental Journal*, 48(December), 4-9.

Runte, A. (1977). The National Park Idea: Origins and Paradox of the American Experience. *Journal of Forest History*, 21(2), 64-75.

Runte, A. (1979). *National Parks: The American Experience*. Lincoln: University of Nebraska Press.

Runte, A. (1990). *Yosemite: The Embattled Wilderness,* Lincoln: University of Nebraska Press.

Salstonstall, R. (1993). Healthy Bodies, Social Bodies: Men's and Women's Concepts and Practices in Everyday Life. *Social Science and Medicine*, 36(1), 7-14.

Spa Popularity Wells Up (1998). *Travel Trade Gazette, U.K. and Ireland*, August 5-29.

Tarlow, P.E. and Muehsam, M.J. (1992). Wide Horizons: Travel and Tourism in the Coming Decades. *The Futurist*, 26(5), 28-33.

Towner, J. (1996). *An Historical Geography of Recreation and Tourism in the Western World 1540–1940*. Chichester: Wiley.

United Nations, Division for Social Policy and Development (1998). *The Aging of the World's Population*. New York: United Nations. Accesses online, <http://www.un.org/esa/ socdev/agewpop.htm>.

Urquhart, R. (2000) Destination: Relaxation. *Harpers Bazaar,* October, p. 210.

Valentine, G. (1999). Consuming Pleasures: Food, Leisure and the Negotiation of Sexual Relations. In Crouch, D. (Ed.) *Leisure/Tourism Geographies: Practices and Geographical Knowledge* (pp.164-180), London: Routledge.

Walton, J. (1983). *The English Seaside Resort: A Social History 1750–1914*. Leicester: Leicester University Press.

Walvin, J. (1978). *Besides the Seaside: A Social History of the Popular Seaside*. London: Allen Lane.

Ward, S.V. (1998). *Selling Places: The Marketing and Promotion of Towns and Cities 1850-2000*. London: E and FN Spon.

Williams, A.M., King. R., and Warnes, A.M. (1997). A Place in the Sun: International Retirement Migration from Northern to Southern Europe. *European Urban and Regional Studies,* 4, 15-34.

Witt, C. and Witt, S.F. (1989). Does Health Tourism Exist in the UK? *Revue de Tourisme*, 44(3), 26-30.

Wolf, N. (1990). *The beauty myth*. London: Chatto and Windus.

Wolff, C. (1992). Checking into Cuba: The Brave New World of Cuban Tourism. *Lodging Hospitality,* May, 35-44.

Wright, C. (1988). *The Global Guide to Health Holidays.* London: Christopher Helm.

Wu, N. (1994). China Offers Health Care Itinerary. *Beijing Review,* 37(38), 31-32.

# Chapter 10

# Virtual Sport Tourism

Joseph Kurtzman
John Zauhar

## OVERVIEW

This chapter demonstrates how human experiences are being expanded, and how powerful instrumentalities are being developed and put into practical use. Men and women are no longer subjected to physical world properties but rather, through effective transformations, can augment, modify, and direct their environmental conditions. These applications can be included in the traditional touristic concept. More specifically, tourism can be qualified within a passive framework whereby physical displacement is no longer the primary criteria. Within the realm of sports tourism this virtual reality nondisplacement is gaining predominance and popularity worldwide.

Sport interactiveness is currently more feasible, possible, and plausible through cyberspace "theatres" amplifying intelligence, perceptions, emotions, experiences, and data—real or fabricated. Presently there exists a number of engineering mechanisms that contribute to the virtual reality of sports tourism.

Furthermore, there are existing response display modes such as light sound entertainment, game silhouettes, adventure architecture, viewer stalwarts, educational fandom, design graphics, and simulation apparta. These seven display modes add to the flavor of virtual sports tourism and indirectly foster and help spread the concept of the virtual reality sports tourism industry.

## Prologue

> Sport permeates any number of levels of contemporary society and it touches upon and deeply influences such disparate elements as status, race relations, automotive design, clothing styles, the concept of hero worship, languages and ethical values. (McPherson and Curtis,1989, pp. 16-19)

> [Tourism is] the sum of the phenomena and the relationships arising from the interaction of tourists, business suppliers, host governments and host communities in the process of attracting and hosting these tourists and other visitors. (McIntosh et al., 1995, p. 4)

> Sport when introduced into a social system has an integrating effect. In essence, sport is a vehicle for improving social relationships in surroundings, for attaining relationships with one another, for strengthening abilities to understand one another and for the well being of peoples. When tourism is linked with sport, Sports Tourism becomes a viable and vibrant contribution to international understanding, appreciation and world peace. (Kurtzman and Zauhar, 1998, p. 6)

## Background

Generally speaking, a tourist is a person visiting a particular place, site, or destination for enjoyment and satisfaction—be it for sightseeing, educational endeavors, health reasons, and/or engaging in specific leisure activities to varying degrees. Such visitation displacements may involve photography, geoexploration, heritage, adventure, sports, etc. Forms of transportation may vary from walking to bicycling, from driving to flying, from sailing to boating, and the like. In essence, tourists take a trip; they displace themselves from their actual physical place of residence.

However, distance criteria classifying the tourist may vary from country to country, from continent to continent. Some tourist authorities consider seven kilometers as the determinant, others twenty-five, and still others sixty kilometers or more. In addition, the duration of time spent at a destination as well as the purpose for the trip may also limit, redefine, or expand the "tourist" definition. Subsequently, words such as "excursionist," "visitor," "domestic," and "international" may categorize people who travel away from their home—affecting the economy as a result of routine local expenditures. Furthermore, without question, the nature of various emotional, psychological, sociological, and physical experiences may well determine the selected physical environment and activities as well as para-activities to be engaged and/or enjoyed.

## TECHNOLOGICAL ADVANCEMENTS

Living in a physical world, people, as tourists, sense an affinity with the physical environment—affording each and every one the opportunity to enjoy, to satiate, and to satisfy. However, modern technology has advanced so that this consensual reality is possible through sensory and stimulation experiences. Electronic media amplifies reality to a state of powerful enrapturement and entrancement. The objective of this technology is to present a virtual reality within the human mind, enabling an individual to perceive and evaluate the actual ongoing experiences. Above all, these technological offerings strain one's imagination, enhance recognition, and introduce "real-time" interactiveness.

### Cyberspace Theatrics

This type of experiential visualization can be applied to tourism—hence, virtual tourism. Here, the individual does not displace himself or herself physically. The technology breaks the necessary traditional touristic criteria by bringing to the person, through computer-generated worlds, an experiencing "theatre" enabling one to absorb, feel, think, and evaluate. In essence, a symbiotic process is achieved through information, challenges, structural display, and sounds.

This responsive technological environment is the medium tremendously enjoyed by a vast number of sports enthusiasts worldwide. For a variety of reasons, these fervent sports people cannot at all times and means attend and/or participate in sports events, sports tours, sports attractions, sport cruises, sports adventure activities, and the like.

Moreover, the experiential caliber presented through this technological media is most often of superior quality and skillfulness. Thus, the interaction between person and machine augers a realm of human experiences—emotional, intellectual, cultural, sociological, and physical. This interactivity helps to create affinities, judgment behaviors, conceptual abstracts, and philosophies. It also enhances and ignites an involvement with the realities presented, inducing relationships between individuals, actions, and results. This same involvement could also unite sports enthusiasts in the sharing of experiences at a particular moment. As such, this cyberspace theatre is a form of communication—communicating space with sensitive and specific physical and spatial boundaries—far away from the individual's home base.

Sports presentations are becoming more accurate and realistic. Electronic media give users the impressions and feelings that they are truly present at the sports activity—as if they have been transported from their physical world to another existing physical reality. This can be said for the highly skilled, the average, and the neophyte user. Modern technology is definitely playing an increasingly meaningful role in the lives of many people.

### To Be or Not to Be

Play and its enjoyment is a vital part of any person's cognitive, social, and emotional development. Think about when that notion of play is computer stimulated; when mental processes will be vital to intellectual construction whereby responsiveness and representational capacities of the computer—on all sports people—to interface with events and happenings of the moment. Think about when three dimensional information using viewing apparatus or glasses will show images of reality situations or simulated realities or both.

On-site sports spectators are bombarded by feelings of anxiety while watching their teams (Wann et al., 1998). Studies demonstrate that among onlookers there exist common motives, collective self-esteem, individual and group escapism, entertainment englobement, aesthetic appreciations, economic results, sports people affiliations, and extended family ties. Fans, in fact, forget about their troubles through spectatoritis. Personal aesthetic values surface, and beauty and grace in performance is admired (Wann et al., 1999).

The values of and in sport are both intrinsic and extrinsic. The former involves health, entertainment, power, etc. The latter value set involves joy, skill, appreciation, mastery of performance, and the like (Braivik, 1998). The basic emotions usually involved are happiness, love, anger, fear, and sadness. The latter three are more negative. Nonetheless, sport watching is a process of socialization. In effect, it is a suitable response for the sport consumer. In sports fandom, all human emotions result from real anticipated, recollected, and imagined outcomes (Huang, 1997).

To what extent can and are sports pilgrimages being replaced by electronic media and advanced technology? Can the sports tourist, seeking experiential fulfillment through on-site living, shared materials, and social contacts, presently be satisfied through virtually attending or participating in an event, an activity, or a happening? Can virtual reality, in all its theoretical dimensions, build necessary affiliative tensions between knowledge possessed by the individual viewer/participant and the knowledge level presented by the organizational media?

Three things occur during experimental visualization. First, sport journalism consists of locating, selecting, ordering, and ranking of immediate events with reality reference. Second, the entertainment factor involves pleasure through action-packed programs, aesthetics, celebrities, and other psychosocial diversions. Third, the aspect of drama reinforces the entertainment value of sports through tremendous stress in action and unpredictability (Zang et al., 1998).

## VIRTUAL REALITY PARTICIPATORY MODES

Different viewer participation modes exist with respect to virtual sports tourism. As such, viewer participation could be categorized according to degrees of interest, involvement, and reciprocity:

- Social
- Business
- Bettor
- Vigorous
- Moderate
- Mild
- Therapeutic

## The Virtual Tourist

The experiential theatre, through virtual sports tourists, has found a new life in our physical world. The results create, in and by themselves, an immersion process that is manifested through different modes. Each mode

- consciously or unconsciously
- deliberately or nondeliberately
- intentionally or unintentionally

is involved with sporting legacies. Each mode acts, in varying degrees, as an interface to the cyberspace sports experiences or cyberspace aspirational experiences. Directly or indirectly, this interface conjures physical, psychological, sociological, and/or cultural attention, inspiration, motivation, and levels of self-esteem.

These modes are not input devices within cyberspace. Rather, they are display material devices mushrooming, most often, from electronic media, reality experiences, and orchestrated marketing. Furthermore, these material-generated devices continue to influence, reinforce, and foster a "psychological collage" for and to the virtual sport tourist as well as, in many instances, the general public. These material objects, oftentimes, appear as constructs emerging and maturing the human senses (Kurtzman and Zauhar, 1999). These aforementioned response modes can be categorized into the following display models (see Table 10.1).

### Light-Sound Entertainment

In such cases, display imaging is achieved through the use of computerized games. Hardware and software are designed to entice sports tourists to challenge their game skills, perfect adroitness, and induce sensual pleasure. Studies, particularly on children, show that games evoke development of certain skills and social characteristics (Roe and Muijs, 1998).

A variety of input devices such as data gloves, joysticks, and handheld wands allow users to navigate through a virtual environment and interact with virtual objects related to sports. Directional sound, tactile and force feedback devices, and other technological hardware are

TABLE 10.1. Outgrowth Physical Models Based on Virtual Reality

| Processes | Display Material Devices | Induced Emotional Response | Examples |
|---|---|---|---|
| **Light/Sound Entertainment** | • Computer games | • Challenging skills<br>• Perfect adroitness<br>• Sensual pleasure | • Car racing<br>• Golf<br>• Interactive football<br>• Interactive paddleball |
| **Game Silhouettes** | • Activity minaturization<br>• On-screen facilities | • Interface reality<br>• Bodily senses<br>• Sense physical presence | • Famous golf locations<br>• Walking trails<br>• Miniature racing |
| **Adventure Architecture** | • Physical sets<br>• Challenging devices | • Self-challenge<br>• Experimentation<br>• Realization | • Housed outdoor sports<br>• Indoor domed skiing |
| **Viewer Stalwarts** | • Cyberspace presentations<br>• Action scenarios | • Experience sharing<br>• Groupie discussions<br>• Judgments and argumentation | • Television<br>• Radio<br>• Internet<br>• Interactive videos |
| **Educational Fandom** | • Sports skill development<br>• Visual lessons<br>• Appraisal clinics | • Constructive correctives<br>• Self-satisfaction<br>• Skill betterment | • Video methodology<br>• Internet<br>• Presentations<br>• Self-analysis |
| **Design Graphics** | • Sport logos<br>• Sport symbols<br>• Sportswear | • Support enhancement<br>• Appreciation<br>• Reinforcement<br>• Sense of belonging | • NFL logos<br>• Nike markings<br>• Animated sports figures |
| **Simulation Apparata** | • Miniature physical replicas<br>• Sports environment culturation | • Tryout testing<br>• Familiarization of apparata<br>• Self-skill concept | • Wall mountain climbing<br>• Abridged racing facilities<br>• Table soccer |

*Source:* Kurtzman and Zauhar, 1999.

utilized to create responses consistent with actual sports experiences (Beier, 2000).

## Game Silhouettes

The sports enthusiast engages in miniature sport games that conjure one or more bodily senses. Such games have a strong symbolic relationship to sports. Television and radio, particularly with their daily twenty-four-hour programming, do have a strong bearing on the lives of people, indirectly enticing participation in miniature games (Colangelo and Sherman, 1999).

## Adventure Architecture

Physical set-ups imitating actual structures designed for practical challenge and experimentation in sport are being imitated in virtual reality. Examples of such structures include: indoor mountain climbing apparata, indoor parachuting, luging on wheels, etc.

Technology is furthermore being employed to develop virtual environments. For instance, artists are employing Internet, robotics, and global positioning systems to create housing developments (Pappone, 1999). These projects are a means to explore relationships between technology and people. Furthermore, expenditures and impacts are created, and future environmental evolvement is to be registered.

## Viewer Stalwarts

Sports enthusiasts with intense interest in a specific sport join others in cyberspace to enjoy their favorite sports. In essence, these participants are "groupies" who share potential happenings and promulgate "action scenarios." Discussions, value judgments, and argumentations form the principal ingredients of this mode. Instant replays, slow motion, and close-up images greatly influence viewers. Interest becomes more focused, intense, and significant. Directly or indirectly, the cyber presentations entice strong loyalties to specific teams or players, events, or happenings. Furthermore, this mode draws on the contradiction between the mediated events and personal experiences—creating alternative meanings (Bruce, 1998).

Groupies, furthermore, are generally looking for a good time, a place to go, and an environment suitable to their liking—yet different from their usual place of encounters, such as work or home. Developing a camaraderie with other devotees for a specific sport activity brings out a relationship and accrues inside information on the sport, athletes and the like (Gmlech and San Antonio, 1998).

It is said that banalities, in this case, sports talk, can carry much social power. In effect, sports talk has become a leading form of expression. Supporting one's team has taken the place of what was once the supporting of one's country—right or wrong (Goldberg, 1998). New communities, through groupie clustering, are created, fostered, and developed.

## Educational Fandom

Individuals and groups following with an interest in instructional elements and aspects of a particular sport fall into this category. Here, fundamentals, helpful hints, and/or corrective measures through audio and visual lessons are of essence.

Among the most common are television sessions, videos, and Internet consultations. These sets, intelligent in the state of the art, know and realize their visitor tastes and as such deliver dynamic information about sports skills, pursuits, and services (Venkatraman and Henderson, 1998).

Motivational aspects are also important. Questions such as "Who do you want to be?" and "What is important to you?", which are generally asked of professional athletes (Balague, 1999), are directly and indirectly revealed in instructional presentation structures, stimulating sports-minded individuals to preserve and appreciate both performance and results.

## Design Graphics

In the world of sports, marketing wizards have thoroughly penetrated the sports viewer audience with appropriate and attractive sweaters, caps, shorts, footwear, stylized logos, and other clothing symbols, thus enhancing, reinforcing, and motivating the virtual sports tourist (Research Unit, 1995).

Communal symbols and memorabilia reinforce cohesion, and affect devotion and hegemony. Culture gives people models of their sense of identity. Such identity is created by public forms through use of symbols, mass media, and marketing which have come to dominate and inculcate an individual's sentiments through visual expression (Price, 1995). It could be that such symbolic expressions are an extension of the mind—creating the present of past things and the future of present things (Strade et al., 1996)—in essence, a timeliness associated with cyberspace.

*Simulation Apparta*

More and more, specific sports apparata that contribute to one's sports skill development are offered through tryout experimentation. Oftentimes, these mechanisms are miniature replicas modeled after a true sports environment. Examples include: stationary rowing, flight simulation, windsurfing devices, etc. In essence, these are applied tools by playing and experiencing in simulated environments—interactive theatres. In cultural and museum applications, robots are found as guides to attract, entertain, and instruct (Camurri and Coglio, 1999). Such a virtual studio was developed and promulgated in Europe (Gibbs et al., 1998).

## FUTURES

There is another dimension to virtual reality that, at the present time, remains mostly in the developmental stages and will have a great bearing on the virtual sports tourism industry. As such, this intensive, interactive experience innovation could be defined as a microscope for the mind—a looking glass constructed in a computer memory device affecting as many senses as possible. It truly is a computation of the electronic realm through which reality is expressed—an out of body experience. Such experiential cyberspace theatres, would allow individuals, to some extent, to navigate within a set world quite independently where computers and humans make contact (Pimentel and Teixeira, 1995).

In this virtual reality technique, the individual involved is taken to a remote environment and may, in various ways, be directly participating in the physical world experimentation. Careful engineering of certain elements permit and, after greater perfection, will enable people to interject in ongoing spectacles, events, programs, and discussions. This telepresence method will allow people to project themselves, to have sensations, to participate, and to increase the situational pace—another form of adventure to be available for the virtual reality sport tourist (Rheingold, 1991).

Virtual reality can incorporate events, symbols, and media from other forms of communication, in addition to revealing what is on one's mind. Every object and its relationship to every other object, including the user, is a design element at the discretion of the virtual reality developer. Among these elements are location, color, shape, and size of environment (Pimentel and Teixeira, 1995).

In essence, virtual reality with respect to sports tourism is a computer simulation that offers the sport enthusiast the opportunity to experience different kinds of preproduced programs in "real time." By use of sound, sight, and touch technology, it is possible to recreate touristic characteristics that enable enjoyment, appreciation, and entertainment (Rimmington and Kozak, 1997). Virtual tourism in its most advanced stages enables users to experience artificial tourism pursuits, productions, and services.

Presently, a number of technologically engineered mechanisms exist that will contribute to virtual sports tourism, for instance, binocular illusions—a head-mounted display with three-dimensional images. Another example terminal, the virtual return display, acts as a camera screen with a series of twin mirrors (Wright, 1998). The personal roving presence called "teleembodiment" where one sees, listens, talks, and hears people he or she meets—can pop up in any world location instead of integrating to one specific physical reality (Brown, 1998). The Eye Trek FMD-150 head-mounted display provides viewers the equivalent of a sixty-two-inch television screen (Yamanka, 1999).

Another Internet experiment exists in which people can augment, modify, or eliminate some or all aspects of a proposed painting, inciting group participation in finalizing a tableau. Hence, through the integration of virtual reality techniques and telecommunication networking, human interaction is and will be more possible in the future through virtual reality. This sophisticated technology will definitely influence the horizons of sports tourists. Enthusiasts will be able to be present at baseball games; they will be able to be on the field and actively involved in the game. Think about the possibilities of bilocating oneself to a sports museum, canoeing in turbulent waters, or exploring caves virtually. The scientific frontiers are increasing and probability will bear out accessibility and directiveness for technological structures.

Walt Disney Company, with its DisneyQuest, a gargantuan virtual theme park, is considering establishing sites in different countries. In effect, it is an ultimate interactive adventure stadium blending technology with story tales in which individuals will embark on adventures such as white-water rafting through the jungle, stomach-turning climbs around a cyberspace mountain, and the like (McNaughton, 1999).

Furthermore, different experimentations and developments that are becoming "futures" of our society, include:

- The cave automatic virtual environment (CAVE), which provides the illusion of immersion by projecting images on walls and floors of a room-sized cube simulating the cave entrance and walking space within the projected area (Beier, 2000).
- Design methodology for automation utilizes multidiscipline optimization. This methodology consists of a robust design, decision analysis and support, concept exploration of diverse systems, and simulation. From this, engineers can develop methods for the description and evaluation of sensitivities inherent within the design of virtual reality (Clemson Research Report, 1997).
- QuickTime virtual reality is a revolutionary technology pioneered by Apple Computers allowing an individual to interact with an image. In effect, one can look up or down, left or right, as if one were there. Tourism Web sites utilize this technology to better illustrate countryside, architecture, cities, and the like (Bain, 1997).
- The practical application of virtual reality centers on its ability to model actual places, buildings, and information in three-dimensional imagery. The commercial use of virtual reality in tourism will be closely linked to developments of broadband telecommunications and telemedia technology for sales and marketing (Cooper and Benjamin, 1995).
- Project virtual reality models have been used to illustrate the virtual protyping of a sailing yacht. This detailed virtual linkage

allows for the study of deck layouts and interior arrangements (Beier, 2000).

- The study of computer-aided design related to rapid prototyping and development of algorithms to improve speed and accuracy has been initiated. The results will lead to the use of virtual reality as a truly three-dimensional computer-assisted design modeler (Clemson Research Report, 1997).
- Virtual reality is often thought of as new technology, but its development dates back almost fifty years to flight simulators built by the aircraft industry. Virtual reality was also influenced by film techniques such as stereoscopic or 3-D cinema, and several widescreen systems that filmmakers experimented with in the 1950s. Cinerama, the best known of these technologies, sought to expand the movie-going experience by filling a larger portion of the audience's visual field. The theory of visual immersion and the 3-D concept went on to become important virtual reality elements (Weiss, 1996).
- A complete virtual tour of Australia takes people on a journey through the country using revolutionary virtual reality walkthrough technology. This virtual reality tour highlights selected beaches, reefs, national parks, etc. The accompanying tourist information is quite extensive and valuable to those interested in journeying to Australia (Virtual Australia, 2000).
- Sports simulation machines are designed to create specific human elements of the particular activity. As an example, windsurfing hardware is designed to create specific movements involving reaction time, muscular strength, endurance, balance, and the like. This virtual reality "boarding" includes counteractions to wind velocity changes that determine a person's ability to navigate and windsurf (Baig, 1996).

As a result of all these interface applications, the virtual sports tourism industry will take on a more distinctive definition and participatory role. These visions and experiences of reality or constructed realities will bear a new entertainment model and societal economy. It is likely that the tourist experience will become more and more a mixture of reality and virtual reality and, thereby, more appropriately satisfy the demands of sustainability (Dewailly, 1999).

Virtual tourism is already possible in limited form, and some say that a more compelling form of virtual reality will eventually replace real travel. The example most widely known would be the Holodeck in the televison series *Star Trek*. In this virtual hologram mechanism, the virtual sports tourist can play any game, tour any sports facility, visit any sports heritage site, perfect skills at the sport resort of choice, or take in a sports adventure that has the greatest of challenges.

### Relevancy

Mihalyi Czikszentomihalyi described six criteria that most often characterize experiences that individuals consider optimal, and that could be applied in certain measures within the sports tourism concept. The experience of individuals, regardless of culture or geographical location, must:

- Require the learning of skills
- Have concrete goals
- Provide feedback
- Let the person feel in control
- Facilitate concentration and involvement
- Be distinct from the everyday world (Czikszentomihalyi, 1990)

### Plausible or Possible Implications

Will these six criteria be met by virtual reality theatres? Will virtual sports tourism gain greater grounds? Will the actual visitations to a sports event or sports attraction diminish? Will touring sports activity participation in sports clinics be eliminated? Will the present sports industry, believed to be valued in the United States at some $35 million, be positively or negative affected (Dennis, 1999)? Will there be any effect on the trillion-dollar international tourism industry? Will sports tourism become a "natural" for virtual reality mechanisms to surpass its current market share of 25 to 30 percent in the international tourism industry (Research Unit, 1994)? Do the answers to these questions lie, without question, in the acceptance of all virtual technology?

Will society fully accept technological advances, endorse non-physical displacement, and will virtual substitution satisfy the wants, needs, and desires of sports tourists? On the whole, what does the future hold for the virtual sports tourism industry?

## Virtual Tourism Examples

Passage to Punta di l'Acellu, Self-Movement of 3-D Views of the Area: http://evm.vr-consortium.com/regions/zzf/panosj club/bavella/bav16.htm

Virtual Tourism, Self-Movement of 3-D Views and User Controlled Movement: http://www.sribascad.com/QTVRindex. html

Virtual Sports Interaction, Full Screen, and Full Motion with Realistic Car Handling: http://203.61.124.10/vsi/game2.htm

Virtual Seaside of Brazil (has a search and many visuals of the seaside): http://www.litoralvirtual.com.br/index_i.html

## REFERENCES

Baig, Edward (1996). *Virtual Sports, Real Sweat.* New York: McGraw Hill.

Bain, Donald (1997*). Geo-Images Virtual Reality Panoramas.* University of California at Berkeley: Geo-Images Project.

Balague, Gloria (1999). Understanding Identity, Value and Meaning When Working with Elite Athletes. *The Sports Psychologist,* 13(1), 90.

Beier, Kenneth P. (2000*). Virtual Reality: A Short Introduction.* Ann Arbor: Virtual Reality Laboratory, University of Michigan.

Braivik, Gunnar (1998). Sport in High Modernity: Sport As a Carrier of Social Values. *Journal of Philosophy of Sport,* 25,103-118.

Brown, Brandon (1998). Trust Me in the Middle. New Scientist, 1253, 30-31.

Bruce, Toni (1998). Audience Frustration and Pleasure. *Journal of Sport and Social Issues,* 22(4), 376-378.

Camurri, Antonio and Coglio, Alessandro (1999). An Architecture for Emotional Agents. *Communications,* 42(5), 25.

Clemson Research Reports (1997). *Engineering and Optimization.* Clemson, SC: Clemson University.

Colangelo, Jerry and Sherman, Len (1999). Sports and the Media. *Management Review,* 10(2), 44.

Cooper, M. and Benjamin, I. (1995). *Virtual Tourism: A Realistic Assessment of Virtual Reality for the Tourism Industry.* Proceedings of ENTER '95. Austria: Innsbruck.

Czikszentomihalyi, Mihalyi (1990*). Flow: The Psychology of Optimal Experience.* New York: Harper Row.

Dennis, Howard (1999). The Changing Fanscape for Big-League Sports: Implications for Sports Managers. *Journal of Sport Management,* 13(3), 79.

Dewailly, Jean-Michel (1999). Sustainable Tourist Space: From Reality to Virtual Reality? *Tourism Geographies,* 1(1), 41-55.

Gibbs, Simon, et al. (1998). Virtual Studios: An Overview. *IEE Multimedia,* 4,21.

Gmlech, George and San Antonio, Patricia (1998). Groupies and American Baseball. *Journal of Sport and Social Issues,* 22(1), 33-35.

Goldberg, David (1998). Call and Response. *Journal of Sport and Social Issues,* 22(2), 216-219.

Huang, Ming-Hui. (1997). Exploring a New Topology of Emotional Appeals: Basic, versus Social, Emotional Advertising. *Journal of Current Issues and Research in Advertising,* 20(1), 23-25.

Kurtzman, Joseph and Zauhar, John (1998). *Product Seminar Guide to Sport Tourism.* Ottawa: Sports Tourism International Council.

Kurtzman, Joseph and Zauhar, John (1999). The Virtual Sport Tourist. *Journal of Sport Tourism,* 5,4.

McIntosh, J. et al. (1995). *Tourism: Principles, Practices and Philosophies.* New York: Wiley and Sons.

McNaughton, Derek (1999). Disney Eyes Ottawa for Theme Park. *The Ottawa Citizen,* May 10, p. B3.

McPherson, Barry and Curtis, James E. (1989). *The Social Significance of Sport.* Chicago, IL: Human Kinetics.

Pappone, Jeff (1999). Under Virtual Construction. *The Ottawa Citizen,* May 24, p. B3.

Pimentel, Ken and Teixeira, Kevin (1995). *Virtual Reality: Through the New Looking Glass,* Second Edition. San Francisco: Intel/McGraw Hill.

Price, Monroe (1995). Television, the Public Sphere, and National Identity. *Communication Research Trends,* 17(1), 10.

Research Unit, Sports Tourism International Council (1994). Sports Tourism Contribution to Overall Tourism. *Journal of Sport Tourism,* 1(4), 36-43.

Research Unit, Sports Tourism International Council (1995). Survey of Sportswear Worn by Tourists. *Journal of Sport Tourism,* 2(2).

Rheingold, Howard (1991). *Virtual Reality.* Toronto: Simon and Schuster.

Rimmington, Michael and Kozak, Metin (1997). Developments in Information Technology: Implications for the Tourism Industry and Tourism Marketing. *Anatolia,* 6(3), 71.

Roe, Keith and Muijs, Daniel (1998). Children and Computer Games. *European Journal of Communication,* 13(2), 181-186.

Strade, Lance et al. (1996). Communication and Cyberspace: Social Interaction in an Electronic Environment. *Communication Research Trends,* 16(3),18.

Venkatraman, N. and Henderson, John (1998). Real Strategies for Virtual Organizing. *Sloan Management Review,* fall, p. 37.

Virtual Australia (2000). Available online at <vraustralia.com>. Accessed July 12.

Wann, Daniel et al. (1998). The Cognitive and Somatic Anxiety of Sport Spectators. *Leisure of Sport Behaviour,* 21(3), 322-325.

Wann, Daniel et al. (1999). Sport Fan Motivation: Questionnaire Validation, Comparisons by Sport, and Relationship to Athletic Motivation. *Journal of Sport Behaviour,* 22(1), 115.

Weiss, Sonia (1996). *Virtual Reality.* New York: Jones Digital Century.

Wright, Gilles (1998). Virtual Reality: Display and Illusion. *New Scientist,* 2146 (August), 33-35.

Yamanka, Toru (1999). Picture Caption. *National Post,* May 22, p. D2.

Zang, James et al. (1998). Relationship Between Broadcasting Media and Minor League Hockey Game Attendance. *Journal of Sport Management,* 12(2), 105.

# Index

Page numbers followed by the letter "i" indicate illustrations; those followed by the letter "t" indicate tables.

# THE HAWORTH HOSPITALITY PRESS®
## Hospitality, Travel, and Tourism
## K. S. Chon, PhD, Editor-in-Chief

**TOURISM IN CHINA** edited by Alan A. Lew, Lawrence Yu, John Ap, and Zhang Guangrui. (2002). "Aside from guidebooks, there are few widely accessible sources in English that address the broad aspects of tourism in China. So, this work constitutes an extremely useful point of departure for those interested in gaining a current and critical understanding of tourism in this important, but poorly understood, part of the world." *Geoffrey Wall, PhD, Associate Dean, Graduate Studies and Research, Faculty of Environmental Research, University of Waterloo, Ontario, Canada*

**SPORT AND ADVENTURE TOURISM** edited by Simon Hudson. (2002). "This book incorporates the most recent information and real-world case studies to inform the reader of the importance of sport and adventure tourism. The publication is rich in knowledge and provides the reader with innovative models, useful resources, and invaluable references for further study and research." *Wayne G. Pealo, PhD, Professor, Recreation and Tourism Management, Malaspina University College*

**CONVENTION TOURISM: INTERNATIONAL RESEARCH AND INDUSTRY PERSPECTIVES** edited by Karin Weber and Kye-Sung Chon. (2002). "This comprehensive book is truly global in its perspective. The text points out areas of needed research—a great starting point for graduate students, university faculty, and industry professionals alike. While the focus is mainly academic, there is a lot of meat for this burgeoning industry to chew on as well." *Patti J. Shock, CPCE, Professor and Department Chair, Tourism and Convention Administration, Harrah College of Hotel Administration, University of Nevada–Las Vegas*

**CULTURAL TOURISM: THE PARTNERSHIP BETWEEN TOURISM AND CULTURAL HERITAGE MANAGEMENT** by Bob McKercher and Hilary du Cros. (2002). "The book brings together concepts, perspectives, and practicalities that must be understood by both cultural heritage and tourism managers, and as such is a must-read for both." *Hisashi B. Sugaya, AICP, Former Chair, International Council of Monuments and Sites, International Scientific Committee on Cultural Tourism; Former Executive Director, Pacific Asia Travel Association Foundation, San Francisco, CA*

**TOURISM IN THE ANTARCTIC: OPPORTUNITIES, CONSTRAINTS, AND FUTURE PROSPECTS** by Thomas G. Bauer. (2001). "Thomas Bauer presents a wealth of detailed information on the challenges and opportunities facing tourism operators in this last great tourism frontier." *David Mercer, PhD, Associate Professor, School of Geography & Environmental Science, Monash University, Melbourne, Australia*

**SERVICE QUALITY MANAGEMENT IN HOSPITALITY, TOURISM, AND LEISURE** edited by Jay Kandampully, Connie Mok, and Beverley Sparks. (2001). "A must-read. . . . a treasure. . . . pulls together the work of scholars across the globe, giving you access to new ideas, international research, and industry examples from around the world." *John Bowen, Professor and Director of Graduate Studies, William F. Harrah College of Hotel Administration, University of Nevada, Las Vegas*

**TOURISM IN SOUTHEAST ASIA: A NEW DIRECTION** edited by K. S. (Kaye) Chon. (2000). "Presents a wide array of very topical discussions on the specific challenges facing the tourism industry in Southeast Asia. A great resource for both scholars and practitioners." *Dr. Hubert B. Van Hoof, Assistant Dean/Associate Professor, School of Hotel and Restaurant Management, Northern Arizona University*

**THE PRACTICE OF GRADUATE RESEARCH IN HOSPITALITY AND TOURISM** edited by K. S. Chon. (1999). "An excellent reference source for students pursuing graduate degrees in hospitality and tourism." *Connie Mok, PhD, CHE, Associate Professor, Conrad N. Hilton College of Hotel and Restaurant Management, University of Houston, Texas*

**THE INTERNATIONAL HOSPITALITY MANAGEMENT BUSINESS: MANAGEMENT AND OPERATIONS** by Larry Yu. (1999). "The abundant real-world examples and cases provided in the text enable readers to understand the most up-to-date developments in international hospitality business." *Zheng Gu, PhD, Associate Professor, College of Hotel Administration, University of Nevada, Las Vegas*

**CONSUMER BEHAVIOR IN TRAVEL AND TOURISM** by Abraham Pizam and Yoel Mansfeld. (1999). "A must for anyone who wants to take advantage of new global opportunities in this growing industry." *Bonnie J. Knutson, PhD, School of Hospitality Business, Michigan State University*

**LEGALIZED CASINO GAMING IN THE UNITED STATES: THE ECONOMIC AND SOCIAL IMPACT** edited by Cathy H. C. Hsu. (1999). "Brings a fresh new look at one of the areas in tourism that has not yet received careful and serious consideration in the past." *Muzaffer Uysal, PhD, Professor of Tourism Research, Virginia Polytechnic Institute and State University, Blacksburg*

**HOSPITALITY MANAGEMENT EDUCATION** edited by Clayton W. Barrows and Robert H. Bosselman. (1999). "Takes the mystery out of how hospitality management education programs function and serves as an excellent resource for individuals interested in pursuing the field." *Joe Perdue, CCM, CHE, Director, Executive Masters Program, College of Hotel Administration, University of Nevada, Las Vegas*

**MARKETING YOUR CITY, U.S.A.: A GUIDE TO DEVELOPING A STRATEGIC TOURISM MARKETING PLAN** by Ronald A. Nykiel and Elizabeth Jascolt. (1998). "An excellent guide for anyone involved in the planning and marketing of cities and regions. . . . A terrific job of synthesizing an otherwise complex procedure." *James C. Maken, PhD, Associate Professor, Babcock Graduate School of Management, Wake Forest University, Winston-Salem, North Carolina*

# SPECIAL 25%-OFF DISCOUNT!

## Order a copy of this book with this form or online at:
### http://www.haworthpressinc.com/store/product.asp?sku=4649

## SPORT AND ADVENTURE TOURISM

_____in hardbound at $44.96 (regularly $59.95) (ISBN: 0-7890-1275-8)

_____in softbound at $26.21 (regularly $34.95) (ISBN: 0-7890-1276-6)

Or order online and use Code HEC25 in the shopping cart.

COST OF BOOKS_____

OUTSIDE US/CANADA/
MEXICO: ADD 20%_____

POSTAGE & HANDLING_____
*(US: $5.00 for first book & $2.00
for each additional book)
Outside US: $6.00 for first book
& $2.00 for each additional book)*

SUBTOTAL_____

IN CANADA: ADD 7% GST_____

STATE TAX_____
*(NY, OH & MN residents, please
add appropriate local sales tax)*

**FINAL TOTAL**_____
*(If paying in Canadian funds,
convert using the current
exchange rate, UNESCO
coupons welcome)*

Prices in US dollars and subject to change without notice.

☐ **BILL ME LATER:** ($5 service charge will be added)
(Bill-me option is good on US/Canada/Mexico orders only;
not good to jobbers, wholesalers, or subscription agencies.)

☐ Check here if billing address is different from
shipping address and attach purchase order and
billing address information.

Signature_____

☐ **PAYMENT ENCLOSED: $**_____

☐ **PLEASE CHARGE TO MY CREDIT CARD.**

☐ Visa ☐ MasterCard ☐ AmEx ☐ Discover
☐ Diner's Club ☐ Eurocard ☐ JCB

Account # _____

Exp. Date_____

Signature_____

NAME_____
INSTITUTION_____
ADDRESS_____
CITY_____
STATE/ZIP_____
COUNTRY_____ COUNTY (NY residents only)_____
TEL_____ FAX_____
E-MAIL_____

May we use your e-mail address for confirmations and other types of information? ☐ Yes ☐ No
We appreciate receiving your e-mail address and fax number. Haworth would like to e-mail or fax special
discount offers to you, as a preferred customer. **We will never share, rent, or exchange your e-mail address
or fax number.** We regard such actions as an invasion of your privacy.

### Order From Your Local Bookstore or Directly From
### The Haworth Press, Inc.
10 Alice Street, Binghamton, New York 13904-1580 • USA
TELEPHONE: 1-800-HAWORTH (1-800-429-6784) / Outside US/Canada: (607) 722-5857
FAX: 1-800-895-0582 / Outside US/Canada: (607) 722-6362
E-mailto: getinfo@haworthpressinc.com
PLEASE PHOTOCOPY THIS FORM FOR YOUR PERSONAL USE.
http://www.HaworthPress.com

BOF02

# Date Due

PRINTED IN U.S.A.     CAT. NO. 24 161     BRO DART